DISCOVERING
PROVENCE

(Frontispiece, overleaf) I *Arles: the façade of the church of St Trophime*

Patrick Turnbull

DISCOVERING
PROVENCE

B. T. Batsford Ltd *London*

First published 1972 under the title *Provence*
© Patrick Turnbull 1972
Second Impression (paperback) 1973

Made and printed Offset Litho in Great Britain by
Cox and Wyman Ltd, London, Fakenham and Reading
for the publishers B. T. Batsford Ltd
4 Fitzhardinge Street, London W1H 0AH

ISBN 0 7134 0180 X

Contents

Acknowledgments   8

List of plates   9

1 Introduction   11

2 Avignon   39

3 Arles   71

4 Aix-en-Provence   111

5 Two Rivers – The Durance and the Verdon   137

6 Marseille   160

7 The Var Coast   183

8 The High Var   203

9 The Côte d'Azur   228

Index   260

Acknowledgments

The author's sincere thanks are due to Mr S. H. Barlow, FLA, of Nuneaton, Patrick Waldberg of the *Beaux Arts*, and Monsieur Philippe, Mayor of Seillans, for their help with his research for this book; also to Geoffrey Wilkinson, author of *The Monkeys*, for allowing him to consult and quote from his notes on Provence's early history.

The author and publishers wish to thank the following for supplying photographs reproduced in this book: Anne Bolt for plates 3, 7–9 and 11; Raymond Broad for plates 10, 12–16, 18–20 and 22–25; A. F. Kersting for plates 1, 2, 4, 5, 17 and 21; Roland Stalencq for plate 26; and Witold Wondrausch for plate 6.

List of Plates

1 Arles: the façade of the church of St Trophime   *frontispiece*

2 Avignon: the ruined bridge and the river Rhône   17

3 Tarascon castle on the river Rhône   18

4 Orange: the triumphal arch   37

5 Arles: the Roman arena   38

6 Les Baux de Provence   55

7 The Château d'If   55

8 Les Saintes Maries de la Mer: the fortress church   56

9 The Camargue: sand dunes and salt lakes   89

10 Horsemen of the Camargue   89

11 Aigues Mortes: aerial view   90

12 Moustiers Ste Marie: the gorge and Notre Dame de Beauvoir   107

13 The Pont du Verdon, near Moustiers Ste Marie   108

14 Moustiers Ste Marie: the church   125

15 Grand Cañon de Verdon: bergerie, Falaise des Cavaliers   126

16 Castellane: Notre Dame du Rocher   143

17 Fréjus: the cathedral cloisters   144

18 Draguignan: Pierre de la Fée dolmen   161

19 Comps: old church   162

20 Bargémon village   179

21 Nice: looking westwards from the Quai des Etats-Unis   180

22 St Paul de Vence   197

23 Maeght Foundation, St Paul: Giacometti statues   198

24 Vence: rue du Marché   215
25 Coursegoules and Cheiron mountain   216
26 Olive trees, centuries old   216

1. Introduction

History

'The country is wild and arid. The soil is so stony that you cannot plant anything without striking a rock. Work is an ungrateful toil, and daily hardships are such that life is truly difficult for these people whose bodies, as a result, are skinny and shrivelled. Women have to sweat like the men. It sometimes happens that a woman gives birth to her child in the fields, covers the little one with leaves, and then returns to her work so a day will not be lost. . . .'

The writer, Posidonius, historian and stoic of the second century B.C., was talking of the Ligurians who, evolving from the Bronze Age, may be termed the first 'natives' of Provence.

This primitive, tough way of life, however, had the compensation of being untroubled by foreign influence, hostile or friendly, till the sixth century B.C.

By that time, nevertheless, the Ligurian coast had already featured in Greek legend; every 24 hours Apollo drove his sun chariot westwards, skirting this unknown shore; Hercules in his journey to the Occident to search for the garden of the Hesperides had been protected by Jupiter's personal intervention from his Ligurian enemies. It was inevitable therefore that the exploring Greeks would eventually reach a stage when they could no longer be satisfied by legend.

The first westward expedition was organised by the Phoceans from Asia Minor. After consulting the goddess Artemis of Ephesus a little fleet was put under the command of Protis, eminent citizen of Phocea, and the spiritual protection of Artemis's high priestess

Aristarche. The long journey was accomplished without incident, continuing till the morning when the explorers found themselves not far from the mouth of a great river (the Rhône), close to a *calanque* (creek), the Lacydon. Here the aspect of the coastline reminded them so much of their native Ionia that they decided that this was the place to disembark and found their first city, Massilia, present-day Marseille, the Mediterranean's greatest port and the second city of France.*

Protis and his men had come to trade, not to conquer. It was to their interest to be on the friendliest of terms with the autochthones. Excellent businessmen, the Phoceans rapidly spread their zones of influence and prospered. Other commercial centres were founded at Nicaea (Nice), Antipolis (Antibes), Athenopolis (St Tropez) and Citharista (La Ciotat). In what could be termed a ribbon development, Phocean basically peaceful domination eventually stretched from Monaco to Catalonia.

During this period another great Phocean navigator, Pytheas, basing himself on Massilia, sailed still farther eastwards between the Pillars of Hercules, turned north, reaching the misty islands where he bartered wine with the primitive Britons for tin before attaining the ultimate mysterious shores of Thule. At the same time other traders making their way up the Rhône penetrated to most of the regions of Gaul.

Inevitably such prosperity aroused the jealousy of the warlike Celto-Ligurian tribes to the north – the spread of Celtic influence southwards began soon after the Phocean colonisation – and in particular that of the Segobrigian tribe. A surprise attack on Massilia led by the Segobrigian chieftain Coman was, however, defeated, and the young chief himself with 7,000 of his warriors died in the battle. The result of this defeat was one of those miraculous eras of peace, lasting for the best part of 300 years, during which time the Massiliots, rich and prosperous, must have come to the conclusion that it was 'better to make love than to make war',

* It has been suggested that Greeks from Rhodes had settled in the Rhône valley – hence the river's name – as early as the eighth century. However, the bulk of existing evidence is in favour of the Phoceans.

and proceeded to put this amiable theory into practice to such a degree that one historian called Massilia 'the great whoreshop'.

However, threats to this state of promiscuous bliss began to develop both from north and south. The southern menace arose from the power of Carthage and materialised when Hannibal, marching from Spain with 60,000 infantry, 9,000 cavalry and squadrons of fighting elephants, crossed Provençal territory and forced a passage of the Rhône before swinging north prior to his semi-mysterious crossing of the Alps. Frightened by the appearance of this enemy army on their land the Phoceans did everything within their power to help Rome, sending men – mostly locally recruited Ligurians – and money.

Carthage's defeat and the alliance with Rome still further increased Phocean power, but at the same time an even more serious threat from the north was taking shape.

In 128 B.C. the Celts, banding together, raised an enormous army which the Phoceans felt unable to resist, appealing to Rome for assistance. In answer to this appeal Caius Sextius Calvinius, at the head of a Roman army, marched into Provence, defeated the Celts after a peculiarly savage three-year war, and then himself founded a city on the ruins of Celtic Entremont which he named Aquae Sextiae, present-day Aix-en-Provence.

The Roman ally, having borne the brunt of the fighting, decided to annex the territories, scenes of his victories, but by way of a magnanimous gesture allowed the Massiliots to retain a coastal strip from the mouth of the Rhône to Monaco.

Twenty-three years later another vast migratory movement of northern barbarians, the wild Teutons and Cimbrians, moved south to wipe out Mediterranean civilisation. This horde was eventually annihilated in 102 B.C. by the Roman consul of Massilia, Caius Marius, in the plain below the village of Pourrières under the shadow of the Montagne Sainte-Victoire, then known as Mount Venturi. Freed of this further danger the Massiliots prospered again, but at the time of Rome's civil war (50 B.C.) made a disastrous choice in backing the claims of Pompeius against Caesar.

Julius Caesar was not a man to suffer enemies gladly. In 49 B.C. he surrounded the city, which he captured after a six-month siege with the help of a fleet built by the citizens of Arles. After the fall of Massilia, most of whose possessions were handed over to the Arlesians, Rome converted the whole of the south of France into a Roman province (the largest) with Arles as its capital and a subsidiary capital at Cimiez, the hill above Nice. It is from this time that the word 'Provence' enters into the current vocabulary.

As in other imperial possessions the *Pax Romana* brought a lengthy period of well-being to the people of Provence, a period which also saw the introduction of Christianity.

Provençal legend insists that the 'Word' first came to this part of the Mediterranean in the persons of those who had been the companions of Christ. To avoid persecution, Lazarus the resurrected, his sisters Mary Magdalene and Martha, together with Mary Jacoby sister of the Virgin Mary, Mary Salome, mother of the apostles James and John, the saints Maximinius, Parmenos, Trophime, Sidonius the blind, and the servants Marcelle and the black Sarah, set off from the shores of Asia Minor in a small boat without sails, and after narrowly escaping death on many occasions eventually ran aground on the sandy shore where, today, is the town of Les Saintes Maries de la Mer.

Mary Jacoby, Mary Salome and Sarah stayed on the coast. The others moved inland, evangelising the local populations, Lazarus to Massilia, Trophime to Arles, Maximinius and Sidonius to Aix, Parmenos to Avignon, Martha to Tarascon. Mary Magdalene, eternal penitent, found a cave in the range of hills above Massilia – today the Sainte Baume – and lived there as a hermit for over 30 years till her death.

Thanks to these first apostles, Provence, by the time of the Roman Empire's fall, was totally converted to the new faith.

The collapse of Rome was the prelude to the barbarian eras. First came that of the Visigoths (476), then of the Ostrogoths, who ceded Provence to the Franks in return for Frankish neutrality when the Ostrogoth king Vitigès came into conflict with the eastern empire.

The area nominally under Frankish rule was, however, so vast that it could not be controlled effectively by a central authority. Successive kings therefore delegated their power to representatives known as 'Patrices' who, in turn, took advantage of their remoteness to create an almost totally independent Provence. In fact they were so obsessed by their love of autonomy that they did not hesitate to ally themselves on occasions, with a new foreign invader from the east, the Saracens, who were to ravage the land systematically for no less than four centuries.

In 712 the Saracens crossed the Pyrenees from Spain, but did not make their first appearance in Provence till 726, having taken fourteen years to subdue Languedoc. The Moslems then advanced as far as the Rhône which they crossed above Avignon, but at this point unexpectedly turned north. There were incursions in 729 but 732 saw the first major attack when two Saracen armies under Abd-er-Rahman besieged Arles. In the battle to raise the siege 'the Franks had scant fortune. Put to flight by the invaders the Rhône engulfed those bodies left on the banks' (Rodriguez de Toledo).

Again turning north Abd-er-Rahman was himself defeated by Charles Martel at Poitiers. Dissatisfied by the half-hearted resistance shown by the Provençaux Charles Martel decided to keep the country under tighter control, appointing a certain Duke Mauronte as Duke of Marseille and Governor of Arles. It is suggested – chiefly on the strength of the name – that Mauronte had Moorish blood in his veins. One does not know for certain. What was soon evident, however, was that Mauronte was ambitious and untrustworthy. No sooner was he established in his fief than he declared himself an independent ruler and called on Abd-er-Rahman for help. The Saracen leader marched at once, returning to Arles not as an ally but as a conqueror. Churches and shrines were sacked, the treasures seized: an orgy of destruction in which Mauronte seems to have taken part, for he is next recorded as commanding one of the Saracen columns which, after Arles, destroyed Saint-Rémy, Tarascon, Avignon, Cavaillon and Apt.

Charles Martel's counter-attack was again successful – in fact from then on one is reminded of the attacks, pursuits, counter-attacks, counter-pursuits, which were the pattern of the war in the western desert from 1940 till 1943 – ending with the recapture of Arles. Unfortunately the Frankish king was as brutal in his treatment of the wretched local inhabitants as the Saracens, and one reads of the recapture of Avignon: 'He (Martel) broke in to the sound of his trumpets and burnt Avignon to the ground, massacring Moors and inhabitants indiscriminately. Thus three times stormed and sacked, more than three-quarters destroyed, burnt, the city died . . .'

As usual Charles Martel returned to the north to meet other threats, and once more the Saracens returned to the attack in 739, moving east along the coast. The monasteries of the *Iles de Lérins* and Nice were their principal objectives. Most of the monks on the islands were slaughtered, the monasteries despoiled and Nice was looted and burnt. Again the Franks raced back to the Mediterranean. In the meantime Charles Martel had died, but his son Pepin le Bref proved to be as able a commander as his father. Not only Provence was cleared of the Moslems but Languedoc as well, and with the fall of Narbonne, last Saracen stronghold, in 759, the armies marching to the crescent banner fell back across the Pyrenees.

From then on the Saracens changed their tactics. No more land invasions from Spain were launched; instead major seaborne raids were carried out which kept coastal communities and all Provence up to a hundred miles inland in a constant state of insecurity for more than two centuries. And as if this were not enough the Provençaux were victims of another scourge. The year 859 saw the first of the Norman invasions. Arles and Nîmes were sacked and the whole countryside was ravaged till the Norsemen were defeated tardily by Gerard de Roussillon. Then 'hardly had the blond giants departed than back came the black demons, raiding again and carrying off numerous slaves', and it was no exaggeration on the part of a contemporary chronicler who wrote: 'This lovely country has become a horrible desert over which wolves and other wild beasts wander freely.'

2   *Avignon: the ruined bridge and the river Rhône*

It was in the concluding years of the ninth century, however, that Saracen hold on Provence reached its apogee. The entire coastal area fell and the raiders reached as far inland as Sisteron and Embrun. In a form of savage hallali the Saracens were joined by pillaging bands of Hungarians who crossed the Alps, infiltrating down the Durance valley until defeated by Hugh of Provence in the passes of the Alpilles in 924, the survivors being exterminated by plague the following year. And it was not until 1032, after a brilliant campaign led by 'William the Liberator', that the Saracen menace was finally eliminated and Provence became part of the Holy Roman Empire under Conrad le Salique.

At the beginning of the twelfth century the country provided the spectacle of a vast area divided into three sub-provinces: Provence-Forcalquier, Provence-Barcelona, Provence-Toulouse, sub-divisions which did not make for unity since each strove continually to absorb the others. At last after a succession of minor wars and campaigns and a temporary aggressive alliance between Barcelona and Toulouse aimed at Forcalquier, the three counties split up definitely. Toulouse became Languedoc, Barcelona was from then known as Catalonia, while Forcalquier evolved into the more restricted Provence of later days.

At the time of the conciliation of these separate and independent states Raymond Berenger was Count of Provence and father of four daughters all of whom made brilliant marriages. The eldest, Margaret, became Queen of France after marrying the Prince, later to be known as Saint-Louis. In 1236 the second girl, Eleanor, married Henry III of England. The third, Sancie, married Richard Duke of Cornwall, later to become the Germanic Emperor, and was crowned with her husband at Aix-la-Chapelle, the modern Aachen. The youngest, *lo gento cacoio* (the sweet last-born), notorious for her looks and charm, had many suitors, among them Raymond II of Toulouse, and Peter, son of the King of Aragon. In the end, however, she became the wife of Charles of Anjou, the French king's brother. This youngest sister Beatrice was at first, so we are told, treated in a rather Cinderella-ish fashion by her sisters as being the only non-crowned queen. However, this

3   *Tarascon castle on the river Rhône*

proved to be only a temporary state of affairs and in 1265 she and her husband were crowned 'King and Queen of the Two Sicilies', a title which was further increased when the ambitious Charles became also King of Jerusalem and later Count Charles I of Provence.

His Provençal subjects, however, were far from amenable. As a *foreigner* they disliked him automatically.

First to rebel was the city of Marseille. Charles attacked the city, temporarily broke off the siege to accompany his brother Louis on a crusade, but returned in 1250 determined to bring his rebellious subjects to heel. Marseille held out till 1257– in the meantime Charles had subdued Arles and Avignon – its fall marking the end of its centuries-old quasi-autonomy.

On his death in 1285 Charles I was succeeded by his son Charles II, ardent supporter of Clement V, first of the popes to install himself in Avignon (see p. 42). He was succeeded by his third son Robert (1309) who in turn on his death in 1343 left the various estates over which he ruled to his granddaughter, Jeanne, a girl of 17 married to her cousin Andrew of Hungary.

Jeanne, often referred to as the 'wicked queen', was nevertheless popular with her subjects, and her wickedness is obviously meant to qualify her private rather than her political life. Where her emotions were concerned she was as unscrupulous as she was beautiful. Her sex life was troubled, turbulent and adventurous. Married four times – Andrew of Hungary, Louis of Tarento, Jaime III of Mallorca, Otto of Brunswick – she probably gave orders for the first to be assassinated, was indifferent to the second, adored the third (11 years her junior, handsome as the traditional Apollo, but unfortunately half mad as a result of having been shut up 13 years in an iron cage) and survived the fourth.

None of these marriages produced an heir.

Her direct heir was therefore her cousin Charles of Durazzo, but disliking him intensely she adopted Louis of Anjou, brother of the French king Charles V, proclaiming him her successor – an action which immediately split the country into two rival and warring factions. Charles of Durazzo went further than raising the standard of revolt. In 1382 he managed to arrange for Jeanne to be kidnapped, carried off to a lonely castle, Muro, in the Appennines, and there, her feet and hands strapped to the four corners of a bed, strangled.

The war which followed was merely a continuation of the permanent strife which then seemed an endemic feature of Provençal life. During Jeanne's reign the country had come near total defeat by Languedoc forces under Duguesclin who had captured Tarascon, besieged Arles and Aix, and was only pushed back after bitter fighting when the Provençal troops had been reinforced by contingents from Naples. Impoverished as a result of these wars Jeanne had felt obliged to restore her finances by selling Avignon to the Holy See in 1348 for the sum of 80,000 gold florins.

The civil war between the rival supporters of Jeanne's adopted and natural heirs only ended after Louis of Anjou's death in 1384 thanks to skilful diplomacy on the part of Louis's widow, Marie of Blois, acting as regent to the eight-year-old Louis II, and the fortuitous murder of Charles of Durazzo while on a visit to Hungary. Louis II grew up to be a capable and much-liked ruler but his principal claim to notoriety is the fact that he was the father of 'Good King René' who eventually became Count of Provence and King of Aragon and of Sicily when his elder brother died childless.

Modern historians tend to decry René's qualities as a monarch. Nobody on the other hand denies that he was tolerant (for those days), affable, a lover of nature and the arts, even though insisting that he was more fitted to play the role of monk, philosopher or scholar rather than that of ruler of war-torn domaines.

It is indeed true that the arts flourished during his lifetime, but equally true that on the battlefield he suffered reverse after reverse. Finally his disastrous campaign against Aragon weakened him so much materially that in old age he was forced to yield to near-blackmail on the part of France's Louis XI, nominate an invalid, Charles of Maine, as his heir and renounce his rights to Anjou.

Charles of Maine died before René, and was succeeded by Charles III, who in turn only lived two years after René's death, long enough, however, to be bludgeoned into leaving Provence to the French crown in his testament which was signed on 10 December 1481. The unification of France and Provence was finally ratified at a meeting of the *Etats de Provence* in Aix in 1486, stipulating at the same time that the former independent state should preserve its ancient customs and a substantial measure of its liberties.

Unification and the sixteenth century, however, did not bring any measure of peace. During the reign of François I, Provence was twice invaded by Charles Quint who before being pushed back had himself crowned king of Arles. Scarcely had the country recovered from these invasions than the religious wars broke out. As usual, atrocities were committed on both sides, but the most bloody record of this sad period has been left by Baron Meynier d'Oppède after his savage repression and systematic massacres of the sect known as the *Vaudois*, inhabiting the Luberon *massif*. It was only a terrible counter scourge, a virulent outbreak of plague in 1582, which put a stop to this fruitless and seemingly insoluble conflict.

The seventeenth century saw a more united Provence but one continually at loggerheads with Paris and the representatives of the central authority. In 1658 Louis XIV in person directed a siege of Marseille, ordering the building after its capture of Fort St Nicholas in order to dominate both town and port, while in 1691 it was the turn of rebellious Nice to be assaulted and occupied by the royal army.

Pre-revolutionary eighteenth century brought a slight improvement in the relationships between Paris and Provence, though only in all probability because France in general was forced to forget her family quarrels under the threat of foreign invasion during the wars of the Spanish and Austrian successions. During these wars both Nice and Toulon suffered severely from the ravages of Austro-Sardinian forces before their final defeat by Marshal de Belle-Isle in 1747. As if this were not enough France's most deadly attack of plague broke out in 1720; before it had run its course it accounted for over 100,000 victims, half of them from the city of Marseille alone.

Never really reconciled to their annexation the people of Provence welcomed the Revolution enthusiastically and with an extraordinary violence, seeing in this new movement – to begin with – more of a political means of gaining still-regretted autonomy than a social upheaval. Throughout the old *comté* there was an 'epidemic' of uprisings accompanied by pillage, arson, and murder, reaching its bloodiest excesses in Marseille. Nor was it long before a guillotine was set up in the city's main street, the Canébière, where heads fell as rapidly as in Paris.

On 11 April 1789, the *Société Patriotique des Amis de la Constitution* was formed in the rue Thubaneau, and it was there that Rouget de Lisle's song *Le Chant des Marseillais* was sung for the first time. And it was from the little town of Martigues, on the *Etang de Berre*, that the new flag, the *tricolor*, originated – Martigues consists of three *bourgades*: Ferrières, Jonquières and the Ile Saint Genest. Each had its own flag, blue for Ferrières, white for the Ile, red for Jonquières. When in the sixteenth century the three *bourgades* united to form the town of Martigues, they also united their colours into a single standard. Thus the tricolor flag had been reflected in the canals of Martigues many years before being adopted by the French Revolution.

At Toulon a young Corsican artillery captain, Napoleon Bonaparte, first came to public notice because of his major part in the successful recapture of the city from an occupying Royalist-Spanish-British force, and three years later, 1796, it was from Nice that General Bonaparte, commanding general at the age of only 27, started off on his first Italian campaign with its attendant glory.

Yet in spite of this major participation in the Revolution's early days the Provençaux reacted violently against Napoleon the Emperor, and were as enthusiastic in their support of the returning Bourbons as they had been for the principles of *Liberté, Egalité et Fraternité*. Nowhere was the 'white terror' to claim so many victims as in Provence, exceeding at times the savagery of the 'red terror' of Jacobinism.

One of the few positive results of the Congress of Vienna following on the Napoleonic wars was that Provence was shorn of much of her eastern territory – Nice, and the land up to the Var river being handed over to Sardinia. Forty-six years later, however, after Napoleon III espoused the cause of united Italy and French troops played the major role in the victories of Magenta and Solferino, these same territories together with Savoy returned to France.

The nineteenth century was the most peaceful in Provence's long history. The revolutions of 1830 and 1848 and their resulting changes in regime roused little interest in the south. When after being plebiscited on to the resuscitated imperial throne Napoleon III visited Aix and Marseille it was easy to forget that in 1814, on his way to Elba and exile, his more illustrious uncle had narrowly escaped being lynched.

Above all the nineteenth century was a period when the arts flourished as they had not done since 'Good King René's' time, when trade boomed, and thanks to the fact that the English aristocrat Lord Brougham, turned back from his winter playground, Italy, and became enamoured of the village of Cannes and its surroundings, a new source of wealth, tourism, was discovered.

Though materially untouched by the 1914–18 war, rural districts were hard hit by the fact that a tragic proportion of village youth died in the trenches of Verdun and the Aisne, accounting for the depression of the inter-war years. Losses were infinitely smaller in the second conflict but the people of the *midi* found themselves in the centre of hostilities for the first time for over 150 years.

On 21 June 1940, encouraged by the French collapse before the German onslaught, Mussolini launched his army in a general offensive against the thinly-held Alpine front. The fighting lasted only four days till the armistice on 25 June, but the Italian mass had made little or no impression on the French outpost line. With the cease-fire the south of France was comparatively fortunate in that it was in the unoccupied zone. But this precarious state of semi-independence lasted only till the Allied north African landings in the winter of 1942, when the Germans marched on Toulon and Marseille and the Italians took over the Côte d'Azur. Ten months later, with the collapse of Italy, the Germans occupied the whole of the area.

From then on war came to Provence in earnest. Resistance groups, active in the mountains east and centre, brought inevitable reprisals on the part of the occupying forces in their wake. At the same time the American Air Force mounted an ever-growing attack on strategic objectives as a preliminary to future landings. Unfortunately for the local inhabitants these raids caused greater damage to historical monuments and private property than to genuine military targets combined, tragically, with considerable loss of civilian life.

Eventually the landings of a Franco-American force consisting of General de Lattre de Tassigny's 1st French and General Patch's 7th armies took place on the flat Dramont beaches just to the east of St Raphaël on 15 August 1944. By 15 September Provence had been cleared of the enemy with the exception of a small pocket in the mountains between Menton and Sospel, finally eliminated by the 1st Free French Division in late April of the following year.

Economic recovery came rapidly after war's disasters, much helped by the tourist rush to re-find the sun, a tendency at first confining this renewed prosperity to the coastal areas. At the same time a certain endemic hostility to 'the government' began to manifest itself and a few small communities in Provence were the only ones in all France to say *non* at the time of General de Gaulle's first plebiscite.

Today this traditional *frondeur* element has been still further reinforced by the numbers of *pieds noirs*, the French from Algeria who, one and all, consider that they were betrayed and ruined by their own government, and who in the vast majority have settled in the *midi*, nostalgically hoping that climate and countryside may bring back memories of their beloved north Africa.

Yet the stress in Provence today is on prosperity. The flood of tourists increases yearly. Industrialisation of the once sleepy south is a feature of national planning and economy. As a result the intensive building programme with its emphasis on characterless blocks of flats has changed – and ruined – much of the country-side and the whole of the coast, while factories have hopelessly disfigured many former beauty spots. Fortunately the government saw the warning light and one of the new preoccupations of local authorities, backed by Paris, is to harmonise development to blend with the traditional style: preserving countryside, historical sites and monuments and – this only just in time – what remains of wildlife.

The People

'Provence was in Europe before France existed' is a favourite Provençal saying, and it accounts for the fact that even today when distance has been annihilated by air travel and *autoroutes*, an inhabitant of Arles feels he has little in common with a citizen of Amiens. The Provençal differs fundamentally, physically and mentally, from the Breton, the Alsatian, the Auvergnat, the Parisian: the last-named being usually designated by the hostile and contemptuous term *Parigot*, while all non-Provençal natives, be they from Lille or Leningrad, are dismissed as *estrangers* – foreigners.

Physically the Provençaux are normally small but robust, dark-haired, dark-skinned, dark-eyed, with a tendency to put on weight with years. Mercurial by nature they offer a mixture of laziness and an astonishing capacity for sustained effort, due to the fact that exaltation and acute depression can alternate within minutes. In the same way their ebullient temperament makes it possible for quarrels to flare up over a trifle in the space of a few seconds, swiftly to be followed by effusive reconciliation, when embraces succeed blows. This characteristic also means that voices tend to be loud and gestures over-emphasised; the stranger from the north on his first visit to the old town of Nice, for instance, could have the uncomfortable impression that all round him the most ferocious quarrels were raging, when in fact the persons concerned were merely indulging in a little gossip.

The original surprise giving way to comprehension it then seems that such volatility is indicative of an easy-going approach to life in general, which in turn is basically deceptive. Below this slightly endearing characteristic is a deep, half-hidden streak of violence and cruelty with a medieval conviction that after all life is comparatively cheap, combined with a near-Moslem fatalism. One has only to watch a typical crowd following a hearse from church to cemetery to realise this. Particularly in villages a funeral is an event and the cortège is followed by scores of chattering, joking, smoking individuals who were barely casual acquaintances of the defunct. Unless the coffin contains a child little or no grief is shown.

It is rather significant too that only in the south of France is the Spanish national sport of bullfighting permitted, and that the great arenas of Arles and Nîmes are veritable Meccas of taur-omachy.

Napoleon, after narrowly escaping being lynched at Orgon *en route* for Elba, though himself a southerner remarked with considerable bitterness: '*C'est une méchante race que les Provençaux. Ils ont commis toutes sortes d'horreurs dans la revolution, mais quand il s'agit de se battre avec courage, alors ce sont des laches.*' ('They're a bad lot those *Provençaux*. They committed every conceivable atrocity during the Revolution, but when it comes to putting up a brave fight, they're a bunch of cowards.') I do not consider for a moment that the accusation of cowardice was justified, but that of violence – particularly in the cities – certainly rings true. On the other hand I find that most Provençaux have the excellent characteristic described in the psalm: 'He that sweareth unto his neighbour and disappointeth him not, even though it were to his own hindrance' – in other words one could not ask for a better, a more loyal friend.

This highly individual character was well summed up in a

speech delivered at a *Fête de l'Olive* held at Fontvieille, a small town near Daudet's mill, in June 1970 – 'With his hot blood and love of *contestation* and freedom, the Provençal is a turbulent individual, but his spirit is proud, his heart generous. We may be sure that if indeed any of our forefathers have spent long periods in purgatory, by now they are in Paradise . . .'

Another characteristic – more noticeable with the older generation and in smaller communities – which causes a certain amount of friction is a marked lack of sense of time, so exasperating to those who base their philosophy on the belief that 'time is money'. A settler in a Provençal village who imagines that mason, carpenter or plumber speaking of 'tomorrow' has in mind a period of twenty-four hours is in for a rude shock – 'tomorrow' may well mean next week, month or even year.*

Undoubtedly climate and countryside have much to do with this outlook. As Posidonius said, 'The country is wild.' In summer the temperature can rise to over 100 degrees Fahrenheit, dropping in winter to as little as fifteen, ice thick on roads. Nice has an average annual rainfall of 754 mm as against 560 mm in Paris, but whereas the fall in Paris is spaced evenly over the year, that in Nice – and Provence generally – occurs almost entirely from mid-October to mid-December with a small subsidiary rainy season usually from late February to mid-April. The result is that, swept as it is by the violent west wind known as the *mistral*, which has an almost unbelievable drying effect, the soil, until the recent introduction of modern farming methods and implements and the creation of huge artificial lakes serving the triple purpose of irriga-

---

* A village butcher, himself a true Provençale born and bred, told me that he had once asked the local carpenter to make him a small chest of drawers. The carpenter warned that he was busy but that he would have the job done by the following week. The butcher, understanding the significance of 'next week', did not show signs of restlessness till ten months had passed. After two years he was aggrieved. Finally after eight years had passed he went to the carpenter and said, 'Now look! I've had enough. I don't want the damn chest of drawers!' The carpenter looked at him horrified and said, 'But you can't do a thing like this to me. I've just bought the wood to make it!'

tion, power production and recreation, was more the enemy than the friend of both peasant and shepherd.

Now that life is becoming so much easier for the Provençal, it will be an interesting study for future generations to decide whether the new era affluence will take away much of the *midi*'s individuality to make way for a progressive national uniformity. Already an element which may prove decisive in this direction is the neglect and gradual disappearance of local dialects and in particular the traditional Provençal, though there are still some who feel that such a disappearance would constitute a sad artistic loss.

For centuries the linguistic barrier separating Aix from Paris was considered as one of the main bastions of the people's jealous independent spirit, but the tendency to be dominated by 'centralisation', heritage of the Revolution, was strongly marked by the middle of the nineteenth century. The young, eyes turned towards Paris, saw little point in learning two languages. In any case who would think of conducting business in Provençal?

The reaction to this trend was the 'Provençal Renaissance' started by Joseph Roumanille, poet and gardener's son, and reaching its apogee under Frederic Mistral, born at Maillane near St Rémy-de-Provence in 1834. On 24 May 1854, Mistral, together with seven other poets, describing themselves as *felibres*, founded the *Felibrige* Society whose object, via its review *L'Armana Provençau* (The Provençal Almanach) was 'to raise up, honour and defend the mother tongue, now so sadly despised and neglected', and 'to bring joy, relaxation and happy hours to all the people of the *midi* . . .'.

Mistral's success was meteoric. It became fashionable even for those who had previously ignored the very existence of Provençal as a tongue to read *Mireille* in the original version. But Mistral's triumph was more academic than demographic. A century after the *Felibrige* Society's foundation, two world wars, the advent of radio and television, together with general industrialisation, seemed to have dealt near-mortal blows to dreams of regional political or artistic autonomy. Yet in the space of the last few years a certain nostalgia, combined with a reborn fear that

Mistral's heritage may be irrevocably dissipated, seems to be showing itself, and paradoxically the movement is more marked among the young of urban than rural communities.

Many of the *midi*'s larger towns have their *Felibrige* groups, and though it would be the grossest exaggeration to suggest that the *farandole* is on the way to becoming more popular than the latest evolution of the twist, there are nevertheless a number of teenagers who enjoy dressing up in the traditional costumes and giving performances of Provençal dances at the various fêtes and festivals following each other in unbroken succession during the summer months.

The Arts

Few French painters, musicians, writers, today or in the past, have not been either born in the *midi* or deeply influenced by the Provençal atmosphere.

In the Dark Ages the troubadours of Provence provided the only light relief in a generally gloomy, savage era, with their love songs a mixture of themes celestial and profane, pure and libertine, and their rhymed epics appealing to all strata of society. In view of the widespread illiteracy of the day the majority of those whose works and reputation have survived were of comparatively noble birth, though there is little doubt that professional strolling troubadours who depended on their art for their living must have been equally, if not more, talented.

One of the earliest of these dilettante minstrels, mentioned by Nostradamus, was Raoulx de Gassin, born in Gassin castle near Grimaud – '*Il fut par le moyen de ses graces et vertus singulières en poésie toujours trés bienvenu entre les plus grands, et même des prelats et gens de l'Eglise ...*' while another, Raimbaud of Orange (in Provence) Nostradamus noted – '*Ce poète s'adonna à poursuivre l'amour des Dames d'Honneur à la louange desquelles il composa et fit merveille ...*' There were in fact over 200 of these troubadours whose works it was claimed laid the foundations of the renaissance of the arts which reached its apogee under 'good' King René's patronage.

Like most artistic movements the troubadours also had their mad genius, Piere Vidal, son of a Toulouse furrier, who was firmly convinced that he was destined to be Emperor of Byzantium and spent much of his time preparing for his future coronation. He had the reputation of being the Caruso – or, if one prefers it, the Franco Corelli – of his day. But if his voice was golden his verses were often vinegary, even abusive, and since he was 'only the son of a furrier' a few injudicious rhymes resulted in him having his tongue slit on the orders of the Chevalier de Saint-Gilles. After this salutary punishment Vidal took shelter with one of his patrons, Hugues des Baux, and was lucky enough to recover. In 1227 he left Marseille in a vessel presumably bound for Constantinople. He got as far as Greece where, in his naïvety, he married a Greek woman 'who pretended that she was the Emperor of Constantinople's niece and that the Eastern Empire belonged to her'. Later, after a sad disillusionment and return to his native land he fell in love with a woman calling herself *La Louve* (the She-wolf). In an original attempt to win her affections he 'dressed himself in a wolf's skin, whereupon he was attacked by shepherds' dogs and so badly bitten that he was carried almost moribund into his She-wolf's castle'.

Petrarch can be said to have evolved from the troubadours. Born at Arezzo, his family exiled for political reasons, he became a Provençal by predilection. Though remembered above all for his love of Laura de Noves which inspired his best-known *canzoni*, others of his works such as *Les Triomphes*, composed largely at the Fontaine de Vaucluse, were equally important. Skipping a couple of centuries, another great writer whose name became irrevocably linked with Provence was François de Malherbe, born at Caen in 1555, who in 1581 married the daughter of the President of the Aix Parliament. Settling in Aix, Malherbe became a great friend of the poet and astrologer César de Nostradame, better known as Nostradamus.

Before Malherbe's day, however, King René, himself a writer and composer of genuine talent, had been a true patron of the arts. If for example a canvas pleased him he would give the artist the right to call himself 'by letters patent, painter Royal to King René'. Two of the best known of these painters Royal were Barthélémy de Clive and Nicolas Fromont, the latter responsible for the superb reredos 'The Burning Bush' which is the greatest treasure of St Sauveur Cathedral, Aix.

The late seventeenth and early eighteenth century Provençal painters regained the fame that had been theirs in King René's day, the first of the new school being Nicolas Mignard and the Pugets, father and son, Pierre and François. They were followed by what is sometimes called the Parrocel tribe, since this family produced no less than thirteen well-known artists, five of whose works still survive. The most famous; Charles, grandson of the first of the 'tribe' painted an equestrian portrait of Louis xv which so pleased the monarch that on the death of the official court artist Hyacinth Rigaud a portion of the latter's pension was bequeathed to his young rival. Charles Parrocel's *Halte des Grenadiers de la Maison du Roi* can be seen in the Louvre today.

Another tribe, though smaller, was the Van Loo.

The original, first of seven, Jacob van Loo, born in 1614, wandered south from his native Holland in search of the sun. Following in his father's footsteps Abraham-Louis married an Aixoise and settled in the country. The last of the family, Jules, died in Paris as recently as 1921. Agreeable painters as were the van Loos they did not reach the same heights as Joseph Vernet, born at Avignon in 1714, rightly considered as one of Provence's greatest artists : or that of the Grasse-born Fragonard, as renowned in his day for his good humour as for his Arcadian portrayal of life's gentler and more refined aspects.

During the nineteenth century artists flocked to Provence in even greater numbers. They came not only for climatic reasons but also to capture the countryside's charm on their canvases, and above all, breaking away from tradition, its dazzling light. The apostles, precursors of the new school, were Van Gogh, Cézanne, Renoir and to a lesser extent Gauguin. Van Gogh, in particular was fascinated by the sun, the explosion of contrasts in stark angry strata of luminosity, after Holland's mellowed tones. Cézanne, born in Aix in 1839, and who lived to see the turn of the century, became the model for those who first dared to defy the subdued effects considered decorous by the Academy, scandalising traditionalists by their use of vivid yellows and reds, those colours which in fact streak the Sainte Victoire's southern slopes and the Gorges du Verdon's formidable cliffs.

Today, however, colour is no longer a novelty, and such great figures of modern art who spend most of their time in the *midi* – Picasso, Max Ernst, Chagall – are no longer attempting to translate the *midi*'s shimmering rocks, the heat-drenched Durance valley, the olive's silver sheen, but rather the plastic reverberations of their own minds.

In the world of music Felicien David, composer of the seldom-performed opera *La Perle de Brésil*, and Reyer, composer of the equally forgotten operas *Salammbo* and *Sigurd*, were both Provençal born, but it was two non-southerners, Bizet and Gounod, who with *L'Arlésienne* and *Mireille* – the former based on a Daudet story included in *Lettres de Mon Moulin*, the latter on Mistral's great epic *Miréio* – who most evoke the whole atmosphere of the Rhône valley and the spirit of its inhabitants. It is a pity that Gounod's *Mireille* is practically unknown to British opera lovers, for it contains music of an infinite nostalgic charm on which Gounod worked in close co-operation with Mistral himself.

From the mid-nineteenth century till the present day Provence has occupied a solid position on the French literary scene. Internationally Daudet is best known for his *Lettres de Mon Moulin* and his *Tartarin de Tarascon*. Both Merimée, and later Zola, were strongly affected by the *nostalgie du midi*, while the present-day authors, Marcel Pagnol, Jean Giono and Henri Bosco, seldom look beyond Provence's frontiers for their inspiration. In Britain's period of opulence the Riviera was richly portrayed by Oppenheimer, while many who have never been near Antibes have probably heard of Somerset Maugham's 'three fat women'; and, more recently, Françoise Sagan's earlier heroines undertook their first journeys on permissive society's sexual *autoroute* under Provence's balmy skies.

The Country

Though the age of jet air travel has made it possible for anyone with only a fortnight's holiday to visit India or Alaska, it has taken away much of travel's intrinsic pleasure. One can be in Nice within an hour and a half of leaving Heathrow, but on arrival there is no feeling of having made a journey. None of the pleasure of going from A to B in the gradual transition from one scene to the next, whetting the appetite like the succession from *hors d'oeuvres* to savoury, has been experienced.

I made my first journey to the south of France in winter, leaving Victoria in fog, the Channel unpleasantly choppy, melancholy northern France's roads mostly icebound. Paris was bitterly cold and the stuffy heat of a crowded second-class *couchette* almost welcome. But when dawn broke the train was already in the neighbourhood of Toulon. Instead of a mere lightening of prevalent nordic gloom the sun rose in a cloudless sky of dazzling blue above an equally azure sea, making one feel that the term *Côte d'Azur* was more than justified. And as one moved leisurely towards Nice there was time to appreciate this vital contrast and to adjust oneself, not only physically but mentally, before the actual fact of arrival.

This gradual sense of a changing world is the reason that makes a journey by road the ideal medium – even more than the train – for a first visit to Provence. A geographical upheaval becomes almost immediately evident after crossing an imaginary east-west line running through Lyon, particularly so on the picturesque highway known as the Route Napoleon which cuts across the Alps' western foothills, through Grenoble, and over the pass known as the Col Bayard.

The summit of this 4,000-foot pass marks what the *Guide Bleu* calls the *septentrional* limit of the Mediterranean climate. It is an accurate if somewhat prosaic observation. Coming from Grenoble and starting on the downward slope, the land of dark forests of giant pines, lush green meadows and luxuriant valleys, carrying with them promise of rain, of swirling mists and an obscured sun, are left behind to emerge into the typical bright sharply outlined

Provençal contours, stunted pines and squat ilexes interspersed with rock outcrops, river-beds of bleached pebbles where for many months of the year the river threads its course through shallow isolated channels of doubtful survival, and the silvery fascination of millenary olive groves.

Yet one of Provence's greatest charms is the infinite variety of its scene. I know of no other region – certainly in Europe – where within so limited an area so many of nature's aspects are presented to please the greatest scale of tastes. From the long coastal stretch with its alternating sandy and stony beaches where the very hardy may swim all the year round, it is only 40 kilometres to the nearest ski-ing resorts. A bare quarter of an hour's drive from the crowded, glaring, perfume-industry city of Grasse, and on the main Draguignan road, is the *fjord*-ish St Cassien lake. St Paul-de-Vence's medieval silhouette surveys stretches of blocks-of-flats-mutilated coastline. The near unbelievable stillness of the walled village of Bargème in the Haut Var is a bare 30 miles from the important road junction of Castellane. When the higher ground is hard and bleak in winter the lower slopes of the Estérel are a blaze of mimosa, fruit blossom, and orange and lemon trees heavy with fruit. In summer when the coast is hot, sticky and dried up, the upper Var hills are first a solid gold from a myriad bushes of flowering Spanish broom, then, as the hot weather is all-embracing, a deep purple from vast fields of lavender. Only a short day's motoring separates the Camargue's steamy atmosphere, swamps and rice fields, from Barcelonnette's crystal clear heady air and brightly dancing Alpine torrents. Provence caters equally for those who like crowded cities, lonely villages, the sea, lakes, stretches of cultivated land, wild and barren vistas, green valleys and snow-capped peaks, those who wish to study Roman remains, medieval castles or art treasures of succeeding ages.

As regards the question, what is the best time of the year to visit the south of France? the answer, unless one is a ski maniac or interested solely in flesh scorching on overcrowded, under-shaded beaches, is May–June or September.

During the two late spring months the countryside is still green

and flower-covered, more luxuriant even than most nordic land-
scapes at the same time of the year. The summer rush has not
started. Accommodation can be found and prices have not leaped
for the benefit of the summer invaders. It is pleasantly warm,
shorts-and-sandals weather; but nights remain fresh, while days
are long, ideal for leisurely motoring. By September it is true the
summer sun has scorched the earth. Flowers, the meadows' green,
have disappeared, making an olive tree's thrown shadow doubly
welcome, but the country has returned, albeit somewhat jaded, to
normal after the hectic artificiality of the holiday months, as have
prices in hotels, restaurants and shops. Furthermore in recent
years September has been more reliable climatically than either
May or early June, blessed with a comforting Indian summer,
warm during the day, fresh at night, yet with no hint or reminder
of the melancholy fact of winter's approach.

4   Orange: the triumphal arch

2. Avignon

'*Qui n'a pas vu Avignon du temps des Papes, n'en a rien vu. ...*' wrote Daudet, and he goes on to say, 'It was without rival for gaiety and endless feasting. . . . Cardinals sailed up the Rhône in stately barges bedecked with wind-tossed banners, the Papal guards sang Latin chants in the squares, the mendicant friars prattled ceaselessly, and all the houses, thronging like bees round the great palace, hummed with constant activity of all kinds. . . . Ah! Happy town! Where the soldiers' weapons were blunt and the wine was stored in the state prisons, where war and want were unknown. . . .'

Today Avignon is still a fascinating and attractive city despite being on one of the Continent's main tourist routes and gnawed by the cancer of a *zone industrielle*. Vestiges of the past more than hold their own with the encroachment of 'progress' and it will, I hope, be many years before the cult of materialism has finally destroyed such superb monuments as the Papal palace and St Bénézet's bridge.

Due to its position on the Rhône Avignon was well known even before the Roman era, yet it would never have attained its international notoriety, but rather have remained subsidiary to both Aix and Arles, had it not been for its brief glory as the centre of western Christianity. After having risen to the status of Roman colony under the Emperor Hadrian it became plunged into centuries of war and bloodshed with Rome's decline and fall. Successive invaders, Goths and Vandals, looked upon it as a keypoint in their supply lines, inevitably passing for preference by the river rather than over the bare tracks glorified by the name 'road'. Then from the first half of the eighth century it became one of the main Saracen targets, and as such was pillaged and sacked not only by the soldiers of the Crescent but by those of the Cross when Charles Martel and his successors came sweeping down from the north in their retaliatory expeditions.

By the time the Saracen menace had been finally eliminated Avignon, and to a slightly lesser extent Arles, became a frontier town when the Rhône marked the boundary between the kingdom of France and the Holy Roman Empire. Till very recent times in fact boatmen could call out 'Reiame!' or 'Emperi!' according to whether they were heading for the western or eastern bank. Yet in spite of war, bloodshed, invasion and counter-invasion Avignon became a centre of the troubadours and the famous Courts of Love which must have been such a welcome contrast to the omnipresent battlefields of past centuries: graced in particular by a certain Adelais, Countess of Forcalquier and Avignon. 'In her person, if we may believe her biographers, this noble lady united all those qualities of physical beauty and mental charm the Troubadours most delighted to sing; and in delicate questions of love and gallantry, in the amorous disputes between knights and dames that came before the Courts over which she presided, her discretion and wisdom were never appealed to in vain . . .' (Thomas Okey, *The Story of Avignon*.)

Furthermore, once freed from the Saracen menace, by skilfully remaining aloof from the internecine squabbles of the great southern families claiming Provence as their fief, the people of Avignon managed to secure a high degree of independence. In 1206 William of Forcalquier confirmed the city's status of autonomous republic which had been granted tentatively seventy years previously.

It was during this semi-official republican period, in 1177, that a youth named Bénézet, a shepherd boy, arrived in the city saying that he had been ordered by God to build a bridge across the Rhône. According to François Nouguier, who recorded the story in 1659, he had been watching his flock when, he said, he heard a mysterious voice which instinctively he knew to be that of Christ saying, 'I will that thou leave thy sheep, for thou shalt make me a bridge over the river Rhône'. The boy answered that as his total fortune amounted to three farthings and he had no knowledge of anything except guarding sheep he did not see how he could ever build a bridge. 'Little Benet,' replied the voice, 'even as I shall show thee.'

The youth then set off, and on the way was met by an angel disguised as a pilgrim who led him to a spot on the river-bank opposite the city, told him to cross by ferry and present himself to the bishop, explaining what was his mission and on whose orders he was acting. The bishop, as can be imagined, was not impressed, accused 'little Benet' of blasphemy, and played with the idea of commanding his hands and feet to be amputated. However, after having called in the Provost it was decided to put the presumptuous youth to trial. 'I know right well that a bridge must be built of stone and lime. I will give thee a stone I have at my palace,' said the Provost, 'and if thou canst move it and carry it away I will believe thou canst build the bridge.'

The 'stone' was a vast slab of rock which forty strong men could not have lifted. 'Little Benet' raised it as easily as if it were a small pebble. 'Then did the Provost kneel before him and kissed his hands and feet and cast down before him 300 pieces of silver . . .'

Hearing of this miracle volunteers flocked to have the privilege of helping to build the bridge, which was completed after twelve years. And since it was the only stone bridge across the Rhône between Lyon and the Mediterranean its completion enormously increased the city's importance.

Unfortunately for the peace of Avignon the city then became involved in the wars against the sectarians known generally as the Albigenses, considered as dangerous heretics not only by the established church but also by the kings of France. The Albigenses, who had a considerable following among all strata of society in Provence, it should be noted, were not as is rather generally believed Protestants or Huguenots. In fact Ford Madox Ford insists

(*Provence*) 'the poor Albigenses were not even Christians'. They had indeed denied most of the basic doctrines of Christianity but one has the feeling that their cause was espoused so fervently by the Provençaux more as an expression of their endemic anti-governmental tendencies than a declaration of faith. But whatever the reason the result was a war more disastrous, more hideous, than at the time of the Saracen invasions; in particular one thinks of the appalling atrocities committed at Béziers when the city fell to the Catholic army from the north. The Albigensien Avignon-nais – it should not be forgotten – had also shown themselves rivals in cruelty when in 1218 they captured the Prince of Orange and flayed him alive.

The city was besieged by Louis VIII in 1226 for several months and finally captured to the accompaniment of such horrors as disease, famine and plagues of poisonous black flies. In January .1227 the Cardinal Legate pronounced sentence on Avignon, among the principal clauses being 'all heretics to be expelled, their property burned, walls and towers to be razed; all arms to be surrendered to the King of France's representatives; 6,000 marks of silver to be contributed towards further anti-heretical campaigns'. The Avignon republican status was abolished and the city came directly under the sovereignty of Raymond Berenger, Count of Provence.

A further tragedy was only just averted in 1247 when quarrels and scuffles broke out between crusaders *en route* to embark at Aigues-Mortes and townspeople, when (Saint) Louis, refusing to listen to his nobles and punish the city, remarked, 'I have taken the Cross to avenge the insults done to Jesus Christ, and not to myself or my father.'

In 1305 Raymond de Got, Archbishop of Bordeaux, was elected Pope on the death of Benedict XI. At that time the situation in northern Italy as well as in Rome was chaotic. The bitter war between Guelfs and Ghibellines was at its height. There was no security for anyone, pope, noble or peasant. Raymond de Got, who assumed the name of Clement V, was a prudent man. A Frenchman, he decided to stay in France, and although crowned at Lyon finally after much hesitation chose Avignon as the Papacy's future city.

This was the beginning of that era of splendour and prosperity which transformed Avignon from a provincial city to the capital of the Christian world and Mecca of the arts.

Dying nine years after his election Clement v was succeeded by Jacques d'Eusse, Bishop of Avignon, under the name of John xxii, who though 72 years old at the time of his election occupied the papal throne for 18 years. It was Benoit xii, however, who inaugurated the work on the huge building, half palace, half fortress, completed during the time of his successor Clement vi, the papal palace described by Froissart as 'the most beautiful and the strongest house in the world', which fortunately for those who can still be impressed by sheer architectural beauty has survived the vicissitudes of time and man. During the same period every form of art suddenly burst into the bloom of a new spring. The leading painters, sculptors and architects, not only from France but the Low Countries and Italy, flocked to the city of the popes. It became an honour to be considered as of the 'Avignon school'. The printers produced illuminated text; blowers the finest glass. From the looms came elaborate and beautiful tapestries and silks.

The Pope's temporal power also increased. John xxii is said to have left more than 25 million gold florins. In 1348 the Pope, Clement vi, agreed to receive Queen Jeanne, accused, with probable justification, of the murder of her first husband, Andrew of Hungary, after her flight from Naples to Avignon to avoid the vengeance of Andrew's brother Louis.

The 'reception' was really an unofficial trial. Jeane was obliged to face the accusations launched at her by various members of the Curia. She did so with such success that Clement declared her not guilty and admitted the right of her second husband, Louis of Taranto, to call himself Count of Provence and King of Jerusalem.

Nobody can really tell, however, whether this papel pardon was connected with the fact that shortly afterwards Jeanne sold the city of Avignon to the Holy See for the comparatively trifling sum of 80,000 florins, a sale ratified on 21 June 1348.

The popes remained 71 years in Avignon, from 1305 to 1376, but the latter half of this period was far from being the earthly paradise depicted so enthusiastically by Daudet. Prosperity continued, increased almost yearly, but there was a dark side including an extraordinary series of trials for witchcraft and pacts with the devil. One of the many but earlier victims of this witch-hunt was no less a person than the Bishop of Cahors, who after being horribly tortured was finally flayed alive and roasted over a slow fire.

In 1361 the Black Death accounted for nine cardinals, 100 prelates and 17,000 citizens, and in 1363 an arctic winter blighted vines, olive and fruit trees. Five years later, in 1366, Avignon was forced to pay 200,000 gold florins to that army of brigands known as the *Routiers*, headed by Bertrand de Guesclin.

Last of the Avignon popes was Gregory xi, successor of Urban v in 1370. By then there were strong influences at work within Italy to bring the Pope back to Rome. In 1375 there was open revolt accompanied by bloodshed. In Italian cities non-Italian prelates were murdered by crowds calling them *demoni incarnati*. At the same time Gregory, not a strong character, was besieged with letters from that strange personage St Catherine of Sienna, imploring him to return to St. Peter's city and who eventually arrived in Avignon in 1376. Though Catherine was only a dyer's daughter she was not afraid to speak her mind – via an interpreter since she knew no Latin and Gregory not a word of Italian – accusing Avignon and the Papal Palace of being a 'hell of filthy vices'. To everyone's astonishment Gregory submitted docilely to these reproaches. One might say more than docilely for after a good three months St Catherine's battering-ram tactics bore fruit. Gregory announced his intention of abandoning Avignon.

His decision caused general consternation. The King of France urged him to stay. The Pontifical Court was horrified. Gregory, however, now clung to his decision with the stubborn obstinacy of a basically weak man.

Bishop Aneilh, who was obliged to accompany the Pope, commented on the departure, 'Hélas! What tears were shed on the day of supreme affliction. On leaving our dear Provence all the travellers gave vent to their feelings. Never had anyone seen or heard such groans, tears, moans, sighs and lamentations. Ah! the pain of being torn from thee, blessed land, exceeds that of a woman in labour.'

The people of Avignon were stunned. Recovering from the shock they refused to admit that theirs was no longer the papal city. When Gregory died the Christian world was suddenly aware of what was to become known as the Great Schism: a Pope in Rome, Urban VI, an anti-Pope in Avignon, Clement VII. The schism was to last 40 years, ending only after the last anti-Pope, a Spaniard, Pedro de Luna, gradually abandoned by all his followers, had shut himself up in the palace with a handful of faithful retainers, resisting a seventeen-month siege by Marshal Boucicault before escaping in the night by a secret underground passage and fleeing to Spain.

Avignon, from then on ruled by a Papal Legate, remained papal property for a further 400 years till, in 1791, an act of formal annexation to Revolutionary France was ratified; though it was not until 19 February 1797 that the Pope, in article 6 of the Treaty of Tolentino, renounced his rights not only to the city but also to the Comtat Venaissin.

The palace was indeed lucky to survive the Revolution. On 1 October 1792, the city council demanded authorisation to destroy it, but the fact that it was serving as a barracks and a prison brought a reprieve. It remained a barracks till just after the First World War and it was only in 1920 that the admirable work of restoration – still in progress – was begun.

On approaching Avignon one's first impression is of the ramparts surrounding the entire city proper. Originally of the fourteenth century they were restored in the nineteenth by Viollet-le-Duc. This – to my mind – well carried out and highly necessary work has provoked much ink-spilling on the part of protesting purists: protests which I find totally invalid. If ancient monuments are not restored they crumble, fall, disappear. An intelligent reconstruction painstakingly carried out which seeks to re-create the original image in every detail is surely preferable to a blank space occupied by a few unconnected stones, or modern buildings bearing a small plaque to the effect that they have been erected 'on the site of the ancient ramparts'.

One may object that these walls in their present form are not high enough to offer a serious obstacle or argue that their geometrical symmetry is too perfect. To the former objection it should be pointed out that the vast and profound moat, major feature of the defence, has been filled in to make a circular road: and to the latter one may quote Viollet-le-Duc's own words, 'To restore a building is to reinstate it in a condition of completeness which could never have existed at any given time . . .'

A visit to the palace seems to be the natural start to a tour of the city. It would be difficult to imagine anyone failing to be moved at first sight, and Froissart's description comes automatically to mind. Indeed in appearance the exterior, with its sheer walls, windowless but loopholed, dominating machicolated towers and massive gateways so obviously designed to resist attack, is pure fortress.

It is a pity on the other hand that the interior can only be seen at set hours, in groups under a guide's direction, which excludes the possibility of lingering over any detail, especially during the summer months when the throng is so great and groups are so big that the guide has finished his set piece and is hurrying on to the next hall or room before those at the end of the queue have had time to indulge in more than a preliminary glance.

Little, sadly, is left of former glories other than the fabulous dimensions. Revolutionary mobs and generations of soldiers, no respecters of art treasures, murals or gothic sculpture, combined blind vandalism with a plunderer's greed.

Today the huge Court of Honour which opens out from the entrance is used as a theatre during the summer months, devoted somewhat incongruously to works of the most modern dramatists and expressions of 'pop' art. From there the guide takes one to the vast *Salle du Consistoire*, the walls hung with five Gobelins tapestries, the most interesting showing the burning of Rome, where once were frescoes which if one can believe contemporary writers were among the most beautiful in the world.

St John's Chapel leads off from this hall, constructed in the tower of the same name, decorated by frescoes showing scenes from the life of John the Baptist and John the disciple, painted between 1346–8 by Matteo Giovanetti da Viterbo, and from there one is taken into Clement vi's kitchen, surmounted by an enormous pyramid chimney. Popular but completely unfounded rumour states that the great fires below were used not only to prepare papal dinners but also to heat Inquisition implements of torture: even, on occasion, to roast heretics.

The Pope's bedroom is surprisingly small and simple in the midst of such surrounding luxury and aura of space, and it seems strange also that the walls of the room known as the *Chambre de Cerf* in the *Tour de la Garde-Robe* should have been decorated with secular rather than religious subjects. Instead of scenes from the lives of saints are portraits of simple rural life. I noticed, faded by time, a fisherman with his net, a pond, rabbits in a field, and even, most unexpected of all, a group of naiads feigning alarm at the approach of a hunter. These murals were also in all probability the work of Matteo Giovanetti and his French pupils.

Parts of the 'Old' Palace are still not open to the public, one of them being the *Tour de la Glacière* adjoining the kitchen where on 16–17 October 1791, sixty people were murdered by revolutionaries, an atrocity still referred to as *La Massacre de la Glacière*.

In the wing to the left of the entrance, known as the 'New' Palace, are the *Salle de Grande Audience* and the Pontifical Chapel, the latter one of the finest examples of French Gothic, whose single nave is 156 feet long and whose ogival vaults rise to a height of 70 feet.

Avignon is certainly a bewildering city. In the summer of 1970 this magnificent chapel was used as a gallery for the latest Picassos,

a large number of them so anatomical that they seemed to be
genial reproductions by a great artist of subject matter normally
associated with pre-war Port Said post-cards.

Adjoining the Palace is the Basilica, also known as the Cathedral
church of *Notre Dame des Doms*, raised in the twelfth century on
the site of an early Christian church, whose clock tower is surmounted by a huge gilded statue of the Virgin dating from 1859, a
statue which generally gives rise to even more acid comments than
Viollet-le-Duc's restored ramparts. The entrance, a mixture of
Gothic and pseudo-classical, is flanked on either side by statues of
St Mary Magdalene and St Martha.

In pre-revolutionary days the cathedral was apparently a
veritable museum, but little remains of the former treasures. On
the left in the first chapel is a romanesque altar used by the popes
but stripped of its original ornamentation. In the second, also to
the left is a nineteenth-century pseudo-Gothic tomb of Benedict
XII. In the choir, to the left of the high altar, is the twelfth-century
marble throne of the Avignon popes, decorated with carvings of
St Luke's ox and the lion of St Mark, and a modern cenotaph to
the 'brave Crillon'.* Of the many statues the most moving is that
of the repentant St Peter, by Puget, to be seen in the third chapel
to the right. Records show that 150 'cardinals, prelates and
legates' were buried in this cathedral church; but of these,
monuments to only two, Domenico Grimaldi and Marini,
both vice-legates, are to be seen today in the third chapel to the
left.

From Notre Dame des Doms one should go up to the *Rocher
des Doms* – now a well-laid-out public garden – on which the
original pre-Roman town was built. Though carefully planned
and well cared for the garden is somewhat prosaic. One finds the
inevitable duck-pond, an oak tree planted by Marshal Canrobert
after his triumphal return from the Crimea, and a somewhat
gloomy snack restaurant offering the eternal *assiette anglaise*.

* A distinguished general, friend of Henri IV, Louis Balbis de Berton de
Crillon, boasted to have taken part in more battles and to have received
more wounds than any man in France (1543–1615).

The view from the garden's north-west corner is, however, far from prosaic.

Rivers have always fascinated me, and though in comparison with American or Asian giants, or even the Danube, the Rhône's course is a short one, it has all the natural attributes, the grandeur, the pride, of the mightiest of streams, and is in addition one of the world's most historic waterways.

From the *Rocher des Doms* one looks down on the river curving in a great sweep in two arms separated by the green *Ile de Barthelasse* which rejoin below the modern bridge to race on towards Arles and the sea. Thrusting out forlornly into the stream is all that is left of 'little Benet's bridge', four arches only out of the original 22, the second supporting the fourteenth-century St Nicholas chapel, built in two storeys so that the saint's relics should be safely above the highest flood level, and which is open to the public. The gradual disintegration of the bridge began as far back as 1602 when three of the arches collapsed, to be followed in 1633 by two more. In 1650 the gaps were linked up by wooden constructions but these were swept away by floods in 1670. Petty squabbles and avarice prevented any serious repairs. Louis xiv and his successors claimed that repair costs should be borne by the papal legates. Rome insisted that responsibility lay with the French government. Little by little therefore the fruits of St Bénézet's miraculously inspired construction were lost in successive floods.

The song, 'Sur le pont d'Avignon', must be known to millions who have never seen, and are not likely to see, the bridge. The words, however, according to all experts give an erroneous impression. The bridge is not and never was wide enough to be danced upon. Fêtes were held beneath its arches on the *Ile de la Barthelasse* and the word *sur* is a French misrepresentation of the Provençal pronunciation of *sous*.

Beyond the river and again best seen from the *rocher* is Villeneuve-les-Avignon, old, unspoiled, protected by the squat but immensely powerful fort of St André spread over the summit of the rock known as Mont Andaon, its approach guarded by Philippe le Bel's tower.

To visit the city itself it is best to return to the *Place du Palais* – even though far from central, a convenient parking place – a short walk only from the city's principal square, officially the *Place Clemenceau* but almost universally known as the *Place de l'Horloge*, at the head of a central avenue, the *Rue de la République*, becoming as it nears the railway station the *Cours Jean-Jaurès*.

The Place, shaded by the ubiquitous giant plane trees – its milling pigeons reminding one of Trafalgar Square or the Piazza San Marco – is lined almost exclusively by cafés and restaurants, some of them remarkably cheap (one can get an extremely 'honest' meal for as little as ten or even eight francs): its centre adorned by an elaborate statue, the work of F. Charpentier, unveiled in 1891 to mark the centenary of the French annexation of the Comtat Venaissin.

Best known of Avignon's museums are the *Musée Lapidaire* and the *Musée Calvet*, the latter one of the most interesting of all French provincial museums.

The *Musée Lapidaire* installed in an old Jesuit College is devoted to mosaics, sculpture and a remarkable collection of sarcophagi dating from Roman times up to the eighteenth century. Of the earliest pieces shown the most remarkable is the 'Tarasque of Noves', said to be of *La Tène* or second Iron Age period. This Tarasque, not to be confused with the Tarascon Monster, is a lion obviously truly carnivorous holding two sturdy Gauls in its claws. In addition Alexander the Great's bust in polychrome marble and a peculiarly lifelike head of the Emperor Trajan should not be overlooked.

The Calvet Museum, named after Dr Esprit Calvet who on his death in 1810 left his vast private collection to the city of Avignon, was officially opened to the public in May 1834. It is one of those museums where it would be possible to spend an entire day, leave with an attack of mental indigestion, and still feel that one had only touched on the fringes.

The ground floor shows a remarkable collection of wrought-iron work and a hall entirely given over to Greek antiquities; but for

me the chief fascination lies in the vast assembly of canvases beginning with the masters known as the 'Avignon primitives' and
continuing through all known schools of art till we come to the
comparatively contemporary works of Toulouse-Lautrec, Utrillo,
Dufy and Brayer. Of the older masters there are two enchanting
Breughels, scenes of village life. Joseph Vernet, most famous of
the Avignon school, deservedly has a room to himself, off which
opens a gallery showing mostly the works of a lesser-known but
equally talented Avignon artist, Hubert Robert (1733–1808), including four extremely beautiful allegorical canvases of 'The Four
Seasons'. Above the main stairway is a curious picture by Horace
Vernet showing a small boat in a mountainous sea with a figure,
that of his grandfather Claude Joseph Vernet, lashed to the single
mast the better to study storm effects.

However, it is to the Avignon primitives I find myself most
drawn, always feeling that if one considers some contemporary
works of so-called genius the term 'primitive' is a sad misnomer.
It would be hard to imagine anything more vivid or so intensely
emotional as many of these pictures, especially those attributed to
Nicholas Froment, *The Annunciation, St Siffrein Bishop of Carpentras*, to Simon de Chalons's *Adoration of the Shepherds* and a
most interesting portrait of Henry vii (of England) by an unknown
painter.

Avignon was also a centre for those brotherhoods known as
penitents. Three of their chapels still stand today. Those of the
Black, White and Grey Penitents are respectively in the Rue
Banasterie, the Place (de la) Principale and the Rue des Tein-
turiers.

The origin of the *confrèries* dates back to the siege of the city by
Louis viii, ended by the city's capitulation on 12 September
1226, when the king obliged the Bishop of Avignon to bring the
Holy Sacrament to his tent. After this ceremony all those who had
acted as escort decided to form a brotherhood, adopting as their
uniform a sackcloth robe and twisted rope girdle. They were
known as the *Disciples et Battus de la Croix* or Grey Penitents. In
1448 Ricasoli, a young Florentine nobleman forced to leave

Italy after the Pazzi conspiracy, founded tl.e Black Penitents brotherhood with a group of fellow exiles. The foundation of the White Penitents dates from 1527 when 13 Avignon noblemen founded the order under the emblem of the 'Five Wounds of Christ'.

These three brotherhoods were, however, only a beginning.

In 1557 dissident groups formed the Blue Penitents at a time when it was fashionable to belong to one or other of these brotherhoods. Cardinal Rivere (later Pope Julius II) was 'Grey', the Cardinal of Armagnac 'Black', the Cardinal of Joyeuse 'Blue', while royalty – including Charles IX and Henry III – adhered to the most exclusive 'White' *confrèrie*. Towards the end of the sixteenth century a colonel of the papal infantry in Avignon, as a protest against the pomp and circumstance of the existing brotherhoods founded the Black Penitents of Pity, whose principal occupation was to look after and try to improve the miserable lot of lunatics, common prisoners and even those under sentence of death. In 1662, 16 protesting Blue Penitents broke away to form the Violet Penitents: finally in 1700 we find the Red – bourgeois or working-class – Penitents.

The Revolution sealed the fate of these diverse brotherhoods and today only the Grey Penitents exist. The Black lasted until 1948 and were then dissolved by their last rector, Charles le Gras, who has written a book, *La Fin des Confrèries des Penitents Noirs et des Penitents Blancs d'Avignon* on their disappearance from the ecclesiastical scene.

The Grey Penitents still talk of the miracle which occurred during the catastrophic floods of the Rhône, Durance and Sorgue rivers in 1443. The night of 29 November flood-waters invaded the city and swept round their chapel. In the morning the rector and several of the brothers reached the chapel in a rowing boat to find that though the waters had penetrated into the building they had divided and piled up to a height of four feet on either side of the nave, leaving a clear dry passage to the altar. This chapel is well worth a visit for its pictures, the most striking a primitive 'St Paul on the road to Damascus' by Simon de Chalons.

A tour of Avignon is not complete, however, unless one crosses the modern bridge to explore the opposite bank and the little town of Villeneuve-lès-Avignon – the *lès* with grave accent, as Archibald Lyall points out, in this case signifying 'near'.

The change in atmosphere is immediate.

Even the ancient quarters of Avignon itself throb with life. The passing of centuries has not enfeebled its pulse. But in Villeneuve's narrow streets one is immediately plunged into the past. It is a town of quiet shadows: not dead, as some suggest, but slumbering, its back turned firmly away from modernity.

This contrast has always existed. When Avignon was one of the western world's most vital centres people exhausted by the hectic round of almost non-stop gaiety would cross the river to the quiet of Villeneuve for a rest cure. Wealthy cardinals built the most sumptuous holiday homes called *livrèes*, 15 in all, which sadly were sacked and razed during the Revolution.

Standing watchdog to the town is the solid fortified tower of Philippe le Bel. The original building dates back to 1302 when the right (Villeneuve) bank of the Rhône belonged to France and the left (Avignon) to the Empire. The King of France, Philippe le Bel, who violently opposed the church's temporal power and is referred to sometimes as the first 'modern' king of France, had the tower built to keep a watch on the imperial city opposite and also to dominate traffic across St Bénézet's bridge. The tower, nearly 70 feet high, is remarkably well preserved and it is worth while climbing the seemingly interminable number of winding stairs that spiral up to reach the terrace; its view – the best – gives over the river to the papal palace, a compact mass above the city ramparts.

The town itself is scarcely older than the tower.

Prior to 1292 a Benedictine monastery, St André, stood solitary on Mount Andaon. In that year the abbot was on such bad terms with the authorities of Avignon, then a republic within the Empire, that he appealed to Philippe le Bel for protection, an appeal to which the monarch responded immediately. In return for this help Philippe was allowed to found a new town (Villeneuve), a rival community to the city, across the river; this rapidly grew in strength and popularity.

The plain but unusually powerful fortified *enceinte* which now crowns Mount Andaon, known as Fort St André, was built by Philippe le Bel's successors, Jean le Bon and Charles v, between 1362 and 1368. It acted as a stronger second line of defence, or offensive base, to the tower, and at the same time completely enclosed the abbey and little township of St André.

Here the interest is almost entirely from the outside.

The main gate, flanked by two cylindrical machicolated towers, is with Tarascon castle the most massive example of the heyday of medieval fortification I have ever come across; the arch of the gateway was so thick as to be defended by three successive well-spaced portcullises. Once through the gates, however, one finds nothing but a waste of ruins and crumbling walls, the atmosphere made all the sadder by the fact that both of the gate's towers were for centuries used as prisons.

The town itself with its narrow, sometimes arcaded streets is best seen on foot; even in August it is not too difficult to find some shaded corner to park a car.

Since 1868, when the municipality took over the seventeenth-century *hotel* of the Marquis de Montanégues for the Villeneuve Museum the show-piece has always been the 'Coronation of the Virgin' by Enguerrand Charonton – born in Laon but who studied and lived most of his life in Avignon – generally looked upon as one of the greatest paintings of the day. To begin with it was thought to be the work of King René himself, then of van Eyck, and later of van der Meere. In 1889, however, an Abbé Requin discovered the original contract for the painting drawn up at Avignon, dated 24 April 1453 between a priest, Jean de Montegnac, and *Magister* Guerandus Quarton (Charonton).

The artist can be congratulated on his draughtsmanship and colour but not on his originality, since it appears from the contract, written in both Latin and French, that the most precise and exact details as to the composition, scenes depicted, figures – and

6   *Les Baux de Provence*
7   *The Château d'If*

their attitudes – to be included, backgrounds, and sentiments suggested, were strictly laid down.

Close to the museum is the church of Notre Dame founded by Cardinal Arnaud de Via, nephew of John xxii, in 1333, the first to introduce the Gothic style, replacing romanesque in Provence, and whose recumbent marble statue can be seen in the second chapel to the left.

The church's most precious treasure, an ivory statue of the Virgin, is kept locked up in the sacristy and can only be seen in the presence of the sacristan.

It was with some astonishment that on entering the sacristy I found myself confronted, not with the statue but the blank faces of two steel safes built into the walls, like a bank strong-box or the cache for ultra-top-secret MI5 documents.

The first to be opened contained a little polychromatic figure of the Virgin holding the infant Jesus in her arms, carved from an elephant's tusk, the back following the tusk's natural curve. It is an exquisite piece of work, perfect and lifelike in detail, the expression on the Virgin's face sweetly gentle, that of the child of the purest innocence. Supposed to be the work of a fourteenth-century Moor converted to Christianity it was carved specially for John xxii whò in turn gave it to his nephew. One notices in fact a slightly Islamic touch about the robes and veils fringing the face.

The other carefully-guarded statue, if less perfect from a technical point of view, is none the less remarkable. Carved from a single block of wood it portrays a double Virgin and Child back to back, the one face depicting joy, the other grief. Sculpted by an anonymous German it was originally presented to the Cardinal of Nuremberg who sent it as a token of his esteem to Arnaud da Via. On the face representing joy the Virgin is smiling and the child holds a dove, symbol of peace. On turning the statue we see the Virgin's features haggard. Her left foot is bare – sign of poverty – while the child holds a minature globe, indicating that all sorrows stem from mankind's imperfections.

From Villeneuve it is a bare fifteen miles to the most imposing of all Roman aqueducts, the Pont du Gard, through attractive

8   *Les Saintes Maries de la Mer: the fortress church*

countryside planted with vineyards, via the village of Remoulins. In view of the fact that the structure is so enormous it is strange that one does not realise its presence till almost beneath its shadow. In former times the surprise must have been quasi-total but today one is warned by the sudden appearance of booths and stalls selling postcards and souvenirs and, lining the road, of hotels, restaurants, *buvettes* and camping sites.

The original aqueduct was built by order of Agrippa, son-in-law of Augustus, with the object of bringing the water of the Eure river from the neighbourhood of Uzès to Nîmes, a distance of 50 kilometres – roughly thirty-one miles. Although about 2,000 years old this section, spanning the Gardon river, is in a perfect state of preservation.

At first view one would say that three bridges had been super-imposed, the lower consisting of six arches, the middle of eleven, and the upper and smallest – supporting the stone canal through which the water passed – of 35 arches. On closer inspection it is noticed that the structure is dry-stone: enormous blocks, most it is reckoned weighing a minimum of six tons, raised, some to the incredible height of 160 feet, by pulleys worked by unfortunate slaves known as 'squirrel men' shut up in a wooden cage and turning a treadmill. It is possible to walk the whole way across on the top of the covered canal. But as there is no parapet, the width here a bare ten feet and the drop into the Gardon river quite sheer, I preferred to cross in the semi-obscurity of the old water canal itself, sloping at the angle of one foot every five furlongs, hoisting myself up to get an occasional view down river through the openings in the arches.

One of Provence's most amusing legends is connected with the Pont du Gard. There was considerable competition after its completion as to who should be the first to cross, since there was a footpath beside the actual canal. Always on the watch, the Devil decided to claim the soul of the person who did so and called in on the Roman-appointed guardian – a man of Greek origin named Andreos – offering every form of earthly reward if he would hand over the individual concerned. Andreos, though indignant and rather frightened, but at the same time being a true Greek and not fearing any rival when it came to a question of trickery, agreed.

The rendezvous was for dawn the following morning. 'When evening fell Andreos crept out of his hut, a sack under his arm, and spent the night in one of the many overgrown gullies, known as *garrigues*, which cut up the hills around the *Pont*. At first light he returned staggering under the weight of the sack which in fact contained a huge hare he had snared during the night. "Hi! Satan! I've brought you your soul!" The Devil of course was waiting impatiently. Andreos then opened the sack; the hare leaped out as though the good God had given him wings and was half-way over the *Pont* in a matter of seconds. But when at the far end he saw the fearsome monster with his cruel black face and eyes like glowing coals who was waiting for him, stretching out eager claws, not wishing to roast in Hell, preferring rather the paradise reserved for hares, the hare did not hesitate. He swung round and hurled himself into the void, striking the eastern *voussoir* of the third arch as he fell, and was drowned in the Gardon (river). The Devil had been really "had", and Andreos thought he was going to die with laughter . . .' (Pierre Jalchot: *Contes de Provence-Languedoc*).

In the summer the Gardon, its banks shady, is a popular bathing-place after a tour of the aqueduct, but I doubt if many, as they splash or swim in the clear water, remember the hare.

Barely 20 miles north of Avignon, astride National 7, is the town of Orange with its Triumphal Arch and ancient Theatre, two of the finest Roman monuments still existing.

Colonia Julia Secondanorum Arausio was the name given to the ancient Celtic city of Arausi, the Cavare tribe's capital when it was a Roman colony and settlement for veterans of the 2nd Gallic Legion. The arch, built by order of Augustus about 49 B.C., is classified as the third largest of the Roman world. Today it stands firmly and aggressively splitting N7 into two traffic streams at the northern exit of Orange, an island surrounded by small lawns in the midst of a constant traffic roar.

Apart from the dangers of crossing the road this necessarily confined space presents great difficulty in the studying of carvings and reliefs, for the lawns come very close to the columns and bristle with notices to the effect that it is strictly forbidden to walk on the grass. This means that after contemplating the higher reliefs – the arch's walls rise to some 60 feet – one departs with a decided crick in the neck.

Most of these sculptures and reliefs are on the north face. Above the eastern and western arches, flanking the main central vault, is a record of Julius Caesar's victory over the Greek-Massilian fleet, won thanks to the fact that the Greeks failed to take advantage of their superior navigating skill and allowed the unbeatable Roman legionaries to board them. The east face is decorated by the figures of six captured Gauls and their arms. On one shield the name Mario can be deciphered. For a long time it was considered that this referred to Marius, victor of the battle of Pourrières in 102 B.C., but later schools of thought have decided that it designates Marion, a barbarian chief, probably one of the six captives recorded on the east face.

At the southern extremity of the town is the colossal Roman theatre which, the *Guide Michelin* claims, is 'the most beautiful, the best preserved, not only in Provence, but the whole of the antique world'. And certainly one is left breathless by the tremendous dimensions above all of the exterior wall, towering a sheer 120 feet, and described by Louis XIV as 'the most beautiful wall in all my kingdom'. On entering beneath the arches and looking at the proscenium one sees above the stage in a central niche a huge statue of Augustus which was found in small pieces, put together again with amazing skill, and returned to its original place in the niche in 1951.

This theatre still plays a part in Provence's artistic life. Each year, continuing a tradition dating back a century, performances of the more spectacular operas are given. In 1970 *Faust, Aïda* and – appropriately – *Mireille* figured in the programme. In 1869 it was Mehul's *Joseph* and in 1874 Bellini's *Norma* which drew huge crowds.

Several British writers have drawn attention to the fact that the name Orange denotes, as well as this ancient Provençal town, a former king of England, a district in Holland and in the South African Republic, towns in California and New Jersey, the Dutch royal family, and an Irish Protestant political party. The name, which has no connection with the fruit (derived from the Arabic), is merely a degradation of the original Arausio. In medieval times, however, the old Roman colony became one of the many hotly disputed territories in the European political scene.

In 1559, after the Treaty of Cateau-Cambresis, the principality of Orange was handed over to William of Nassau, Stadtholder of the Low Countries, confirming devious claims resulting from marriage alliances with the house of Les Baux. In 1622 Maurice of Nassau decided to turn the city into a vast fortress and for this purpose used the stones of the many Roman buildings still standing which had survived Alaman and Visigoth ravages. When Louis xiv declared war on Holland one of his first moves was to storm Orange, ordering his army commander, the Comte de Grignan – Madame de Sévigné's son-in-law – to raze the fortifications to the ground, and only good fortune, or an oversight, prevented the theatre, on which one of the main bastions was based, being totally destroyed. It was not till 1713, by the Treaty of Utrecht, that the Dutch, on the suggestion of their legal ruler by inheritance, the King of Prussia, finally renounced all claims to Orange, but transferred the title – Principality of Orange – to a part of Gelderland.

Vaison-la-Romaine lies seventeen miles to the north-east of Orange, an easy run across rolling country which is one vast vineyard, the southern horizon broken up by Mont Ventoux's volcano-like silhouette and the jagged hills known as the Dentelles de Montmirail, reminding one very much of Monsarrat above Barcelona or the Cyprus *Pentadactylon* range, two of whose peaks, the *Crête du Turc* and the *Crête du Clapis* – like the *baous* near Vence in the Alpes-Maritimes – are considered excellent training grounds for budding alpinists.

Before the Roman invasion the area round Vaison was occupied by a Germanic tribe, the Voconces, who seem to have been a level-headed, practical people: for when the Romans started infiltrating north after Marius's great victory they realised that Roman domination was inevitable, co-operated with the foreign colonisers and provided levies to swell the ranks of Roman armies in their wars against the Gauls, thereby earning the official title of 'ally' which enabled them to preserve an almost total local autonomy as well as freedom of worship of their various gods.

Called Vasio Vocontarium after the establishment of the Empire in Rome, Vaison was the capital of the upper valleys watered by the Ouvèze and Aygues rivers, becoming the province of Narbonne's most opulent city. '*La ville la plus agréable à voir, la plus élégante, celle qui sait le mieux jouir des fastueuses douceurs de la paix romaine . . .*' (Abbé J. Saintel – *Vaison-la-Romaine*).

The Romans themselves were particularly fond of Vaison, since, often homesick, it reminded them of their native Italy. 'The sky's brilliant blue beneath which the grey of the olives blends with the green of vines', wrote a contemporary, 'the local inhabitants' inbred charm, the abundant richness of the earth, take us back to the fertile plains of Lombardy and Venetia. . . .'

Though after the collapse of Rome most of the barbarian invasions bypassed Vaison, where learning had been kept alive by a series of powerful and highly intelligent prelates, the centuries of comparative peace came to an end in the Middle Ages.

In 1060 Raymond, Count of Toulouse and Marquis of Provence, demanded that the town and *châteaux* dependant on it be handed over to him, and on this demand being refused took the place by storm.

The city was won back for the church in 1178 by Bishop Bertrand de Lambesc, and recaptured a few years later by Count Raymond, who on being excommunicated promptly put every priest he could lay his hands on in prison. By the middle of the fourteenth century the insecurity of daily life was such that the unfortunate citizens decided to abandon their homes on the right bank of the Ouvèze and build a new, more easily defended town on the steep hill dominating the left bank, which eventually, protected by a double line of ramparts, became known as the *Haute-Ville*.

It was a move which paid. The *Haute-Ville* was never stormed.

Three centuries later many of its inhabitants, tired of the rather cramped accommodation within the walls, drifted back to the original town.

Again, being off the beaten track, Vaison was spared the Revolution's worst excesses, and with the return of peace after the Napoleonic wars a new modern town sprang up on the site of the old Gallo-Roman city.

Excavations are still going on in the area and gradually, as at Glanum near St Rémy-de-Provence, much of the Roman city is being reconstructed, such as the villa with its bathroom, its kitchens, its reception room: the column-lined street with its original pavements and the monument *Portique de Pompée*. The museum, just beyond the excavations known as the *Quartier de Puymin*, is best known for its four statues: an unknown emperor clad in armour, the Emperors Hadrian and Tiberius and the Empress Sabina.

It is also the original Roman bridge which crosses the Ouvèze river and connects the two – or rather three – Vaisons. Though two thousand years old this bridge was so skilfully and so strongly built that though today it supports the mass of heavy traffic, there is no question of any reinforcement being necessary. It consists of a single arch of 55 stone blocks reposing on the natural rock foundation of the river-banks.

Abandoned for many years when massive fortifications had lost their *raison d'être*, the Haute-Ville is gradually being re-inhabited.

The dilapidated church, formerly cathedral, half-way up the hill towards the ruined château and seldom mentioned in guide books, is in an unusually bad state of repair – though there are indications that restoration is to be undertaken– which is surprising, for the interior is full of interest. Just after the entrance at the foot of the aisle facing the altar, a show-case divided into two compartments, contains on the right a number of original documents including a Papal Bull of Clement vi, and on the left elaborate vestments decorated with spring flower motifs currently used during the sixteenth to eighteenth centuries.

On either side of the altar rails are two chapels. The one to the right shelters two wooden shields, primitively and rather crudely painted, commemorating St Quentin and St Theodore, both Vaison born, bishops of Vaison in the mid-sixth century, while in the chapel to the left hang three similar shields in memory of Ste Rusticule, Abbess of Arles, St Barthe, Bishop of Vaison – but not Vaison-born – early sixth century: and St Albin, martyred in Vaison in 262.

Before leaving the Avignon area there is one journey which should be made without fail and which could almost be considered a pilgrimage: to the *Fontaine de Vaucluse*, spiritual home of the poet Petrarch where so many of his outpourings of love for Laura were written: Laura, whom the youthful Petrarch first met outside Avignon's *Eglise des Cordeliers* on 6 April 1327.

'Lifting his eyes he beheld a sweet young damsel of Provence, modestly arrayed in green and decked with violets, whose fine eyes bound him captive and drew him into the labyrinth of a passion whose vicissitudes he has celebrated in 5,000 lines of a lover's plaints and praises. . . .'*

This love remained strictly platonic. Laura, of the Noves family, was the wife of Hugues de Sade (ancestor of the Marquis de Sade known for his pornographic writings) and it is possible that the two never even exchanged a word. But before she died of plague in Avignon in 1348, by which time she was the mother of 11 children, Petrarch had lavished all his genius on the portrayal of this ideal love.

* There is a theory that Laura was not the unique love Petrarch extolled but that his heroine (Laura) was a composite figment of his imagination. Yet in Milan's Ambrosian library there is a note undoubtedly written by the poet himself which states, 'Laura, so long celebrated by my poems, first appeared to my eyes in the time of my early manhood in the church of St Clare at Avignon (also known as the *Eglise des Cordeliers*) in the year of our Lord 1327 in the early morning of the 6th day of April.'

It was only the fact that his father had been forced to leave Italy because of political intrigue and take refuge in the city of the popes that Petrarch lived most of his early life in Avignon, a city he came to detest, becoming as he grew older a fanatical supporter of those who urged the return of the popes to Rome, and liking to refer to his foster home as 'the modern Babylon'.

He was a strange man, poet, diplomat, mystic, and it must be admitted, something of a hypocrite; for though his verses mentioned only spiritual love, purity and nobility of spirit, he was none the less father of two illegitimate children by an Avignon girl who has, to this day, remained anonymous.

It was his friend Philippe de Cabassol, Bishop of Cavaillon, who first invited Petrarch to stay in his château near the head of the valley from which the Sorgue river springs: one of the most remarkable river sources in Europe.

The poet was delighted by the calm, the green cool of woods and grassy slopes, the silence broken only by the Sorgue's chatter, after the noise, dust, heat, intrigue and intense social life of Avignon. In 1333 he bought a house and two gardens near the bishop's château. Though during the next 16 years he made a number of journeys, notably to Paris and Rome, it was always to his house in Fontaine de Vaucluse – his 'Transalpine Parnassus', as he called it – that he returned, and where most of his important works were written: among them *The Triumphs*, *De Vita Solitaria*, and of course his impassioned *canzoni* to Laura (*Bucolicuum Carmen*).*

Soon after Laura's death in 1348 Petrarch, with his two illegitimate children, Giovanni and Francesca, returned to Italy to settle in Arqua, a scenic replica, it is claimed, of *La Fontaine de Vaucluse*, where he died in 1374.

The undoubted beauty spot which is this *Fontaine de Vaucluse* has been very much despoiled. The approach to the village is a

* His existence at Vaucluse was described by a contemporary: 'Living in a small house, his only companion a dog given him by Cardinal Colonna, dressed like a peasant, living on the simplest food, the only sounds that greeted his ear in that sylvan silence the song of birds, the lowing of oxen, the bleating of lambs, the murmuring of the stream. . . .'

repetition of that to the *Pont du Gard*, only on a vastly exaggerated scale. The ranks of post-card and souvenir sellers must extend for well over a mile. The agglomeration of hotels and restaurants all bear the names 'Petrarch', 'Laura', or 'Petrarch and Laura'. The river's right bank – the left, dominated by the ruins of Philippe de Cabassol's château is fortunately too precipitous – is occupied by a series of open-air restaurants and *buvettes* where provided one buys a drink one can take a picnic. Yet I would not go as far as to look upon a visit as a mistake never to be repeated.

The *buvettes* have a smug, rather *Belle Epoque* air about them. The river, sweeping over brilliantly white symmetrical pebbles and trailing dense green weeds like silky tentacles, gurgles at the foot of the terraces. Here on the hottest day it is cool and shady. There is space, and an invigorating freshness in the air. One could say that the environment is not overwhelmed by the tourist mass; it absorbs it.

From the *buvettes* to the river's source is a sharp scramble along a dusty track looking down on the Sorgue's first ebullient bubbling over a series of rapids split up by huge boulders. In spring after the rains and when the snows melt the rush of water is terrifying, but to get an idea of the source one should go during the dry summer season, looking up at twisted fig-trees well above one's head which yearly resist the flood waters' frenzied efforts to uproot them.

There is something Dantësque, unbelievably sinister, about the deep cavern and the deep black pool which is the Sorgue's womb, its surface so still that it might almost be a slab of black marble. One can feel the presence of vague monsters, of creatures born of the shadows, the incarnation of sun-frightened protoplasms communicating their horror by the very chill which pierces one in these eternal shades, even through the most blistering of Provençal summer hours. In fact one is not in the least surprised to learn that the *Fontaine de Vaucluse*, like Tarascon, had its man-eating monster known as the *Coulobre*.

In Cavaillon cathedral behind the high altar is one of Mignard's pictures showing Bishop Véran getting the better – after the manner of Ste Martha of Tarascon – of the monster; though others insist that it was slain by Petrach when one day it was rash enough to attack the poet when he was walking arm-in-arm with Laura along the river-bank.

After the *Fontaine de Vaucluse* it is a short run to follow the course of the river to the small attractive town of *L'Isle-sur-la-Sorgue*: sometimes, but with a considerable stretch of imagination, called the Provençale Venice. For though the actual town is built round the ten banks of the Sorgue river which splits up into a number of canals there is no question of waterways predominating, and a visit to the town is made either on foot or by car.

Off the square, *La Place de la Liberté*, is a church unusually ornate for Provence, filled with seventeenth-century paintings (Parrocel, Mignard, Levieux), and purely Italianate gilded wooden statues. From the church also in the old quarter and rather difficult to find, is the hospital, the old *Hôtel-Dieu* where side by side one finds modern wards, a stylised eighteenth-century garden and fountain, and the old pharmacy with Moustier-labelled medicine and powder containers, including the inevitable *nux vomica* and an enormous mortar – the pestle is missing – used in the seventeenth century for mixing potions.

Ten miles due north of *L'Isle-sur-la-Sorgue* is Carpentras, ancient capital of the Comtat Venaissin, ceded to the Pope in 1229 and remaining papal territory till the Revolution. The name is derived from the word Karpenton, meaning a two-wheel cart drawn by two horses, and for years the city was famous for its waggoners. Though the waggoner has little place in the latter half of the twentieth century Carpentras is still renowned for its library, its cathedral and its synagogue.

The library, the most important in Provence, was founded by Malachie d'Inguimbert in 1746, 11 years after he had been nominated bishop of the city. It contains 150,000 books, among them rare editions of Petrarch, and 2,300 manuscripts, as well as a music library with an autographed score of J. S. Bach.

The church, pure late Gothic, formerly, like so many in Provence, a cathedral, is dedicated to St Siffrein and shelters the remains of the saint and the Saint Mors, or Holy Bit, though neither is on view to the public.

Siffrein or Siegfried is one of those mysterious saints whose names figure in few, if any, classified hagiographies. Most of his life was spent apparently on the *Iles de Lérins* off Cannes, till, already advanced in years, he was sent by the abbot as Bishop of Venasque, a small hill village to the south of Carpentras, then the only bishopric in the immediate neighbourhood, from which the Comtat Venaissin took its name. On his death he was buried in Venasque church. Soon afterwards his body was stolen by thieves who, however, are supposed to have been blinded *en route* by Divine Vengeance and who promptly abandoned the corpse on the Carpentras road. We are told, but without satisfactory explanation, that the relics were brought to Carpentras on 12 July 980.

Though both during his lifetime and after his death St Siffrein had the reputation of possessing healing powers it was the Saint Mors, the Holy Bit or Nail kept in a transparent shrine beside the saint's reliquary which drew enormous crowds to Carpentras. The 'bit' was indeed a genuine horse's bit but legend insisted that it had been made from two of the nails from Christ's cross.

It was Helena, mother of the Emperor Constantine, who originally discovered the three nails used for the crucifixion. One of them she threw into the sea to abate a storm threatening to sink her ship. With the other two she had a bit made which she gave to her son and which according to some legends Constantine later offered as a gift to St Siffrein. More probably, however, it was brought back to Carpentras from Constantinople by crusaders.

This extraordinary relic which Pope Clement vii insisted could drive evil spirits from the human body as well as cure neuralgia, eye diseases and hæmorrhages, is brought out twice a year – on Good Friday and every 27 November.

The tympan above the church entrance from the *Place St Siffrein* known as the Jews' Gate is decorated by a marble sphere being gnawed by rats, and whose exact symbolism is much discussed. The most satisfactory explanation seems to be that the rat, responsible for the terrible outbreaks of plague which ravaged the country, is portrayed as the instrument of God's anger with the world as symbolised by the sphere, the whole being the illustration therefore of Thomas Thayre's words – 'God has inflicted the Plague upon His people to punish them for their sins and impiety.'

The church's interior boasts of a number of statues mostly by Jacques Bernus, but my most lasting impression is of the richness of the stained glass above the Jews' Gate, to the right of which can be seen a little balcony connecting directly with the bishop's palace.

Behind the church and facing the *Hotel-de-Ville* is France's oldest synagogue, built in the fifteenth century, restored in the seventeenth and again in 1929, all that remains of a ghetto which once counted 1,200 inhabitants. You have to ring the bell beside the front door – which might be that of any large town house – for the curator, though no entrance fee is charged. The interior is small but very light and the liturgical candlesticks, only decoration visible, seem arranged haphazard. Still existing in the basement is the *cabussadou*, the bath or pool in which young girls take a ritual bath the day before their weddings.

During the time the Comtat Venaissin was the property of the Papal States the Jewish population enjoyed complete immunity from the persecutions and pogroms, both endemic and epidemic, part and parcel of the political life of Continental countries. Not even the Inquisition troubled their peace.

There is one illustrious son of Carpentras who has most undeservedly been forgotten.

Elzear Genet – known in Italy as *Il Carpentrasso* – was born in the late fourteenth century and like Mozart was already a brilliant composer while still a child. After a stage in Italy where he was always more appreciated than in his native Provence he moved to Paris where he became a court favourite and was described by Rabelais as 'one of the gayest composers of the day'.

However, the still youthful Genet, far more drawn towards religious music, was noticed by Pope Julius II and finally appointed *Maître de Chapelle Pontificale* by Leon X. In Rome his work was so much admired that Giovanni Pierlugi, better known as Palestrina, admitted that he had adopted *Il Carpentrasso* as his model. When Genet died, comparatively young, in 1548, he was Canon of St Agricol in Avignon and hailed in Italy as 'one of the greatest benefactors of musical expression especially where vocal scores are concerned'.

But who today has heard of Elzear Genet?

3. Arles

Of all the cities of Provence Arles is, in atmosphere, in aspect and by tradition, the most Provençal. In summer the surrounding sweep of plains becomes yellow, dried up; the straight roads shimmer with rippling mirages. Olive groves glow and cornfields are the flaming gold captured by Van Gogh.

The city itself – partly surrounded by ramparts considerably less impressive than those of Avignon – although inevitably fringed with blocks of flats and industrial constructions has preserved a secretive, almost nostalgically Islamic aura – and one cannot deny the subtle spiritual link between Provence and the Maghreb – within the dark centre, the *Place du Forum*, in permanent twilight beneath heavy intertwining branches – so much more agreeable for an aperitif than the clamorous circular *Boulevard des Lices* with its incessant traffic roar – a maze of narrow streets, walled courtyards, the occasional stark, solitary date palm standing out in the strange hush descending with evening. All is in sharp contrast with Avignon's pure feudalism, Aix's donnish reticence, and Marseille's aggressive modernity.

Arles owed its earliest prosperity to the famous Pro-Consul of Massilia, Marius, who in 104 B.C., a couple of years before his great victory over the Teutons, built a canal linking the town with the Gulf of Fos so that trading vessels could reach Arles direct. This was also a political move on the Roman's part to undermine predominantly Greek Massilia's overgrown opulence, thus distributing – we see the birth of the principle 'divide and rule' – the region's actual and potential wealth more evenly.

Fifty-five years later this policy bore fruit. The people of Arles provided a fleet of vessels to help Julius Caesar in his attack on Marseille. In return for this – the fleet played a major part in obtaining the surrender of the Phocean city – Arles became a Roman colony and a major port with the great advantage of being so far from the sea that vessels could lie at anchor even in the stormiest weather in total security. At the same time most of Massilia's possessions were handed over to Arles. As a result prosperity came so quickly that the population rose to 100,000 inhabitants, and public buildings and monuments were so magnificent that the poet Ausonius described it as *Gallula Roma*, the little Gallic Rome. In fact the Emperor Constantine was so enamoured of the city that he made it almost a second capital.

By the fifth century a contemporary described the Arles market as a centre in which could be found 'in abundance' all the best produce of the Orient: Arabia, Africa, Spain and Gaul. At the same time the city itself was a hive of industry, glass, fabrics, weapons, while its olive oil and wines – today our *Cotês du Rhône* – were already famous thoughout the civilised world of Rome.

Because of this material well-being Arles became a major attraction for the 'barbarians' with Rome's decline, and later for the Saracens. When in 480 the city was finally occupied by the Goths these rugged northerners found it so much to their liking that instead of razing it to the ground they made it their new capital, remaining there till 536 when they handed it over to the Franks in return for the latters' help in a campaign against Rome.

The Saracens first occupied Arles in 730 and remained there for five years. When Charles Martel arrived outside the city walls on his victorious counter-offensive the Saracen garrison put up a desperate resistance, finally falling back on the old Roman arena which in the meantime they had turned into a redoubt. Only after the destruction of part of the aqueduct had cut off their water supply did the remnants surrender. Charles Martel was so enraged by his losses that the city's inhabitants were massacred irrespective of their religion. The Provençaux, never in sympathy with people from the north, asked themselves which indeed were the lesser evils.

However, in 879 in the midst of the Saracen wars Arles became the capital of a kingdom of the same name, a kingdom which was integrated with the Holy Roman Empire in 1032. In 1150, like Avignon, Arles's status changed to that of quasi-independent republic until it was claimed by Charles of Anjou as part of his dowry from Beatrice, fourth daughter of the Count of Forcalquier. When the Arlesians tried to resist this annexation Charles marched against them, entering the city after a brief siege.

United with France – with the rest of Provence – in 1482, Arles was threatened by the armies of the great Charles Quint, Emperor of the Holy Roman Empire, in 1536. Charles Quint had had himself crowned King of Arles in Aix, but failed to enter into his arbitrarily annexed kingdom thanks to the courage of the Arlesians who, in a solid block, men, women and children alike, took up arms to resist the invader.

Although the later wars of religion with all their attendant horrors raged within a couple of days' marches, Arles itself was comparatively untouched, and even at the time of the Revolution and during both 'Red' and 'White' terrors, atrocities were more infrequent than elsewhere in the *midi*.

First impressions being often so lasting it is better to enter Arles from the north, skirting Les Baux, Fontvieille and Montmajour Abbey rather than by the normal N113 main road from Salon, these days almost as traffic-bound as the N7. This quieter approach cuts across the Place Lamartine where stood the house, shared by Van Gogh and Gauguin during the hectic months of their strange love-hate relationship, unfortunately destroyed during the 1944 air raids. Thence one goes through a gate in the ramparts known as *La Porte de la Cavalerie*, skirts the arena, the narrow streets leading to and from the Place du Forum, reaching the city centre, almost inevitably the Place de la République. This, one of the loveliest of squares in any city, is also the most convenient place – if one is lucky – to park.

To study the city's development through the ages one should resist the temptation to visit St Trophime Cathedral, which looks on to the Place, immediately: instead begin at the beginning with the antique monuments, the arena and Roman theatre.

The arena, built about 46 B.C. at the time when the city became a Roman colony, one of the biggest in existence and slightly larger than that of Nîmes, consists of two storeys of sixty arcades each. In its original form – there was a third storey or cornice but this has disappeared with the centuries – it could hold 26,000 spectators on festive occasions when gladiators hacked each other to pieces, a democratic performance available to all classes of society. The height of the wall which encloses the arena proper, 440 by 350 feet, shows that animals also featured in the programmes: wild boars, specially trained fighting dogs and bears, though 'stars' such as lions, tigers or elephants could only take part if the Emperor himself were present. On days when gladiators only were featured, a lower circle was put up so that wealthy spectators could enjoy a closer view of the wounds inflicted.

From the highest seats the drop is almost enough to bring on vertigo and one can appreciate the reasons which caused the building to be converted into a citadel in the Middle Ages, the outer ramparts being further strengthened in the thirteenth century by three towers still standing today; while within the walls were clustered 200 houses and two churches.

Work on clearing the arena of this unhygienic slum was begun in 1809 and continued spasmodically till 1830. In 1846 the actual restoration was started by the archaeologist Quenel, to be continued over the years by Formigé and Véran.

Though not in the Roman style, the towers have fortunately escaped destruction by zealous purists, and from their terraces one has an unequalled view over the city, surrounding countryside and the Rhône, here even wider and more majestic than at Avignon, flowing between low banks, part wooded, part green fields, with a near static beauty suggesting the canvas of an old master. To the east Montmajour Abbey stands out on its bluff; a point to the north a bare jagged crested line of hills, the Alpilles, breaking up an otherwise monotonously flat expanse of alternate stony desert, the Crau, and the Camargue marshland.

Close by the arena is the Roman theatre, not so grandiose as that of Orange and in a poor state of repair. Even after restoration barely half of the original construction still stands. But the setting is pleasant in a quiet garden brightened by apparently haphazard clusters of flowering oleander.

The church of St Trophime, already mentioned, is dedicated to the saint of the same name, a Greek from Asia Minor who is said to have known both St Peter and St Paul and to have promised the latter to 'bring the word of Christ to all the countryside from the Alps to the Rhône and between the Durance and the sea'.

Faithful to his promise St Trophime set out on his journey, travelling west till one day he arrived at the top of a small hill and looked down on a rich town beside a river, which he was told was called 'Arelas-the-White', deriving this name from the fact that 'Arelas' denoted a lake-covered land, qualified as white in this case because of the hundreds of white sails dotted along the great river's course.

St Trophime went down into the city and came to a crowded square. In the centre was a huge altar and at its foot stood three youths, almost naked, arms bound behind them. Somebody in the crowd explained that the youths were to be sacrificed to the Queen of Hell because if such a sacrifice were not performed yearly, and people and houses sprinkled with the victims' blood, the altar would shrink; when its level reached that of the surrounding roofs the whole city would crumble into ruin. At that moment appeared the priest who was to carry out the sacrifice, clad in white, his face covered by a flame-coloured veil.

The outraged St Trophime harangued the crowd so violently, calling on them to give up their pagan ways to 'worship only the one God', and 'not to kill but to love one another', that the priest fled, the youths were set free, and the saint was mobbed by those anxious to be baptised.

This legend is hotly denied in some quarters by those who insist that Christianity did not reach Arles till the third century. It is, on the other hand, so deeply embedded in local legend as to be considered sacrosanct by many.

The original church was probably Carolingian but during the course of the eleventh, twelfth and thirteenth centuries and by then a cathedral it was transformed rather than restored. It was in this cathedral in 1178 that Frederic Barbarossa, Emperor of the Holy Roman Empire, had himself crowned King of Arles, and here too 'Good' King René married his second wife Jeanne de Laval – not to be confused with 'wicked' Queen Jeanne – when he was in his forty-seventh year and his wife only just 21.

However, before entering the church it is worth while looking round and appreciating the richness of the square.

In the centre is an obelisk of Egyptian granite which it is suggested might be the altar mentioned in the legend of St Trophime's conversion of the Arlesians. To the right of St Trophime's church is the archbishop's palace, now sheltering the tourist office (*Syndicat d'Initiative*). The northern end of the square is taken up by the *Hôtel de Ville*, a seventeenth-century building erected round a sixteenth-century clock tower, while to the left opposite St Trophime's church is that of St Anne, meridional Gothic, built in 1621, now housing the *Musée Lapidaire* with its collection of sarcophagi and mosaics.

The entrance to the church is remarkable, a masterpiece of Romanesque art. Immediately above the actual door is a group representing Judgement Day. Christ, surrounded by a halo, holds a Bible in one hand, the other being raised in blessing. On either side of him are the symbolic representations of the four apostles: an eagle (St John), a winged man (St Matthew), a lion (St Mark) and an ox (St Luke). Below the ornate tympan the lintel shows the 12 apostles. On either side is a prolongation depicting to the left a group of 'good' people, fully clothed, being welcomed to Paradise while their souls are entrusted to Abraham, Isaac and Jacob. To the right a melancholy procession of naked sinners is being turned away from the Gate of Heaven and led in chains by demons to hell. On the main left pillar at the inside is the figure of St Trophime in bishop's robes, his mitre supported by two angels; opposite is a grim representation of the stoning of St Stephen.

Within, the church is dark and the sense of height from the middle of the nave can give one an ant-like feeling; this is indeed the tallest vault in Provence, just over 65 feet. High – almost too high to make out details – the walls are decorated with eleven Aubusson tapestries of scenes from the life of the Virgin Mary, replacing the usual wealth of pictures, a normal feature of most Provençal churches. But if canvases of the Provençal masters are lacking there are in compensation three sarcophagi of earliest Christian days. To the left of the entrance is one of the fourth century used as the font, another is behind the altar in the Chapel of the Holy Sepulchre which can be illuminated, surmounted by a magnificent group in marble of Christ being lowered into his tomb. Also in this chapel is the recumbent statue of Pierre de Foix, Cardinal-Archbishop of Arles, who died in 1464, and the tomb of Robert de Montcalm (died 1625) decorated with four graceful little statues representing Justice, Hope, Faith and Charity. Finally the third sarcophagus serves as the altar in the Chapel de Grignan; it is sculpted with scenes of the crossing of the Red Sea and is probably of the fourth century.

The cloisters, which should not be missed, can be reached by turning left on leaving the church then taking the first turning to the left at the bottom of the *Place de la République*. For an ex-cathedral of such importance the cloisters are comparatively small and the gardens prosaic and surprisingly neglected, but the quality of the carving on the pillars and in particular those of the northern cloister, decorated with reliefs of the apostles and depicting the stoning of St Stephen, the Resurrection and the Ascension, is outstanding.

On the far side of the *Boulevard des Lices* and beyond Arles' most luxurious hotel, the *Jules-César*, are the Alyscamps'*

---

* The popular interpretation of this name is that it is a corruption of *Elysii campi* (the Elysian Fields). However the old spelling, Aliscans (prior to twelfth century) contradicts such a hypothesis. No one knows what Alyscamps really means. – André Pezard.

described as 'one of the most celebrated necropoles of the western world'. Originally the Alyscamps, lined by rich sepulchres and tombs, formed part of the great Roman road, the *Via Aurelia*, but for most of the early legends concerning this rather melancholy avenue one must again return to the story of St Trophime.

The saint was old and felt the end of his life approaching. He determined, however, that before his death the pagan burial ground, the Alyscamps, must be converted into a Christian cemetery. Before the actual consecration he invited St Maximinus, Bishop of Aix, St Eutropus, Bishop of Orange, St Martial, Bishop of Limoges, St Saturnin, Bishop of Toulouse, and St Paul Serge to come to Arles to discuss the matter. The bishops accepted and agreed with the suggestion, but each in turn through modesty declined to carry out the service. St Trophime was profoundly disturbed, also being too modest, and 'turning in the direction of Jerusalem, fell on his knees and began to pray for guidance.

'His prayer was barely ended when another figure appeared on a rock facing Trophime, bathed in brilliant light, hands raised to bless the Alyscamps and assembled bishops, and saying, "Because of you, Trophime, from now on this is holy ground." All present recognised the figure of Christ. It was found that the hard rock on which He had knelt bore the imprint of His knees, and St Trophime ordered a chapel built on the spot, called *La Chapelle de la Genoullade*, which – though in ruins – still stands today.'

Another story concerning the Alyscamps is that St Trophime had been mocked by the goddess Venus, saying, 'You have driven me from my temple, but I reign over the dead, over my servants lying here in their tombs.' But when the figure of Christ appeared horrible creatures immediately came writhing up from these same tombs, snakes, toads, fork-tongued lizards, and fled into the night, leaving the once pagan ground purified.

Up to the twelfth century people vied with each other for the honour of being buried in a cemetery consecrated by Christ. Many insist that Roland and the heroes of Roncevaux lie there. But from the thirteenth century the rulers of Arles adopted the strange habit of offering a sarcophagus as a present to their more distinguished guests, while the monks themselves, whose work it was to look after the site, used tombal stones to build new chapels, even walls for their gardens.

Today the Alyscamps present a sad spectacle: a single tree-lined alley, a double row of sarcophagi beneath the trees, leading up to the ruined St Honorat Chapel, formerly dedicated to St Genest, an Arlesian judge decapitated in the third century for refusing to draw up an order to persecute the Christians. In addition the original cemetery has now been carved up by a canal, the railway and a part of the *zone industrielle*. When so much good work has been done regarding the preservation of old monuments it seems strange that this almost unique site should have been wantonly despoiled. One can only be thankful that many of the more elaborate sarcophagi were removed to Arles museums before it was too late. Most of them are to be found in the *Musée d'Art Chrétien*, once the Jesuit Chapel, which it is generally admitted contains the finest collection of sarcophagi in the world after Rome's Latran Museum. Others are exhibited in the *Musée Lapidaire Paien* on the Place de la République.

For me, however, by far the most fascinating museum in Arles is the *Muséon Arlaten* or *Palais du Félibrige* installed in the *Hôtel de Laval Castellane*, an early sixteenth-century building converted into a Jesuit college in 1648. The Arlaten, which owes its existence to the poet Mistral, who devoted to its creation the money from his Nobel Prize awarded in 1907, is one of the most complete and most perfect examples of folkloric museums in the world. It consists of no less than 29 rooms and is so packed that after several hours, as with the Calvet Museum at Avignon, one leaves footsore and exhausted with the irritating fear that half has been missed. There are perhaps two minor complaints one may make. Each room contains too many exhibits; and most directions, explanations and texts are in Provençal and therefore largely unintelligible except to the chosen few.

If one had to make a selection I would pick out the Costume Galleries IV-VI where one sees every imaginable variation of the classical *Arlesienne* dress: long pleated skirt in heavy brightly coloured Provençal material, a fichu either of the same material or muslin crossed over the breast, hair piled up on the crown and kept in place by a band of velvet, usually black. They are portrayed by such well-known artists as the Parrocels and Horace Vernet, and also in a delightful waxwork reproduction of a seamstress's workroom of 1706. On the same floor is the Gallery of Rites, Costumes and Legends (viii) with a reproduction of Tarascon's fabulous monster, the Tarasque, the *Chevelure d'Or*, a strand of almost pure golden hair found in a medieval tomb in the church of Les Baux, and a number of Provençal Christmas crêches with *santons*, the little red clay figures of the Provençal Christmas legend described later in the chapter on Marseille. On the second storey in the José Belon Salon (xii) hangs an enormous canvas showing Mistral acknowledging the applause of the crowd at a performance in the Arles arena to mark the fifthieth anniversary of the publication of *Miréio* (Mireille). *Salles* xiv, xv and xvi contain works of contemporary painters and above all Van Gogh. In the *Galerie de Crau et Camargue* (xxi) there is a reproduction, life size, of a Camargue *gardien's* hut, white stucco walls, thatched roof and rush-fenced yard. A black bull has pushed his head through the rushes and regards one with soulful eyes while the *gardien* himself, ignoring the bull, looks out over the swamps.

No. xxii, the *Salle de la Visite à l'Accouchée*, shows the gathering of relations round the bed in which lies a woman with her newborn baby. Both mother and child look singularly unaffected by the drama of birth as the mother is handed the traditional symbolic gifts: salt, an egg, a piece of bread and a matchstick.

Que fugue toun enfant
Sage coume la sau – Bon coume lou pan
*Plen coume un iou – Dre coume un brouqueto.**

The *Salle Calendal* (xxiii) has a superb reproduction in the most complete detail of a Christmas Eve family gathering round the dining-table in a Provençal *mas* (country house).

* May your child be as wise as salt – as true as bread – as full as an egg – as straight as a matchstick.

There are finally the *Salles Fredéric Mistral et du Félibrige* showing Mistral's cradle, photographs and paintings of the poet, extracts and illustrations from his works, and portraits of other founders of the *Félibrige* movement.

Almost suburbs of Arles are Montmajour Abbey and the little town of Fontvieille, close to the windmill which keeps alive the memory of Alphonse Daudet and his *Lettres de Mon Moulin*.

The abbey is yet another of those Provençal clerical edifices suggesting a fortress rather than a house of prayer. Built on a wooded bluff it rises like a castle above the surrounding expanse of rice-fields, with its sheer unadorned walls and blunt machico-lated towers. The Benedictines inherited the site in 949 from a pious woman named Teucinde, and after settling down the monks not only busied themselves with building the abbey but also attempted the semi-impossible task of draining the surrounding marshes. Their efforts were unsuccessful but with commendable obstinacy successive generations stuck doggedly to this labour of Hercules for the best part of 200 years. They earned fame, how-ever, not because of their unrelenting efforts but through a *pardon* held on 3 June every year – the first in 1021 – the feast of The Finding of the True Cross, which attracted armies of pilgrims. After its heyday in the fifteenth century a gradual decadence set in till, in 1786 on the eve of the Revolution, this nearly 800-year-old institution knew a dramatic end; the abbey was closed due to the fact that its abbot *commendataire* was Cardinal de Rohan, so heavily involved in the scandal of Queen Marie Antoinette's neck-lace.

At least half of the original monastery was destroyed during the Revolution but today work on restoration is proceeding. The twelfth-century cloisters are not only beautiful but interesting for the subjectes sculpted on the column capitals, mostly profane and Old rather than New Testament. One sees the Tarasque, a horse-man being attacked by a lion (St George and the dragon?), Jonah and the whale, Solomon and the Queen of Sheba, and even the allegorical mistral, cheeks blown out like the bad wolf 'huffing and puffing'.

The windmill that one discovers on the crest of a small rocky, scattered, scrub-covered hill on the right of the road between Montmajour Abbey and the little town of Fontvieille is another stronghold of postcards and souvenir booths, and as a site scarcely deserves its present-day fame, for it seems almost certain that Alphonse Daudet did not live there but in the nearby Château d'Amboy belonging to friends, and that much of his *Lettres de Mon Moulin* was written in Paris in 1865. It is possible, however, that the writer may have spent a few hours in the mill, then derelict and sail-less, to impregnate himself with local colour.

The conversion of the mill into a museum has been well carried out. On the ground floor is a bust of the author, with manuscripts, portraits of Daudet, Zola, Mistral and Lamartine: a few caricatures. Upstairs a stuffed owl, supposed to have kept the writer company in his solitary hours of inspiration-seeking, occupies the place of honour; and above on a terrace a *table d'orientation*, giving the names – in Provençal – and directions of the 32 winds which afflict Provence.

Inevitably Arles reminds one of the poet Mistral, and as from Avignon one makes the pilgrimage to Fontaine de Vaucluse, so it is inconceivable to leave this part of the world without spending some time in Maillane, Mistral's birthplace and the village where very happily he spent his long life.

The drive is through a sunny and rich countryside, leaving the Alpilles on the right. The long straight road leading to St Rémy de Provence is lined with giant cypress trees, serving as a windbreak against the prevalent mistral and protection for a series of nursery gardens in which gladioli of every colour predominate. Against this lush background the Alpilles, a prolongation of the Luberon *massif*, stand out jagged and bare, dragon-back ridges quivering in the heat haze, giving the impression of far greater height than in actual fact they can claim: a bare 1,500 feet.

Turning left before arriving at St Rémy the road is bordered by orchards, each with its rectilinear anti-mistral barricade of closely planted cypresses, all the way to Maillane, a large village of 1,354 inhabitants which perhaps more than any other merits the epithet 'sleepy'. And with an overwhelming relief combined with surprise one finds that the post-card souvenir vendors who have so despoiled Fontaine de Vaucluse, the Pont du Gard and Daudet's mill have overlooked this little Provençal gem. Maillane must also be one of the few places untouched by the tentacles of a *zone industrielle* or excrescent skyscraper blocks of flats; it remains much the same, but for the increase of motor traffic, as it was in Mistral's later days.

Near the village square, quiet even at the height of the tourist season, and almost opposite each other, are the two houses associated with Mistral. In the one he lived with his widowed mother until she died; this is known as the *Maison du Lézard Vert*, a solid seventeenth-century construction; the other is a pleasant nineteenth-century prosperous bourgeois home with its small garden which he built on marrying and which today is the Mistral Museum.

The poet was born in a big country house, the *Mas du Juge*, on 8 September 1830, but his mother moved to the *Maison du Lézard Vert* after his father's death – which occurred when he had finished his law studies at Aix-en-Provence university. However, the young Mistral was not interested in law either civil or criminal. All he wanted to do was write, and in his mother-tongue Provençal which he had spoken always in his conservative family circle, and which, seemingly threatened with extinction, he was equally determined, crusader-like, to preserve.

At a period when influence counted for so much in the art world Mistral was lucky to make friends with Lamartine, inspiring him with a real enthusiasm for his struggling efforts. The correspondence between the two men especially after the triumph of *Miréio* (Mirielle) in 1857 recalls, though in far more homeric and flowery phrases, that published recently by two writers of the present day :

'*O Poète de Maillane,*' wrote Lamartine, to whom Mistral dedicated *Miréio,** '*tu es l'aloes de la Provence, tu as grandi de trois coudées en un jour, ton âme poétique parfume* Avignon, Arles, Marseille, Toulon, Hyères *et bientôt toute la France. Mais plus heureux que l'arbre d'Hyères, le parfum de ton livre ne s'évaporera pas en mille ans . . .*' ('Oh Poet of Maillane. You are the aloe of Provence. In a single day your renown has trebled. The poetic perfume of your soul breathes o'er Avignon, Marseille, Arles, Toulon, Hyères, as soon it will over all France. Yet more fortunate than the tree of Hyères, a thousand years will elapse before the aura of your book. . . .') And Mistral, not to be outdone by this effusion, replied at great length, including such phrases as '*. . . vous avez détaché de votre épaule le manteau radieux de l'immortalité et vous m'en avez couvert . . .*' and again '*. . . si humble et petit que soit le grain de blé, lorsqu'il monte en épis sous la rosée du ciel, il peut encore faire honneur à la main que l'a sémé. Votre parole magnifique vient de créer ma gloire et peut-être mon génie . . .*' ('You have taken the radiant mantle of immortality from your shoulders only to cover mine with it . . . however tiny, however humble may be the seed burgeoning under the dew from heaven, it can still honour the hand which has sown it. Your superb eloquence has (just) created my glory, perhaps even my genius. . . .'

Louis le Cardonnel went as far as to say '*On dit Mistal, comme on dit Homère*', a remark immortalised by a plaque on the west façade of the *Maison du Lézard Vert*.

In 1876 the poet married a girl 20 years younger than himself, and the couple moved across the road to the house now the Mistral Museum. As a museum it is perhaps a trifle amateurishly arranged but is nevertheless highly evocative, intimate and moving. There is the desk at which Mireille was written, in the darkish room whose walls are a solid mass of photographs: the poet, his young wife (she survived him by 29 years, dying sadly in 1943 during the

---

* '*Te consacre Miréio; es uoun cor, es moun amo*' – (*Je te consacre Mireille, c'est mon coeur et mon âme*).

German occupation), the faithful female servant always at their side, Mistral talking with Daudet, photographs and portraits of the handsome Lamartine, a naïve *image d'Epinal* stylised triptych showing the young poet in his garden being visited by a blond 'spirit' bringing him inspiration for *Miréio*; a rather incongruous and curious gift, an enormous bow presented by a genuine Red Indian chieftain, 'Silver Eagle', a member of Buffalo Bill's touring Wild West Show, and the photograph of a dog, also heritage of the Wild West Show, which Mistral adopted and called *Pas Perdu*. Apparently the dog had been callously abandoned, and seeing Mistral followed him because of the very striking physical resemblance between the poet and William Cody.

Upstairs is the bedroom, very simple, and the bed in which Mistral died on 25 March 1914.

In the garden with its oleanders, slightly disordered flower-beds and rose bushes, is a rather flamboyant statue by Achard (1924) with the inscription *Lou soléu mi fa canta*, recalling the fact that Mistral – unlike Giono – was a great sun-lover and in the habit of saying, 'I'm like the cicada. The sun makes me sing.'

There are still some villagers who remember Mistral from their extreme youth. Two old men in one of the cafés told me over a leisurely *pastis* how the poet used to call out to the children on their way to school always in Provençal, as he resolutely refused to utter a word of French. He must have been an imposing figure with his leonine head beneath the eternal wide-brimmed black hat, his burly frame clad in a black frock-coat.

Although one's primary reason for visiting Maillane is to enter a little into the life of Provence's greatest poet, one should not leave without looking round the church, *Notre Dame de Grace*, in which Mistral was christened.

Close to the pulpit is a small statue of the Virgin Mary, clothed in an immaculate white robe, enclosed in a small glass case which – as I was told by a 90-year-old lady who insisted on being called *Tante Jeanne* – had been famous since the terrible cholera epidemic of 1854. People were dying like flies, when the priest called for volunteers to form a procession and carry the Virgin to the village square. The few who were not stricken responded eagerly and the procession had made the tour of the square three times when miraculously all the sick, even the dying, were cured simultaneously. *Tante Jeanne* assured me that her own mother-in-law had been an eye-witness of this miracle, still remembered in a festival held every year on 28 August.

The nearby town of St Rémy, also largely unspoiled, linked with memories of Nostradamus and Van Gogh, is close to the Roman remains of Glanum which rival those of Vaison-la-Romaine. Apart from the main road cutting through the town St Rémy strikes me as a larger edition of Maillane because of its intrinsic quality of peace bathed in the purest Provençal atmosphere: dark, narrow winding streets of the old town, the huge main square with its secular plane trees, its glowing colour and subtle sense of aloofness.

The town owes its name to St Rémy, Bishop of Rheims, who performed a miracle in the little anonymous township in the year 500 while accompanying Clovis on his way to besiege Avignon, and through the centuries it has been singularly fortunate in that it has seldom been a bone of contention between warring factions or served as a battlefield. Those born, or settled, in St Rémy have occupied themselves, not with war, temporal power and destruction, but with peace and the arts.

Michel de Nostredame, better known simply as Nostradamus, was born in St Rémy in 1503, grandson of a rich Jewish cereal merchant whose father had become converted to Christianity, adopting the family name of Notre-Dame after the parish in which they lived: Notre-Dame-la-Principale. Michel was at school in St Rémy and from there went to the faculty of arts at Avignon to study Greek and Latin. Later, mixing astrology with medicine and literature, he indulged in a passion for travel till he married for a second time and settled at Salon-en-Provence, half-way between Aix and Arles, today best known for the fact that it is the Cranwell of the French Air Force. After having acquired a very considerable reputation as a doctor who also dabbled in the concoction of love philtres and all forms of magic potions, it was at Salon that Nostradamus began to acquire the reputation of an 'Old Moore', indulging in prophecies which were printed in a volume called *Les Centuries*.

This volume vastly increased his renown all over France – except in Salon, where indeed the prophet was without honour in his own country and where, accused of a pact with the devil, his effigy was burned by respectable citizens in their houses. Fortunately for Nostradamus his book caused such a sensation that the outraged *Salonnais* could not burn him in person, for in August 1555 he was summoned to Paris to appear before Henri II and Catherine de Medici in order to compose the horoscopes of the royal children. He returned to Salon more hated than ever by his fellow citizens but a rich and famous man, and it was also in Salon that nine years later he was visited by the same Catherine de Medici, widowed Queen Mother, with her son King Charles IX. During this visit, 'On seeing in the hall a child* with his tutor, he (Nostradamus) expressed the wish to examine him also . . . then did Nostradamus whisper conspiratorially in the tutor's ear that this young prince would also one day rule over France. Because of this he was highly favoured by the kingdom of Navarre.' (*Histoires de la Provence – André Bouyala d' Arnaud*).

By the time he died in 1566 even the *Salonnais* had come round to thinking that perhaps after all he *was* a man endowed with supernatural powers. For many years it was firmly believed that he had been buried sitting upright at his desk on which were his papers and a little oil lamp, and that he was still continuing his writing while the lamp beside him glowed for all eternity.

Many people these days are inclined to look upon Nostradamus as a clever charlatan whose prophecies if closely examined were always found to be couched in such devious terms that they could be interpreted to fit in with any eventuality. However, Marie Mauron in her book *Hommes de Provence* comments, 'believe or disbelieve, respect or mock the legend, but both for believers and unbelievers, for Provençaux and non-Provençaux, Nostradamus

* The child was the infant King of Navarre, the future Henry IV.

lives and will live, fascinates and will continue to fascinate even his most violent detractors . . .'

Although Mistral's was the name which really launched the Félibrige movement its real founder was Joseph Roumanille (1818–91), son of a St Rémy gardener who would have followed his father's trade but for the fact that because of his poor physique any form of manual labour was impossible for him. So as to be in a position to earn a living he was allowed to go to school, study Latin and Greek, eventually becoming a clerk in the office of a lawyer, Monsieur Gautier, a post he held only a very short time before joining a private school in Lyons as professor. This school was later transferred to Avignon where one day a certain Fréderic Mistral was admitted as a student. As Roumanille was a passionate advocate of the Provençal language and had already written a number of unpublished verses and poems, master and pupil soon became firm friends when Roumanille discovered Mistral writing down *ad hoc* Provençal translations of the psalms.

When the older man died in 1891 Mistral wrote, 'He' (Roumanille) 'has done so much for our tongue, Provençal. To bring it back before the eyes of the world he devoted so much love, such a profound knowledge, such a natural wit combined with determination, that all respected his authority as father of the movement, his charm as a poet, his talent as an author, his sound commonsense of an old master . . .'

After his disastrous attempt to found an artistic colony in Arles with Gauguin and the over-exaggerated incident of cutting off his own ear to offer it as a present to a local whore, Van Gogh was housed in the asylum at St Rémy known as St Paul de Mausole, originally a church (twelfth century) with a monastery attached which had been used as an asylum since 1605. With the Revolution the church was closed and the monks of the Observantine order who looked after the lunatics were driven out. However, in 1806 the asylum was reopened after the buildings had been bought by a Doctor Mercurier, a well-known alienist and citizen of St Rémy. It has remained an asylum ever since, being today in charge of the Sisters of St Joseph of Aubenas.

9   *The Camargue: sand dunes and salt lakes*
10   *Horsemen of the Camargue*

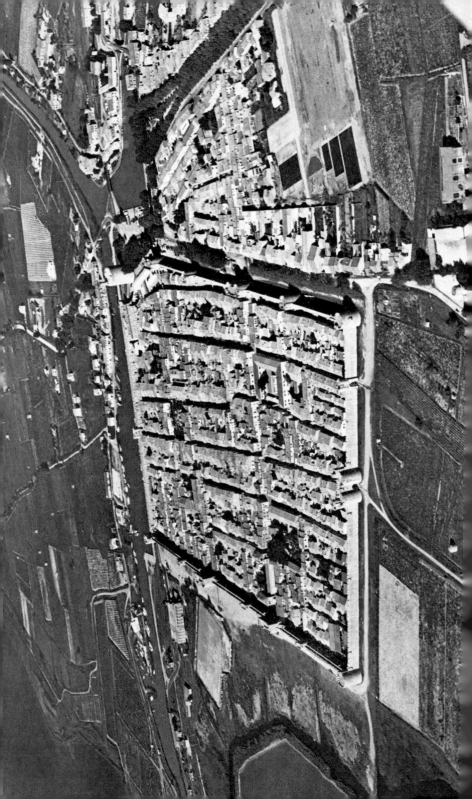

The Dutch painter, who spent almost a year as an inmate (1889–90), was probably far happier – well looked after yet at the same time enjoying an almost total physical freedom – than in Arles itself. Some of his best canvases were in fact painted during this time. Perhaps if he had not been so prone to a growing nostalgia for northern climes which urged him to leave the asylum's friendly shelter he might have lived longer, and not succumbed to the suicidal depression which overtook him fatally at Auvers-sur-Oise.

Music lovers will note in St Rémy the *Hotel Ville Verte* on the *Place de la République* opposite the comparatively modern *Eglise St Martin*, an incongruous classical style edifice at the foot of a clock tower dating back to the year 1330. It was there in close collaboration with Mistral that Charles Gounod composed his opera *Mireille*. Entering the old town to the left of the church by the *Rue Carnot* is the *Maison Roux* – marked by a plaque – where the composer played a piano version of the principal airs and choruses to an enchanted Mistral.

In Glanum on the *Plateau des Antiques* one is plunged back to a distant silence where Roman presence was first felt when the legions of Marius occupied the country after the Pourrières victory in 102 B.C. Two of the monuments, the triumphal arch and the mausoleum, are in a remarkably good state of repair, while excavations show the important role that this comparatively short-lived city of Glanum Livii with its four to five thousand inhabitants played in the general life of the colonisers until Germanic hordes destroyed it in 270.

A smaller Greek community had occupied the same site before the Romans and latterly excavations have brought to light several Greek houses – the only examples known in France – two of which appear to be in the same style as houses on the island of Delos. The largest, known as the *Maison des Antes*, with its Doric columns and probably built in the second century B.C., is the first of the semi-restorations one sees to the left just after the entry.

11   Aigues Mortes: aerial view

However, the two monuments already mentioned are the most rewarding. The arch, of a single vault, has none of the majestic proportions of that at Orange. The *Guide Michelin*, however, claims that it is without doubt the most ancient of Gaul's Roman arches and dates from the first years of Augustus's reign. Others suggest that it was built to commemorate the capture of Marseille by Julius Caesar's general Trebonus in 49 B.C.; but though as usual the reliefs include figures of chained prisoners much of the ornamentation is devoted to fruit and flower motifs, attractive but not helpful historically.

The mausoleum built between the years 5–10 of the Christian era and now definitely considered a cenotaph rather than an actual tomb is on the other hand one of the best preserved monuments of the Roman world. It towers above the arch, rising to a height of 62 feet from a square base, each side measuring 20 feet. Built up in three storeys, the first two square, the third a rotunda, its roof is supported by ten Corinthian columns crowned by a cupola.

For many years it was considered that this memorial had been raised to the memory of an extremely wealthy Glanum citizen, but the latest school of thought is of the opinion that in fact it was erected as a cenotaph to the Emperor Augustus's two grandsons, Caius and Lucius. Caius was killed in an ambush while campaigning in Armenia; Lucius, aged only nineteen, died on his way to Spain. If this theory is correct then the two toga-clad figures on the rotunda are statues of the two youths in question and the bas-reliefs, in Greek style – among them the death of Adonis and Greeks and Trojans fighting for the body of Patroclis – bear an allegorical relationship to their brief careers. The inscription to be seen on the north façade, SEX. L.M. IVLIEI. C.F. PARENTIBPS SVEIS – which can be roughly translated 'Sextus Lucius Marcus of the family of Julius, son of Caius, to their parents' – is taken to be a naïve gesture on the part of some rich Glanumian hoping to be suspected of royal connections.

From this dead plateau it is only six miles, cutting across the Alpilles by the road winding above the *Val de l'Enfer*, to the weird city known as Les Baux, built along a rocky spur, a narrow peninsula of sheer and barren cliffs rising straight as any castle walls from the desert-like surroundings where one has the feeling that since the Ice Age never a blade of grass has grown nor a flower bloomed.

The approach is highly dramatic. To begin with there is the abrupt disappearance of all forms of vegetation so that one is suddenly in a lunar landscape of completely barren hills, hewn and carved in a series of galleries and colonnades as though in the dim past this had been the home of a tribe of primitive yet artistic cave-dwelling giants.

As usual the explanation is less romantic.

In 1822 it was discovered that the rocks of the Alpilles round Les Baux contained a most precious mineral from which aluminium is produced, a mineral which appropriately was called bauxite. These vast galleries are therefore merely disused quarries which have nevertheless added a pseudo-mythical atmosphere to the environment of the city itself.

Unfortunately Les Baux is far from being the haven of peace that is Maillane. The eulogies bestowed by official guide-books have resulted in a positive invasion during the summer months with attendant parking problems necessitating the permanent presence of traffic police, and of course the inevitable post-card and souvenir pest. I cannot help feeling that the best time to see this gaunt relic of robber baronry and bathe in its grim, slightly sinister atmosphere, would be at the height of a *mistral* in mid-winter when one would almost certainly be alone, and the true savagery of its spiritual past combining with the stark present of the natural setting would make the deepest impact. I feel also that Les Baux, like Fort St André at Villeneuve-les-Avignon, and Carcassonne, is best seen from a distance as a silhouette, rather than on the more intimate terms within the city walls, despite the incredible views from the château, and the monument to the Provençal poet Charloun Rieu – who bears a striking facial resemblance to Mistral – a point from which on a clear day there is

spread a vista of the Rhône delta extending as far as Les Saintes
Maries de la Mer.

Les Baux takes a prominent place in local history from the
tenth century when a feudal family took advantage of the superb
strategic and tactical position to build a castle, from then on calling themselves the Lords of Les Baux after the rock (Baou) on
which it was built. Then, feeling established in so impregnable a
position, they had the incredible impudence to claim descent from
Balthazar (one of the Three Kings), thereafter incorporating a
silver 'star in the east' in their coat of arms. Local wars, usually
against the Counts of Provence, established in Forcalquier, seem
to have been the *Baussanques'* principal occupation till the middle
of the thirteenth century, when for a brief period the city on the
rock became famous for its Courts of Love.*

But this philandering renown was replaced from 1375 onwards
by that of Raymond de Turenne – not to be confused with the
seventeenth-century Minstrel of France of the same name – the
very prototype of noble bandit, soon named 'the scourge of Provence'. Towns and villages were raided, people held to ransom.
Those who could, or would, not pay were pushed over the top of
the castle walls to fall the best part of 700 feet while Raymond de
Turenne watched 'crying with laughter at the sight of this
anguish'! It was not till 1400 that he and his men were defeated
near Tarascon by a combined Papal and French army. When one
thinks of the very rough justice of the day it was perhaps lucky
for Raymond de Turenne that he was drowned in the Rhône trying to escape his pursuers.

Alice, niece and ward of de Turenne was the last of the Baux
family. On her death Les Baux was taken over by King René and
given as a present to his second wife Jeanne de Laval. Loss of
independence marked the beginning of an inevitable decline and
fall, the downhill trend being accelerated when the city, deeply

* Tragedy crept in occasionally to mar this artificial romanticism. One
of the Lords of Les Baux suspecting his wife's interest in a popular
troubadour of going beyond the composition of verses and frontiers of
lofty words, had the troubadour in question killed and his heart torn out
and sent to his lady as a choice *hors d'oeuvres*.

involved in the seventeenth-century religious wars, was sacked first by the Protestants and then in revenge by the Catholics. Finally siding with the Protestants it was captured and largely destroyed on the orders of Louis XIII, who then (1632) gave it to the Princes of Monaco, whose fief it has remained ever since. Today the reigning prince's eldest son bears the title *Marquis des Baux*.

Beneath the shadow of past magnificence France's present gastronomic glory is strongly represented. Just before the ascent to the ramparts and below the D27 road is the famous hotel and restaurant *La Baumanière*, one of the few in all France to earn three rosettes for its cooking in the red Michelin Guide: but not, needless to say, to be recommended to those travelling on a limited budget.

Retracing one's steps past Daudet's mill to Fontvieille, then turning north, it is a bare ten miles to another city rich in tradition and popularised by the author of *Lettres de Mon Moulin*: Tarascon and its rival on the Rhône's opposite bank, Beaucaire.

For centuries across the Rhône's broad flood, empire and kingdom as personified by these two cities watched each other with mistrust and latent hostility. In those days Beaucaire was probably the better known principally due to the great annual fair inaugurated by Count Raymond of Toulouse in 1217, a fair which remained a pole of attraction till the railway facilitated travel and such cities as Marseille, Toulon, even Paris became attainable after a matter of hours rather than days of journeying.

Old Beaucaire was constructed rather after the style of an eastern city – Fez, Damascus, Peshawar – each street in the commercial centre being given over to an individual trade, like the *souks* or bazaars. Again like its oriental counterparts at the times of the great fairs it became the centre of the little world of strolling players, acrobats and musicians who considered it the ideal setting to test popular response to a new 'number'. Traders came from India, Turkey, Egypt, Greece, Italy and Spain, displaying their goods side by side with more local products, pottery from Moustiers and perfume from Grasse. To quote Mistral:

A l'égard de Beaucaire en temps de foire
Le grand Caire d'Egypte n'était rien!
On voyait tant, jusque fondre les cloches!*

One great speciality – and very popular – were litle glass rings
which lovers offered to each other, symbolic of love's fragility. The
story also goes that in 1797 the Marquis de Sade tried to start a
private lottery with his advocate Gaufridy and his two sons. It
was not a commercial success; not a single ticket was sold!

Recently Beaucaire has become very much an industrial centre,
and passing through one's chief impression is of factory chimneys
rather than of an ancient city. In fact the best way to recapture
some fragment of the past and allow one's mind to dwell on
pictures of Nicolette wandering the dark streets in search of her
Aucassin is to gaze at the city through half-closed eyes from the
heights of King René's great castle in Tarascon.

When after the miraculous grounding of Lazarus's sail-less
craft on the Camargue shores Martha with her servant Marcelle
penetrated inland following the Rhône's course, they found the
inhabitants of the dilapidated town of Jarnegues, formerly the
Roman settlement of Jovarnica, living in a state of terror because
of the depredations of a monster known as the Tarasque, an
amphibious creature that devoured fishermen, shepherds and
workers in the fields with equal gusto.

To begin with the frightened people mistook Martha for a
reincarnation of the goddess Diana and implored her to rid them
of the pest. 'Martha much moved by their entreaties went off
alone to the dark forest, her only defence a little wooden cross and
a phial of holy water. She was guided to the Tarasque's lair by the
terrifying noises the monster was in the habit of making . . .'

This Tarasque we are told had 'the head of a lion. His teeth
were as sharp as glaives. On his neck bristled a shiny black mane.

* Poème du Rhône (French translation). 'The great city of Cairo in
Egypt was nothing compared with Beaucaire at the time of the Fair. There
one could see enough to make the clock towers melt.' (A highly Provençale
metaphor connected with that of the flight of church bells to Rome at
Easter.)

From head to tail the bones of his spine broke through his scaly skin standing up like a hundred iron spikes. His flanks quivered like the timbers of a storm-tossed vessel. His six twisted paws had claws like those of a bear which furrowed the soil on his passage. Far behind his belly trailed a tail which might have been said to resemble an asp had it not been thick as a man's waist and long as the trunk of a cedar. His strength was that of twelve fighting elephants harnessed together . . .'

At the sight of the frail Martha the beast reared up. The remains of a fisherman he was eating dropped to the ground as he opened wide his jaws. 'His eyes darted flames, his beating tail flayed the soil. He was gathering himself together to leap on his prey when the saint held up her cross and sprinkled him with holy water. Immediately the creature was seized with convulsions and fell writhing to the ground; but little by little as his fury passed he grew calmer, then began to crawl timorously towards the girl's feet, his eyes, moist with a tender fervour, fixed upon her. Martha undid her girdle, passed it round his neck and led him gentle as a lamb back to the town . . .'

I have both heard and read several versions of the end of this story: that on his arrival the Tarasque, patient and unresisting, was either torn to pieces by dogs (or stoned to death by the men); that he voluntarily leapt into the Rhône and drowned himself in expiation; that he lived tamely in the town and loved playing with the children. One can only hope both from the sentimental and fair-play points of view the last-named is the most probable.

Just opposite the entrance to King René's castle is an old rather tumbledown wall, pierced by a series of doors.

Above one is a notice – VISITEZ LA TARASQUE.

Through a small porch is a room housing a papier-maché 20-foot-long reconstruction of the monster as he was seen through historians' eyes at the time of King René, the present model being an 1840 reproduction of the original. I have to admit that the efforts to create a terrifying image have produced a comic rather than dramatic result. More than of a lion the face is that of a mixture between an angry Pekinese and an anguished nigger minstrel, while the body suggests an overgrown tortoise which has been used as a pincushion.

On 14 April 1474 King René decided that Saint Martha's miracle should be commemorated by an annual fête, and created the order of *Les Chevaliers de la Tarasque*. Usually on the morning of Ascension Day the Tarasque was brought out into the streets carried on the shoulders of 16 of his knights, eight on the outside, eight inside the hollow body. 'The procession was a great success,' one reads. 'The Tarasque seemed to be alive. It breathed fire through its nostrils by means of small rockets called *serpentcause*. It twisted and turned, charged the crowd and its swinging tail swept people off their feet.' Commenting on this 'success' the same writer goes on to say, 'In earlier times it was unthinkable that the fête should end without a few deaths.'

This somewhat robust humour does not appeal either to the modern holidaymaker or present-day citizens of Tarascon. The procession now takes place on the last Sunday of June. The Tarasque, fitted with wheels, is pushed by eight men instead of being carried by 16, and there is of course no question of charging the crowd.

Leaving the Tarasque's lair, turning left then left again, one comes to St Martha's church. The saint's body was discovered in 1187 on the site of the original Romanesque church which from 1197 for many years became the scene of a yearly pilgrimage as important as that of Lourdes. Unfortunately during the American 1944 air raids the church was very badly damaged. The fifteenth-century campanile was totally destroyed and the roof torn off. However, restoration work is being carried out. Damage to the interior has been completely repaired and has resulted in a most helpful innovation. The church is rich in pictures which miraculously escaped destruction; re-hung in their original sites they bear an inset in their frame's bottom panel giving the title, artist and date. This is all the more helpful since the huge canvases are chiefly the work of C. van Loo, P. Parrocel, Mignard and Viens, whose style, for the layman, has a marked similarity.

At the top of the stairs leading down to the crypt sheltering St

Martha's tomb, and to the right, is a recumbent statue of Jean de Cossa seneschal of Provence (died 1476), the work of Francesco Laurana. In the crypt itself is first a large stone sixteenth-century tomb showing the saint lying in state on her death-bed, clothed in nun's robes, with that almost uncanny flesh and blood quality typical of the statuary in Genoa's Campo Santo, work of a Genoese sculptor commissioned by Domenico Marini, Archbishop of Avignon. And finally half hidden can be seen the fifth-century sarcophagus in which the remains of the saint were found in 1187.

King René's castle is the finest example of *château fort* in France: the finest, in fact, I have ever seen. It has a solid beauty, a rugged strength which combine to lend it something of the Pyramids' air of time-defying eternity. Its drama is enhanced by the fact that the western walls drop a sheer 150 feet to the Rhône while the other three faces are still moat-surrounded.

The actual building begun by Louis II of Provence and King of Sicily in the closing decade of the fourteenth century was finished some 150 years later by King René, who in his old age divided his time between Aix and his Tarascon castle.

Even today all the splendour of the Middle Ages is reflected within these gargantuan ramparts: the great *cour d'honneur*, parade ground of the armour-encumbered men-at-arms, the banqueting hall with vast open fireplace, the royal apartments, the chapel, all are there, not dilapidated, not crumbling, but with a superb actuality merely mellowed by time.

It is a melancholy but probably justified supposition that one of the reasons for this remarkable state of preservation is the fact that for centuries the castle was used as a prison, up to 1926 in fact, and its walls must have left bitter memories in the minds of a number of English sailors of the eighteenth century.

Looking at the curious *graffiti* I noticed the names Simpson and Tucker, and a mournful doggerel with the scratched date 1778:

> *Here is 3 Davids in one mess*
> *Prisoners we are in Distress*

> *By the French we was caught*
> *And to this prison we was brought*

These unfortunate prisoners who could look out tantalisingly through the loopholes across the river to Beaucaire and the open country – a free world ignorant of, indifferent to, their miseries – were British seamen from the vessels *Zephyr* and *Constantine* captured off Toulon during the Seven Years War and sent to Tarascon as a really safe place of custody.

The high castle terrace should not be missed even though it means climbing 136 steep stairs. The view can only be qualified by the rather hackneyed term 'panoramic', to Beaucaire, along the Rhône's course, down into the older quarters of Tarascon itself, and to the north to a little outcrop of hills known as *La Montagnette*: the setting, the guide tells me, for Tartarin's famous shooting expeditions.*

One must also be indifferent to heights not to feel giddy looking down the 150 feet of wall, its base washed by the turgid river, from the exact spot where in 1794 18 Robespierrists were thrown over the battlements, each with a large stone attached to neck or ankle; an awesome fate; but when one considers the atrocities committed almost daily by the 'Sea-green Incorruptible's' followers, sympathy is somewhat mitigated.

Poised above the countryside one contemplates other visitors, reduced to pigmy proportions, in the elliptical cypress-protected garden at whose northern end King René and his young wife Jeanne used to sit enjoying the fresh air, effectively sheltered from the mistral.

To the south of Arles and well to the west of Marseille the Rhône spreads into a huge marshy delta covering an area of 150,000 acres, known as the Camargue.* Till 1941 most of this

---

* *Tartarin de Tarascon*, published in 1872, infuriated the Provençaux in general, and the very mention of it is still capable of rousing indignation.
* Declared a National Park in 1970.

plain apart from a few scattered vineyards and rice-fields was the home of a rich variety of bird life, peopled by herds of little black bulls (*manades*) and tough little horses, usually an off-grey, descendants of Arab chargers captured from the Saracens.

In 1941, however, when food in unoccupied as well as occupied France was becoming frighteningly scarce, draining followed by irrigation was undertaken on a major scale. Vineyards and above all, rice-fields, spread to such an extent that by 1961 instead of the 2,700 acres under cultivation 20 years previously, 50,000 acres were producing a yearly crop of 120,000 tons of rice.

This agricultural expansion and the vertiginous increase in the number of post-war tenants posed a major threat to the Camargue's wild life which could well have proved fatal, but for the creation of game reserves which today cannot be visited without a special permit, and the fact that the Camargue, thanks to the revival of the popularity of riding, has become sprinkled with pseudo-ranches, joy of the young, and in many cases not-so-young.

The main game reserve, including the vast marshy lake, the *Etang de Vaccarès*, is enclosed by the *Grand Rhône* to the east and the *Petit Rhône* to the west, with the *Parc Zoölogique* in the immediate vicinity of the town of Les Saintes Maries de la Mer. Anybody who can summon up the patience to drive slowly from Albaron to the coast will be able to see a mass of birds settling on or circling above the reedy water: duck, avocets, cormorants, herons, cranes and pink-legged flamingoes.

One's first impression on entering the Camargue after skirting Arles by the *Boulevard des Lices* and the N113, then cutting — dangerously – across the main Nîmes–Marseille road, is of the oppressive flatness so foreign to Provence, in general a hilly, even mountainous land. Roads run in long straight lines bordered by bamboo hedges and for most of the year the tarmac shimmers in a continual mirage. There is the odd copse of stunted trees leaning east at a perilous angle, the result of centuries of resistance to the mistral's uncurbed fury. Houses, whether they be old or modern, cabins of the *gardians*, the Camargue cowboys, farms, villas,

hotels, are squat bungalows or at the most one-storeyed, a uniformity due both to the practical aspect in such a wind-swept
region, and government decrees which have stepped in just in
time to prevent this almost unique landscape from being ruined
by the desecration of the *immeuble* or individual fantasist.

Running parallel to the west of the reserve the road between
Albaron and Les Saintes Maries, especially after the hamlet of
Pioch, is lined by hotels, restaurants or *auberges* advertising
promenades à cheval. Purists resent these rather phony ranches
but they have probably proved a major factor in preserving the
Camargue from the industrialists' clutches. In any case they are
not offensive to the eye, being constructed on classical *Camarguais* lines, while the very reason for their existence has preserved
two local species from extinction: the horse and the *gardian*.

On my most recent visit I was surprised by the number of horses
tethered in each ranch's open stables and the large groups of
horsemen and horsewomen of all ages clip-clopping down the road
or winding in and out of the marshy tracks on conducted tours to
catch a glimpse of the black bulls who, the *Guide Bleu* tells us in
all seriousness, '*sont de nature debonnaire; se gärder, bien entendu,
de les inquiéter . . .*'

As for the *gardians* themselves, they provide the nearest image
that most European children are liable to see for themselves of the
cowboys of 'Westerns'. Their normal work is to watch over the
manades, but today this rather meagre existence is comfortably
supplemented by the added job of acting as riding instructors and
as guides for equestrian expeditions during the long season lasting
from Easter till the end of September. These *gardians* are a
colourful race, highly individual with their wide-brimmed black
hats, gay Provençal shirts and close-fitting slacks cut in the old
cavalry 'overall' pattern. Some still live alone in the typical thatch-
roofed, one-room, stucco-walled hut like that shown in the *Musée
Arlaten* but the majority are now housed on ranches or in normal
village homes.

Les Saintes Maries de la Mer, a characterless and rather smelly
little town, depends for its existence on the attraction of the severe

fortress church around which it has grown in concentric circles.
As with the papal palace in Avignon it is rather difficult to make
out, at first glance, whether the church is indeed church or fortress.
The walls for example are not windowed but pierced by loop-
holes, their summits battlemented. The small entrance (north) and
high tower at the west end are machicolated. Defence rather than
prayer seems to be the motif.

Even the interior, gloomily dark because of the absence of
windows, presents the same fortress-like aspect. There is a high
single nave. Side chapels in the accepted term are non-existent.
There are practically no statues, no carvings, no pictures. This
rigid austerity can be understood when one learns that by reason
of its position so near to the sea on a once-lonely stretch of coast,
the church with its precious relics was frighteningly vulnerable
to the Saracen *razzias* and in the ninth century when the raids
were at their height, its walls were actually part of the little fishing
town's outer ramparts, superimposed on the original oratory built
on the site of a pagan temple.

It was enlarged in 1140 after the Saracens had been finally
defeated, and again on the orders of King René, when after the
discovery of the bones of the saints it began to draw large numbers
of pilgrims.

The crypt containing the reliquary of Sara, gypsy patron saint,
is the church's main attraction, but before reaching its steps in the
middle of the aisle in front of the altar there is a recess in the
north wall sheltering miniature statues of Marie Jacobé and Marie
Salomé surrounded by votaries. One expressing gratitude for a
miraculous escape in 1960 is written at the foot of the photographs, the upper that of a middle-aged man, the lower showing
the wreck of his car, a 2CV Citroën, taken just after the accident
and from which one can see that his survival was, indeed, a
miracle. On the right, nearer the altar, an iron grill surrounds a
fresh-water well. Out of place, one might think, in a church's
aisle, but the well, which is said to be on the spot where a miraculous gush of fresh water saved the lives of the saints after, adrift
without food and water for so many days, they had run ashore,

was of inestimable value during the many sieges to which the town was subjected by the Moslems.

Stone steps lead down to the crypt's blackness. Legend insists that Sara was a dark-skinned Egyptian who of her own free will accompanied the Maries on their dangerous journey. 'During the evangelisation of the Camargue she used to go begging amongst the shepherds in order to buy such things as were necessary for the material well-being of her mistresses. If one may believe a devout work of the sixtenth century it is because of her self-assumed role that the gypsies adopted her. The same tradition adds that Sara's death occurred about the same time as that of the Maries and that she was buried with them . . .' (*Guide de la Provence Mystérieuse*).

The roof is low, the darkness in these depths of the earth lightened only by guttering candles is eerie; in summer the atmosphere is stifling. At the far end the lid of a sarcophagus (probably third century) serves as an altar. To the left surprisingly enough is a queer pagan altar whose details are difficult to determine in the pervading gloom, but which, a pamphlet on sale outside the church assures us 'was later used for Christian worship'. To the right is a small statue of Sara, black of face, clothed in spotless white robes, at her feet a small box with glass sides filled with photographs, offerings of cheap artificial jewellery, surrounded by bouquets of faded wild flowers: expressions of simple faith and as stirring as a *flamenco* lament.

The most important pilgrimage takes place every 25 May, attended by gypsies from all over Europe, but there is an unfortunate tendency these days for it to degenerate into a fair rather than a predominantly religious gathering, to all but the truly initiated, in a setting dominated by booths and portable juke-boxes, with the gypsies themselves almost indistinguishable from the *Roumi* in both dress and methods of transport. Elderly Mercedes and Cadillacs have replaced horse-drawn caravans, the men's blue jeans seem to be almost a world uniform, and the women's full skirts vary little from *avant-garde* 'maxies'.

But despite this drift to commerciality the real heart of the gypsy life remains, kept more or less secret from the outsider. One may watch on the fringe the procession on the 25th – provided one does not suffer from gregarophobia – when relics and statues are carried through the streets, the dancing which follows after vespers, listen to the wild singing, the guitars – one might be lucky enough to hear Manitas de Plata – but the news-hound, the inquisitive fact-finder, the earnest student of folklore, are not popular. During the actual ceremonies the prevalent fear that by mixing with a gypsy crowd one is liable to have one's wallet removed, is unfounded. But once relics and statues have been returned to their niches, as Archibald Lyall says, 'Watch your pockets from now on, for the "truce of God" is over.'

In recent years Les Saintes Maries suffers another annual invasion but unconnected with holy places: that of the summer tourist and holidaymaker. The small *plage* is as crowded as that of St Tropez and the large parking space, backed by a stone dyke and almost below sea level, is invariably packed and not improved by two stark public lavatories, a permanent overflow spreading from the actual premises in a doubtful stain across the cement.

Ethnologically and climatically therefore the best time to visit the Camargue is spring and early autumn. The winter weather can be bitterly cold, summer stiflingly and stickily hot. Most of the year mosquitos are a scourge, but late spring, after the May pilgrimage, is also an opportune moment to see such purely local fêtes as the *ferrade* and the *courses à la cocarde*.

In the first, the mounted *gardians* separate young bulls from the main herd, then throw them in classical rodeo style for the branding. The *courses à la cocarde* is the Camarguais version of the *corrida*, in some ways just as exciting as the infinitely more sombre, more dramatic stylised Spanish national sport; at the same time so much more humane since the heavy shadow of death, dark heritage of the Spaniard's basic character, is absent.

Like their more massive Spanish counterpart the Camargue's little black bulls are bred for the ring rather than the grill, but are never killed or even wounded. On the other hand the *rasetteurs** or local toreadors may sometimes be gored – one *gardian* to whom I was talking recently had a wicked-looking horn scar beneath his navel, proudly shown off by his hipster slacks – and often badly bruised.

The rules of the game are simple. A bull, a cockade attached to its forehead, is let loose in the arena with several *rasetteurs* immaculately dressed for the occasion in white shirts and slacks. The prize goes to the one who snatches the cockade.

These little Camargue bulls cannot be compared in strength and ferocity with the monsters of bone and muscle armed with the wickedest horns who appear, to meet their death, often to kill before being killed, in the arenas of Spain, Mexico and southern France – notably at Nîmes and Arles. But this very smallness gives them a surprising agility demanding a corresponding nimbleness on the part of their opponents.

Between the Camargue proper and Marseille (the *Etang de Berre*) is a 120,000-acre expanse of dead flat ground, the Crau, in contrast with the Camargue utterly unproductive and totally devoid of wild life.

Legend gives as explanation of this stony waste a dispute or battle for life waged by Hercules on the spot when he was attacked by two giants. The hero was on the point of collapse when Jupiter decided to take a hand in the matter by crushing the giants beneath an enormous shower of stones and rocks which he had ripped from both sea and river-beds. Less romantic is the geologists' theory that the layer of pebbles, sometimes 50 feet thick, is the work of the Durance river which once flowed direct into the sea but which as a result of various natural upheavals over the course of centuries, ending with the Durance's confluence with the Rhône, swept the accumulating shale across the flat delta country.

The Crau is also the setting for Mireille's fatal wanderings in search of Vincent before, blinded by the sun, suffering from heat exhaustion she manages to reach the Saintes Maries church –

* *Raset* denotes the pirouetting half-turns made by the *rasetteurs*, much after the style of a *matador* placing the *banderillos*.

Gounod's opera stages the final scene on the *Place* – to die in the arms of her would-be lover to the accompaniment of her parents' lamentations.

After crossing the Petit Rhône, and on the Camargue's western edge, one comes to the former port of Aigues Mortes, one of the few European towns still completely surrounded by medieval ramparts. Lovers of the Age of Chivalry argue the respective visual merits of Carcassonne and Aigues Mortes. Probably the distant view of Carcassonne is the more evocative, but close up Aigues Mortes has the considerable advantage of standing on its own with no modern quarter to mar the aspect of the rectangular thirteenth-century *enceinte*, pierced only by four main gates: a magnificent façade with the geometrical perfection of a child's magnified cardboard fort.

At the time of the town's foundation by St Louis in the early thirteenth century the sea, today a good five miles distant, was up to the site on which the French king chose to erect a fortified base for his crusading ventures, and it was from Aigues Mortes that he sailed in 1270 on his last journey, eventually reaching Tunis where he died of plague, caught from his own stricken soldiers whom, with a complete disregard for personal well-being, he insisted on visiting.

One can make a complete tour of the ramparts on foot – it took me 50 minutes – a walk best undertaken in the evening when the surrounding marshes are plunged in vague purple shadow, the dull hum of voices from the neatly laid out little town below replaces the more strident crescendos of internal combustion engines, and even the solid clouds of mosquitos rising from a thousand stagnant pools seem more of a stage prop than a pest.

The only architectural break in the town's rectilinear monotony is a turret at the north-west corner, still moated. Known as the *Tour de Constance* it is just over a hundred feet high, dominating the rest of the ramparts; it served not only as a watch tower and lighthouse but also for nearly 500 years as a prison in turn for the Knights Templar and Huguenots. Best known of the latter was Marie David, shut up in one of the cells for 37 years. Never very

13 The Pont du Verdon, near Moustiers Ste Marie

robust, her health was completely undermined by this incarceration but her indomitable will-power so impressed the Prince de Beauvan when on a tour of inspection that he ordered her immediate release together with ten other imprisoned Protestants.

The Prince's gesture in such an age of intolerance makes pleasant – perhaps optimistic – reading.

4. Aix-en-Provence

Quand passait une belle fille
Les Aixois, la trouvant gentille
Un peu distraits dans leurs discours
Se retournaient le long du Cours.

Although astride the N7 main road and linked by *autoroute* with Marseille only 20 miles distant, the centre of Aix has retained the calm one associates with old university cities. Less flamboyant than Avignon, less folkloric than Arles, it can claim to be the heart of Provençal cultural life, and one can understand why René, the king who loved the arts and shunned war, chose it as his capital.

For many centuries before King René, however, Aix had enjoyed the reputation of a cultural centre. It owed its foundation not to a dominant strategic position but to the quality of its springs, so much appreciated by the Romans, and as Marcel Brion points out, 'A watering-place implies the influx of a culture-ridden population seeking amusement.'

In 731 Aix shared the sombre fate of all the principal Provençal cities, towns and villages during the gloomy four centuries overshadowed by the Saracen scourge; but soon after the Moslems' final defeat the city became the favourite playground of the Angevins when Provence and Anjou were united by marriage (see p. 19), blossoming with 'Good' King René into a first golden age.

René 'by the Grace of God King of Aragon, Jerusalem and

Sicily, of Valence, of Majorca, Sardinia and Corsica, Duke of
Anjou, Duke of Bar, Count of Barcelona, of Provence, of Pied-
mont' was probably the most amiable of absolute rulers of all
time. Significantly he took the greatest pleasure in and showed the
most love for one of the humbler of his fiefs, Provence. As
historians reproach with justification he was a feeble commander
on the battlefield, but no other monarch of his day spread so much
happiness among or was so sincerely mourned at his death by the
poor.

To compensate for his lack of strategic vision, King René was
fluent in Latin, Greek, Italian, Hebrew and Catalan. A brilliant
musician, painter, and writer of verse, he was also an accomplished
achitect, agriculturist, and keen gardener. His library in Aix was
considered one of the most complete in Europe. Not only was he
so highly talented himself but he loved nothing better than helping
other gifted people in their careers. To him also was due the
inauguration of a number of picturesque festivals, such as that of
the Tarasque and the procession of the *Fête Dieu* (Corpus Christi),
some of which are still carried on. Nor should it be forgotten that
thanks to King René's piety the relics of the Holy Marys were
discovered.

'He cherished his people, protected the humble, encouraged
the workers. He encouraged the re-inhabitation of villages emptied
by incessant war. He rewarded and enobled the deserving bourgeois. He organised agriculture. King-peasant, king-shepherd, his
home at Gardanne with its flock of 3,000 sheep was a veritable
model farm. It was he who decreed the height of the Aix fountains
so that sheep might drink from them. His great pride was to watch
his plants of Sicilian muscatel vines flourish, then distribute
them. . . .' The king's chronicler Bourdigue noted, 'He used to tell
princes and ambassadors who came to visit him that he preferred
country life to any other because it was the only genuine way of
life and the most removed from all ambitions . . .'

This love of the arts and the simple life, of festivities of a cheerful, friendly nature, went even deeper than the satisfaction of a
natural benevolence. René was also a philosopher endowed with

social wisdom. 'He' (René) 'nourished a secret aim: to assemble political parties, families, social castes, the great, the lowly, friends and enemies in one great joyous crowd . . . And men? If they hated each other it was because they did not know each other, because prejudice and misunderstanding separated them. A monarch's duty was to bring about this reconciliation, to force them by means of a general happiness to get to know and love each other . . .'

Poor René was an idealist living many centuries ahead of his time in a singular age of hate and violence rivalling that of the second half of the twentieth century.

Soon after his death Provence was united with France. By then the cultural reputation of Aix was such that the city became – and for three centuries remained – capital of the province, seat of parliament, the *Etats Provinciaux* and a governor, and though the sixteenth century was troubled and made bloody by Charles Quint's invasions and wars of religion, a second even if less brilliant golden age dawned in the eighteenth century, lasting till the Revolution: an age when it became fashionable to have a home in Aix and the aristocracy vied with each other in the building of the most elegant private *hôtel*.

The Revolution was much less of a bloodbath in Aix than in Marseille but nevertheless it destroyed the city's status as a capital, reducing it to that of a *sous-prefecture* even though bringing to the fore a figure in Aixois history whose fame almost rivals that of King René, though for totally dissimilar reasons. This was Count Honoré-Gabriel Riqueti de Mirabeau, whom Taine called a *satyre colossal et fangeux*, born on 9 March 1749 in the Château de Bignon. He was often referred to because of the violence of his nature as *Monsieur Ouragan* (tempest) and first came to the notice of Aix citizens because of his scandalous behaviour which set the whole town gossiping. Extremely plain, almost ugly, he nevertheless was attractive to women and when at the age of 23 after quarrelling with his father he found himself almost penniless, he had no difficulty in seducing – and marrying – Aix's richest heiress, Mademoiselle de Marignane.* However, the more money he had the more he spent, till he soon found himself owing the best part of 200,000 *livres* to indignant Aix shopkeepers.

At this point the old Marquis de Mirabeau intervened, and had his son shut up in a series of prisons, while the wife indulged in a temporary adventure with a certain Monsieur de Gassaud. This prison life lasted for several years, the younger Mirabeau growing not only to hate his father but his own class in general and all that they stood for. While behind bars Mirabeau showed himself as facile a writer as he was to prove orator, composing alternately scathing anti-government tracts* whose publication only increased the disrepute attached to his name, and bawdy fiction after the style of the Marquis de Sade, his cousin whom he loathed, fellow-prisoner at the time of his incarceration in Vincennes.

Finally released and becoming notorious after a speech in court during a case brought against him by his wife, in which, rounding on her advocate, he said, 'A man like you is merely a vulgar trader in words, lies and insults' – the advocate in question fainted before the speech was ended – he decided to go in for political life, not as a member of the aristocracy but of the *Tiers Etat* : the people. Hate had made the aristocrat a demagogue, but an able and for a time popular demagogue, producing such slogans as *les privilèges finiront mais le peuple est éternel.*

In 1789 his popularity was so great that he was elected both by Aix and Marseille – but chose Aix – as their representative at the *Etats Généraux*. In spite of his over-advertised democratic sentiments he still had flashes of pride and self-satisfaction combined with a growing tendency to snub social inferiors – *ils* (the people) *ne me pardonneront jamais ma supériorité* – which might well have cost him his head had he not died suddenly from an attack of acute nephritis on 27 March 1791.

It is a fitting tribute to these two figures, king and demagogue,

* After a reception in the Marignane home Mirabeau slipped up to the girl's bedroom, spent the night with her, and next morning appeared almost naked on her balcony to inform passers-by in the street below of his amorous success.

* One of the first, *Essai sur le Despotisme*, was a ruthless attack on royalty.

that Aix's principal thoroughfare should be named the *Cours Mirabeau*, while at the top of the Cours as if giving it his blessing is a statue of 'Good' King René, a modern (nineteenth-century) work of David d'Angers. The good king, crown balanced on his long hair dropping to his robed shoulders, holding a sceptre in his right hand, has a bunch of his beloved muscat grapes in the left, a pile of books at his feet; and he stands on a column in a fountain round whose base four stone lions spew water through their open mouths.

One cannot but agree with the general consensus of opinion that the *Cours Mirabeau* is one of the finest streets in any town. Sloping gently from the east and King René's statue, it runs between four ranks of plane trees down to the *Place de la Libération*, the city's main cross-roads where the traffic is split up by the central *Fontaine Grande*, while in the centre of the Cours itself – just over a quarter of a mile long – are two other fountains, the *Fontaine des Neuf Canons* (1691) and the *Fontaine Chaude* (1736), the latter fed by the same spring whose medicinal properties first attracted Caius Sextius a hundred years before the Christian era.

A peculiarity of the *Cours Mirabeau* is that its two sides have nothing in common. The north pavement is occupied mostly by cafés and restaurants, the most well-known being the *Café des Deux Garçons* at the upper end near King René's statue – popular meeting-place for the international crowd of students from Aix's 500-year-old university. The south pavement is lined with the famous *hôtels* of Aix's later heyday, still preserving their original façades and beautiful old doors. The most striking is No. 38, the *Hôtel d'Espagnet* with its caryatides; while No. 10, with a magnificent door strengthened by wrought-iron bars, is the *Hôtel d'Isoard de Vauvenargues*, where in 1784 the Marquise d'Entrecasteaux was murdered by her husband.

St Sauveur Cathedral to the north of the Cours is another of those vast medieval buildings found in so many of Provence's principal towns and cities inspiring both awe and a personal sense of insignificance. Concerts of sacred music are given in the cathedral during the July festival and I was told by one atheist critic that the most moving experience of his career was a performance of Verdi's Requiem in this perfect setting.

The great masterpiece sheltered by the cathedral walls – and it would be worth making the journey to Aix if only to see this and nothing else – is the Nicolas Froment triptych, 'The Burning Bush'. Colour, detail and symbolism are exceptional in this work painted specially at King René's request.

On the central panel and in the centre of the Bush, here shown as a green carpet formed by the intertwined branches of a small copse rising from a rocky outcrop, is seated Our Lady with the child Jesus on her knees and holding in his left hand a mirror reflecting their two faces. At the foot of the rocks and in the foreground the elderly Moses looks up, shading his eyes with his right hand, while with the left he is taking off a shoe, traditional sign of respect. Opposite him in the left foreground kneels an angel whose robes are held together by a large cameo brooch on which can be made out Adam and Eve and the serpent. Above this central panel, framed by a frieze of the 12 kings of Judah, is an inscription which could be translated, 'In the bush which the (fire) could not consume seen by Moses, we recognise, Holy Mother of God, the preservation of thy miraculous virginity'.*

The side panels are equally impressive, for the kneeling female figure on the right has the features of René's young second wife Jeanne de Laval. Behind her are St John, St Catherine and St Nicolas de Myre wearing his bishop's mitre: at his feet two children whom he is supposed to have brought back from the dead. To the left, also kneeling, is King René – one notices his delicate artistic hands, contrasting with his double chin and generally rather porcine features – and immediately behind him are St Mary Magdalene, the white-bearded St Maurice, and a dark-bearded man in full armour, right hand resting on the hilt of a double-edged sword.

* Froment based his interpretation of the legend of Moses and the Burning Bush on the dream of a monk, Adam of the St Victor Abbey (twelfth century) in Paris, who claimed to have seen the Virgin in the midst of flames.

Completed in 1476 this work was not exposed in the cathedral till 1803, being originally part of the decoration of the church of the *Grands-Carmes* where King René's heart was buried.

Interesting from the point of view of a visitor from north of the Channel is a series of 17 Flemish-school tapestries in the east end, originally a gift to Canterbury Cathedral: a gift which does not seem to have been appreciated, for they were sold and bought in Paris for the Aix Chapter.

In St Mitre's chapel behind the high altar is the fifth-century sarcophagus containing the saint's relics, a picture on wood graphically depicting the martyred man standing bolt upright holding his head in his hands, probably painted by Nicholas Froment, and stained glass panels by Guillaume Dombert.

Mitre (probably a gallicised version of the Latin Demetrius) was a farm labourer in the pay of a moneylender by name of Arvendus. As Mitre was highly virtuous he was in the habit of lecturing his master on the error of his ways, a habit which so irritated Arvendus that one day he went out into his vineyard, cut most of the grapes and then accused Mitre of stealing them. The pious Mitre prayed all night, and the following day the enraged Arvendus found that the grapes had re-grown. His counter move was to denounce Mitre as a sorcerer. Virtue in this case was unrewarded; Mitre was seized, tortured, tried, condemned to death, and beheaded on what is today appropriately the *Place des Martyrs de la Résistance*.

However, no sooner had his head fallen than Mitre rose to his feet, picked up his head and carried it across to the cathedral. This unusual sight, we are told, 'made the soldiers laugh till they cried, while the children screamed with terror'.

The former archbishop's palace which can be reached through the cathedral cloisters has been a tapestry museum since 1909. Divided into six galleries, these Beauvais tapestries show scenes from Don Quixote, a series called 'Grotesques' – stylised figures in feathered headdresses – and three *Jeux Russiens*, depicting fur-hatted (presumably the reason for the qualification 'Russien') young men and girls disporting themselves on a snowy landscape.

The model for the Don Quixotes was a series of cartoons by Charles Natoire published in 1735 which can be seen now in Campiègne.

During recent years the palace courtyard has served as an open-air theatre for performances of lighter operas – by Mozart and Rossini – during the July music festival.

Aix's principal museum, the *Musée Granet*, named after the painter Granet who contributed 502 canvases to the original collection and who died in 1849, is in the newer part of the town known as the *quartier Mazarin* lying south of the Cours Mirabeau, the Mazarin in question being the famous cardinal's brother, himself an archbishop in the mid-seventeenth century. Installed in a former priory of the Maltese order restored in 1671 it is generally considered as one of the richest in provincial France. Given over mostly to painting it does indeed contain a considerable and varied collection, but in general I found it less rewarding than the *Musée Calvet* in Avignon. This does not mean that it can be ignored, especially by those who are archaeologically rather than picture-minded, as the ground floor contains a collection of pre-Roman Celto-Ligurian sculptures, the oldest yet to be unearthed in France. Among them are a number of death masks, a grim bas-relief of a mounted warrior, a human head attached to his charger's arched neck, and three armoured busts. From abroad there is a beautiful statue of a Persian soldier, work of the Pergamo school second century B.C. brought back from Italy and presented to the museum by the Aixois sculptor Giraud.

Since I last visited the *Musée Granet* work has been going on enlarging and rearranging the interior. Four more rooms will be opened. A further archaeological *salle* is to occupy the basement and the second floor will be entirely devoted to the works of Dutch-Flemish painters, including two Rubens, a Holbein (school) portrait and a Van Coxyen, *Toilette de Venus*. The works of a number of French painters comparatively unknown outside their own country figure in the *École Française du XIXième Siècle* and *École Provençale* collections – none of those I saw could, to my lay mind, compare with the Avignon Vernets – and it was surprising that Aix's most famous painter, Paul Cézanne, was hardly represented other than by a few water-colours of his favourite subject, the *Sainte-Victoire* mountain, and a vague *Paysage de la Campagne d'Aix*. The reason may well be the astronomical value of a Cézanne today which might also explain the absence of both Van Gogh and Gauguin.

Before leaving the *musée*, the Italian gallery (sixteenth-eighteenth centuries) should be visited for the brilliant but gruesome canvas by Polidoro Caldara, better known as *Il Caravaggio*, of Salome being handed John the Baptist's head. Those attracted by the macabre will also be interested in one of the sculptor Chastel's creations, *L'Assassiné*, displayed in the *Musée Paul Arbaud* in the *Rue Mazarine* close by. It shows the lifeless body of a good-looking young man, all the more lifelike in that quite by accident the artist saw the squabble which ended fatally for this posthumous haphazard model. The little museum, opened in 1911, is mostly concerned, however, with less eerie subjects of strictly Provençal interest: portraits of Mirabeau, of the Félibriges, Mistral, Roumanille and Aubanel, a self-portrait of Granet and drawings by Fragonard and Puget.

Near the *Palais de Justice*, opening on to the *Place des Prêcheurs*, is the *Eglise Sainte-Marie-Madeleine*, originally a Dominican monastery rebuilt and enlarged between 1691 and 1703. Now the church is a veritable picture gallery; the chapel of *Notre Dame de Grace* – fifth traverse to the left of the entrance – shelters a fifteen-century triptych of the Annunciation, cause of considerable controversy. To begin with, of the three panels only the central is original: the others copies.* The identity of the painter responsible has been hotly disputed. First considered to

* Even over these panels there is a divergence of opinion. The *Guide Bleu* and Archibald Lyall state that one of the originals is to be found in London, the other in Brussels. Jean-Paul Clébert on the other hand agrees that the right panel is in Brussels Museum but considers that on the left, figuring Isaiah in a green robe, to be in the possession of a Vierhouten collector. The third version regarding the left panel is that of Marcel Brion who says that half of it is in an English private collection and the other half in the Amsterdam Rijksmuseum.

reveal without any possible doubt the hall-mark of the Flemish or Burgundian schools it would now seem to have boiled down to a choice between Jean Chapuis (or Chapus) known to have lived and worked in Aix in the mid-fifteenth century, or Guillaume Dombert. Finally there is a school of thought which would have one believe that the picture was painted with subtly impious intent. A monkey on the cornice – a creature of supposed ill-omen – is said to be in the way of the Lord's redeeming breath descending on Our Lady's head, while the flowers in the foreground are basil and aconite, much used in witchcraft. Having studied this picture closely I cannot see any justification for this interpretation. The breath, shown in light rays, falls directly on to the Virgin's head while the flowers in the vase – to me at any rate – seem remarkably like lilies; it is best perhaps to look on it as a very genuine and beautiful piece of work and leave it at that.

Like the poet Mistral, Paul Cézanne (1839–1906) – whose studio can be visited; a little house with a garden on the *Avenue Paul Cézanne* – was born, lived most of his life and died in the same place; but unlike the poet, the painter knew moments of mental torment aggravated by professional doubts and domestic upheavals. On the other hand, another common link was that both began their adult lives studying law, and both were influenced by famous writers, in the case of Cézanne the brilliant novelist Emile Zola, who on receiving a letter from his friend hesitating to choose between the safety of a legal career or the hazards of an artist's life, wrote, *Sois véritablement avocat ou bien sois véritablement artiste, mais reste mon ami, c'est tout ce que je désire.*

Probably it was this letter which persuaded Cézanne to give up his legal studies, and with a reasonable father's permission – Monsieur Louis-Auguste had started off life as a hatter but ended a banker – was able to go to Paris to plunge himself into a semi-sophisticated *vie de Bohème* in the company of that band of rebels calling themselves Impressionists, Pissaro, Sisley, Monet and Renoir, whose ideals he adopted enthusiastically, not rising to the top spectacularly but slowly, surely, as a result of intense study and hard work. But though intoxicated, unlike Mistral, by the atmosphere of the capital he could never forget his native Provence, and it was the Provençal landscape which gradually obsessed him as the subject for his work.

His first real exhibition was not held till 1874 – a joint exhibition with other Impressionists – and was more of a public scandal than a public success. Most of the visitors were either shocked or amused, but – major step forward – the famous canvas *La Maison du Pendu* was bought by a rich amateur collector, Count Doria. Even so, despite this very real encouragement, Cézanne – refused entry into the Academy – became more or less a recluse for the next 18 years, painting but not showing his pictures, his life further complicated by a mistress, Hortense, and their illegitimate son Paul, whom Cézanne kept comfortably but secretly at Marseille, not daring to admit this liaison to his bourgeois banker parents.

Unfortunately a letter addressed to *Paul Cézanne, peintre* and sent to the *Jas de Bouffan*, the family home, was opened by his father who could hardly believe his eyes on reading references to a 'wife and child'. The result was a serious quarrel. Cézanne left the *midi* to install himself at Melun, but though his father refused to see him he still, fortunately for the painter, continued to pay his allowance. However, 1866 at last saw a family reconciliation on the understanding that Cézanne married Hortense, a condition to which, apparently rather unwillingly, he agreed, finally moving to Gardanne, subject of one of his best-known canvases, with his wife and the young Paul.

The same year the old Cézanne died and Paul found himself a comparatively wealthy man. He moved into the *Jas de Bouffan*, painted more furiously than ever but still unknown to the general public, making a few excursions into the (for him) foreign world of Paris, gradually growing more disillusioned, more misanthropic till his death in October 1906: his deepest hurt his conviction that it was on him that Zola had modelled the hero of *L'Oeuvre*, the novel of a painter who failed.

For Cézanne the subject nearest to his heart was the long granite ridge looking down on Aix from the east, known ever since

Marius's defeat of the Teutons as the *Montagne de la Sainte-Victoire*. This was his favourite model, as real to him as if it had been flesh and blood, and which he painted it is said at least a hundred times without once being really satisfied with the result.

The round tour of this strange barren mountain is known as the *Route Cézanne* and leaves Aix by a minor road to the village of Tholonet. It is from Tholonet, where there is a small statue of the painter, that one gets the first real view of the mountain face to face, more cliff than slope, rising straight from a tumble of scrub-covered foothills.

The *Sainte-Victoire* always reminds me of the body of a monstrous headless, tail-less dragon, and from Tholonet it is the chest and shoulders with which one is confronted, towering blunt and forbidding, and round which the road swings narrow and winding to the tiny hamlet of St Antonin, thence straightening to continue parallel with the southern flank – the monster's 'ribs' – by far the more impressive. Indeed all Cézanne's painting were of this southern aspect, never the northern and gentler.

Moving slowly along the road, stopping from time to time, it is easy to sympathise with the artist's fascination. Geologically the Sainte-Victoire is a limestone dragon's back ridge whose highest point, the *Pic des Mouches*, rises to 3,300 feet: sides precipitous, denuded, furrowed by deep jagged ravines like the open lips of petrified scars, at first sight harsh, almost repellent. Yet one has only to remain a few minutes on the same spot to become aware of the extraordinary play of light and shadow violently flinging into relief an incredible gamut of colour. This chain of rock for so many days of the year with the clarity of a steel blade against an equally sharp steely blue sky, can assume a tigerish gold, a blood-less grey, a mourning purple, a molten glitter, in succeeding moods as rapidly changing as those of an over-pampered pop singer. It is difficult enough to describe; to capture on canvas must be practically an impossibility, conducive to melancholia or frustration complexes. It may well have been responsible for Cézanne's ever-increasing irritability.

Approaching the ridge's eastern extremity is the tiny village of

Puyloubier, a narrow main street, a little square with fountain, two cafés much frequented by inhabitants of the home for Foreign Legion invalids and old soldiers – a rural Chelsea Pensioners' establishment – the *Domaine de Capitaine Danjou* (see p. 181), a couple of miles east of the village itself on the road to Pourrières (see p. 13). The *Domaine* occupies over 1,000 acres and is something of an eye-opener regarding what a (genuinely) grateful government is prepared to do for those who have faithfully served France. The old Legionaries, either physically incapacitated or merely finding themselves with no other ties either of family or country at the end of their service, afraid of being cast out into the jungle of civilian life, are lodged in a huge semicircular building, completed in 1958, known as the *Hemisphère*. They are housed and fed – a half-litre of wine a day is included – free. If they wish for a few extra privileges such as a private sitting-room, they can pay a comparatively small sum. To give them an interest, a trade, there are workshops, watchmakers, a book-bindery, a pottery. The men wanting to take part in one of these occupations are paid for their work and get a share in sales. Additionally the Domaine produces its own fruit, vegetables and wine and has its own flock of sheep. These old soldiers do not feel themselves abandoned, rejected once they have served a purpose. Better still, they are happy.

The north face of the Sainte-Victoire is devoid of drama, its only interest being Vauvenargues *château* close by the village of the same name. For centuries this was the home of one of France's oldest families, the De Clapiers, of whom the best known is probably Luc de Clapiers born in 1715, who turning his back on a military career in order to write, produced such works as *Maximes* and *Méditations Sur la Foi* before his death in 1747, and of whom Marmontel said, *Pour soutenir l'adversité on n'avait besoin que de son exemple.* The château, looking over a wooded valley and dating back to the sixteenth century, is in typical Provençal style, square-proportioned and flanked by two circular towers; it was bought by Picasso in 1958.

Running more or less parallel with the Sainte-Victoire, the

southern side of the plain split in two by the Arc river and the N7 road is the eight-mile-long ridge, the *Massif de la Sainte Baume*, taking its name from the cave or *baume* where Mary Magdalene is reputed to have spent the last years of her life.

According to the legend, after landing on the Camargue coast Mary Magdalene, 'the eternal penitent', determined to pass the rest of her days in solitude. She set off on her own, following the course of the little Huveaune river, and turning south began to climb the steep slopes of the range before her. It was dangerous country. Though only the same height as the Sainte-Victoire, the Sainte Baume is split by deep gulleys, the few paths winding along the edge of precipices. The surface is slippery and a misplaced step could be disastrous, but at last she found a tiny cave, damp and in semi-permanent darkness, which she decided to inhabit and where she lived for 30 years, her only nourishment roots and rainwater.

The story of Mary Magdalene also records that after seven years' solitary existence had passed God called on her to say a prayer. She looked at her hands, caked with seven years' dirt, and begged for some fresh water, at which a spring gushed from the floor of the cave. Mary Magdalene rubbed her hands together vigorously and seeing them again soft and white could not stop herself from exclaiming *O lei bellei maneto!* (Oh, what pretty hands!) God then realised that she was still not purged of her former worldliness and condemned her to a further 23 years' reclusion. She burst into tears, and from her tears were born the Latay, the Issole, the Caramy, the Cauron and the Peruy rivers.

The Hostellerie de la Sainte Baume which can be reached by the D80 road is the best place to stop to refresh oneself before making the final climb on foot to Ste Mary Magdalene's cave, a walk ending with a winding stairway of 150 steps carved out of the hillside. The actual cave with water-sweating sides has been a chapel since the thirteenth century, when Pope Boniface VIII gave permission for the Dominicans to build a small monastery on the site, a monastery which was falling into ruins after revolutionaries had driven the monks out till its restoration was taken in hand in 1822 and the Dominicans returned in 1859.

14 *Moustiers Ste Marie: the church*

Just behind the altar, steps lead to a little terrace called the Place of Penitence, and above this, on a straight cliff face 500 feet above the cave is the deserted little chapel of St Pilon, on a rock pillar looking out over the sea. To this pinnacle, inaccessible in those days to anyone but a skilled mountaineer, angels carried Mary Magdalene every day to pray.

Botanists, as well as students of hagiography, will be interested in the Sainte Baume forest. For centuries tree-felling has been forbidden with the result that as Marcel Brion says, 'The forest reminds one of those paintings of the earthly paradise in which "Velvet" Breughel amused himself by including on one canvas trees of every known kind from all types of climate'.

To the north of Aix across the Durance river is a compact area which is in itself a land apart, an area composed of two low ranges of hills, the *Massif du Luberon* and the *Plateau de Vaucluse*. Through the high valley between them, like a knife, cuts the N100 road, a long unfrequented route through forgotten country running from Avignon to the Italian frontier on the *Col de Larche* and then on to Cuneo.

With the upper Var (see Chapter 7) this region of Provence is the least touched by the July-August tourist invasion, but whereas the upper Var, though beautiful and unspoiled, has little to attract the historian, every square foot of the Luberon and the Vaucluse is steeped in history, most of it of a tragic violence. Again while the upper Var presents vast uninhabited expanses, a visual luxury becoming increasingly rare in western Europe, the Luberon and surrounding country are dotted with villages, each one with its château whose story goes back to the mists of the early Middle Ages.

It is only 15 miles from Aix to the village of St Christophe on the Durance river, facing the little town of Cadenet on the far bank. At Cadenet instead of taking the direct road to Apt, the only town of any size in the area, it is worth turning right to visit the *Château d'Ansouis*, a classified historical monument still today after 600 years the home of the Comtes de Sabran-Pontèves, raised

15   *Grand Cañon de Verdon: bergerie, Falaise des Cavaliers*

paternally above Ansouis village – just on 500 inhabitants – built on the projecting ledge of a rocky spur.

The actual château, which can only be visited with a guide and from two to six in the afternoon, is a seventeenth-century construction, though the original fortress was probably raised in the early twelfth century. The dining-room, used by the family and not merely a museum piece, is hung with Aubusson tapestries of scenes from the story of Dido and Aeneas. Beyond it is a bedroom where François 1 passed the night after the battle of Marignan (Melegnano); on one side of the bed is a Rubens of the young Louis xiv and on the other a Murillo.

In the older part of the château is the room devoted to the memory of Elzéar de Sabran and his young wife, Delphine de Signes, whose story dates back to the mid-thirteenth century. In those days of arranged marriages, Charles ii of Naples hoped to strengthen his position by uniting the two families of Sabran and Signes, both of whom had shown themselves to be his loyal supporters. Delphine, who had been brought up in a convent, though only 15 years old had already taken a vow of chastity. However, she agreed to the marriage if her proposed husband would do the same. Elzéar accepted her conditions and in this room – now called *la chambres des Saints* – one can see the two very small chairs in which they sat when after the marriage ceremony their vows were mutually renewed. The truth about this strange marriage was kept secret till on his death-bed Elzéar, just 40 years old (1285–1325), was persuaded by the priest administering the last rites to make the astonishing history public so as to set 'a shining example of virtue to the Christian world'.

Delphine survived her husband 37 years during which time she lived in a state of absolute poverty, eating and drinking only just enough to keep her alive, never speaking, and sleeping on a bundle of straw.

It was on her insistence, however, that Pope Clement vi canonised Elzéar. On her death she was buried beside her husband in an elaborate tomb built for them in the *Chapelle des Cordeliers* in Apt, which most unhappily was destroyed by revolutionary vandals. Today the busts of the two saints – Delphine was herself canonised – are kept in the little Romanesque church built into the foot of the castle walls. This tradition of adherence to the true principles of Christianity was again in evidence when the Sabrans refused to participate in the abominable St Bartholomew massacre.

The château chapel, which contains a thirteenth-century sculptured figure of Christ and an altar gift of Louis xv, also has a link with the present day: a memorial tablet to Jean de Vallambrosa, mentioned in dispatches for gallantry, killed in action 11 June 1940.

The gardens, sometimes described as 'hanging', complete the very considerable charm of this living present monument to the past and future. It is a good description, for the alleys of clipped hedges give the impression of being suspended in space with tremendous plunging views down over the village roof-tops and the vine- and olive-cultivated valleys.

Still on the Luberon's southern slopes, just over 10 miles to the west of Cadenet, is Merindol, a small village built below a sad mass of ruins on the upper slopes. It is a place of no actual interest, one of the few villages in the region without a château or church worth the briefest of halts. Yet in 1545 it was the scene of one of the bloodiest atrocities in French history. This was the time of 'The Heresy of the Vaudois'.

The originator of this sect was a certain Pierre de Vaux, born in the mid-twelfth century at Vaux-en-Dauphiné, who before being excommunicated by the Concilium of Latran in 1179 had founded the brotherhood of 'The Poor of Lyon', soon called 'The Vaudois'. According to Emmanuel Davin, 'Walking barefooted, wearing a black robe, they used to move from door to door begging and arousing sympathy. To begin with they declared themselves to be against the Albigenses and many Roman Catholics became 'Vaudois' thinking that by so doing they were not straying far from the old religion (*La Vaudoisie en Provence*).

The Vaudois did in fact believe in Communion and adult baptism but they did not believe in most of the Roman Catholic precepts, among them baptism of children, marriage, and the Cross.

As early as 1332 the sect was declared heretic by the Avignon popes and throughout the fourteenth century to admit to being a Vaudois was more or less the equivalent of signing one's own death warrant: death by burning at the stake. Repressive measures took on a further severity and amplitude in the early sixteenth century, particularly from 1528 to 1533, when a Dominican, Jean de Roma, was appointed Inquisitor for the Luberon area, having as his lieutenants Jean de Grossi, the judge at Apt, and Pierre de Sade. It is not the purpose of this book to go into details of the appalling tortures inflicted on miserable individuals on the orders of this trio but it is perhaps of interest to note that Jean de Roma died in Avignon in 1542 'after the most cruel sufferings, his body covered with ulcers, his soul tortured by remorse'.

The final act of this sad drama began when in 1540 the Aix parliament passed the Merindol Act, so called because Merindol village was the religious capital of the 10,000-odd Vaudois in-habiting the Luberon region. The Act decreed that at all costs the heresy must be exterminated and confided the task to Baron Jean Meynier, Lord of Oppède, a fortified village on the Luberon's northern slopes and seat of the Meynier family.

By 1545 Baron Meynier had recruited an anti-heretical army of 4,000 men-at-arms, including primitive artillery pieces, and launched his attack on 16 April; Merindol itself was razed to the ground on the 18th. By the 21st no less than 22 villages had been wiped off the map; the official number of dead was quoted at 1,840 while 255 survivors were condemned by Aix parliament to be burned at the stake and another 666 to the slow death of the galleys.

News of this massacre aroused such indignation throughout France that Henri II repealed the Merindol Act and Meynier d'Oppède together with most of his henchmen was brought to trial in Paris in 1551. The Baron was found not guilty thanks to various and devious machinations of the legal apparatus of the day, only victim of the trial being Guérin the *procureur-*

général who was hanged, and whose head was then sent to Aix to be exposed on a pike in the *Place des Prêcheurs*. The Baron, however, did not as one might say get away with it. Five years later in 1556 he was poisoned by a Protestant doctor and *trépassa d'un mal d'intestin merveilleusement douloureux.*

From Cadenet the Apt road passes through Lourmarin in whose cemetery the Nobel literature prizewinner Albert Camus is buried. Before crossing the spine of the Luberon *massif*, half-way to Apt, it is better rather than carrying straight on, to turn left to Bonnieux, one of the many fortified villages on the northern slopes from where there is a superb view of the whole area: the Luberon itself, the Coulon river valley, the Vaucluse plateau, and above, the volcanic silhouette – rather like a giant Vesuvius – of Mont Ventoux.

For anyone who for business or family reasons is obliged to take a holiday in July or August, this to my mind is by far the most agreeable area of all Provence, combining as it does natural beauty, historical interest, good climate, freedom from crowds and the infuriating seasonal rise in prices endemic to most other regions. Furthermore the principal villages, Bonnieux, Lacoste, Menerbes, Oppède, Gordes, Roussillon, are now attracting an international circle of writers and artists who find the surroundings so conducive to work that they are settling there semi-permanently.

Bonnieux, a village built up in three tiers, almost like the bridge of a mammoth battleship, is famous for its cherries and the good humour of its inhabitants, who are inclined to feel a certain sense of superiority *vis-à-vis* the neighbouring villages. Popular rumour is that this near-smugness is due to the fact that, at the height of Avignon's glory as city of the popes, the offspring of any amorous accidents of members of the papal suite were farmed out permanently to Bonnieux families. These little 'accidents' and in turn *their* offspring were fully aware of their origin and looked upon themselves as belonging to a social level considerably higher than that of their rustic playmates: a naïve snobbism preserved to this day.

Also on this northern flank of the Luberon is Menerbes, important Protestant stronghold towards the end of the sixteenth century,
with a sixteenth-century castle presently being restored, and a
church of the fourteenth century in which one can see two anonymous but beautiful primitives, St Hilary of Arles and St John the
Baptist, and the bust of the poet Clovis Hugues (1851–1907) born
at the *Moulin du Castellet* in the *commune* of Menerbes, son of
farm labourers. Intended for the priesthood Clovis Hugues became a rabid left-wing republican whose works – *Jours de Com-
bat, Madame Phaëton, Le Sanglot de Jehanne* among others –
had so strong a political bias that he is often qualified as *le poète
rouge.**

A little farther on in the direction of Cavaillon, Oppède-le-
Vieux, ancestral home of the sinister Baron Meynier, clings high
on the slopes above the nondescript modern Oppède. The old part
is a most highly dramatic, once fortified emplacement, till recently
almost totally abandoned and in ruins, a real phantom village.
Today, however, its unique position commanding a view even
more vast than that from Bonnieux has attracted a number of
young artists who have restored unaided many of the ruined
houses on the lower level. Now this movement is being followed
up and some of the larger medieval houses higher up towards the
sixteenth-century church are coming into the hands of professional
builders and architects.

Oppède-le-Vieux first became the fief of the Meynier family in
1480 when it was bought by Accurso Meynier, famous legal ex-
pert, for many years the King of France's representative in Venice,
who at the time of the purchase obtained from Pope Alexander vi
– since Oppède was in papal territory – the right to call himself
Meynier d'Oppède. Jean, the butcher of Merindol, was born in
1495 at Aix and created baron by Pope Clement vii in 1529. He
married twice, Jeanne of Ventimiglia and Magdalene of Castel-

* In the little public garden is a marble statue to a Danish captain
Charles von Rantzau who went into voluntary exile in Menerbes in 1781,
dying there eight years later after being involved in a conspiracy against
the Minister Struensee, lover, if rumour is to be believed, of Queen
Matilda.

lane, had one son and two daughters by the first marriage, the second being childless. At a time when the question of an heir and the preservation of family was of such vital importance his fanatical hatred of the heretics can perhaps be explained by the fact that his son, also Jean, became a Vaudois principally because of his love for a young Vaudoise, Mademoiselle de Boulier de Cental, who in turn realising that there was no hope of parental blessing for their marriage, committed suicide by jumping out of a window.

Some two centuries later another equally shadowy name became associated with the village: that of the horrific Marquis de Sade, author of the so-called novel – in fact more of a diseased treatise – on obscene and brutal sexual perversions, *Justine*. Having escaped from Valence the original sadist arrived in Oppède in August 1778 and was hidden for a time by the *Chanoine* Vidal. Uneasy, he returned to his château in Lacoste – between Bonnieux and Menerbes – where he was re-arrested on the 26th of the same month and immediately taken back to his cell in Vincennes.

Lacoste is still dominated by the ruins of the *Château Sade* but here again restoration in progress should resurrect this castle which in 1778 counted no less than 42 rooms. The village itself is shut in, shadowy, rather silent, rather sad, as though still oppressed by· the ghost of the marquis, for it was in Lacoste that Donatien-Alphonse-François de Sade was arrested for the first time after a peculiarly revolting sexual crime committed in Marseille in 1772.

The southern flank of the Vaucluse plateau also has its collection of picturesque and interesting villages. Strangest is Roussillon 'the red' standing on a small hilltop in the middle of brilliant red earth, outlined like a giant blood-clot in the midst of a generally grey-green landscape, whose houses also are of vivid red, more glowing than those of Marrakesh. The reason for this extraordinary coloration is that the surrounding earth is impregnated with iron oxide, and as such Roussillon is one of the few places in the world where the ingredients for painters' red ochre can be found.

Only some six miles to the west is another hilltop village, Gordes, which like Oppède-le-Vieux was till recently deserted. As

I write it is being rapidly restored thanks to the efforts of a number of artists who have done such good work as to make it a popular tourist centre.

Like the majority of the villages here, Gordes is dominated by a magnificent Renaissance château, from the exterior the most majestic and the most impressive in the whole region, its sense of impregnability enhanced by two enormous round machicolated towers on the east front dating back to the thirteenth century and incorporated into the newer building.

The low scrub-covered hills round Gordes are dotted with *bories*, small huts built entirely of drystone. These *bories*, used as shelters by shepherds and cultivators, are possibly the oldest type of human habitation known in Provence, their design that of pre-Roman days. However, there is a tendency to go into ecstasies when confronted with a *borie*, imagining oneself to be contemplating a 2,000-year-old dwelling, whereas in actual fact it is considered that few if any of them date back further than the seventeenth century. A painter now resident in Gordes, has had the original idea of buying up a number and converting them into rather unusual guest bungalows.

Still farther into the heart of the Vaucluse plateau is the former Saracen stronghold of St Saturnin d'Apt, a rather busy little town reached after a short but steep climb, built at the foot of a cliff crowned by the old fortress ramparts which one enters by a wonderfully preserved pure Moorish arch. Within the ramparts is a reservoir, invaluable in times of siege, and a fortified chapel in the saddest state of disrepair where at the end of a crumbling passage I came across what might have been a monk's cell. On the floor lay an abandoned wooden cross and a shroud-wrapped figure of Christ, pierced hands and feet projecting from the shroud's white folds. There was no way of telling whether this disarray was the work of an enthusiastic Jacobin or the result of sheer neglect. In either case it was a melancholy and depressing spectacle.

From the ramparts there is another typical panoramic view, but the village itself is singularly lacking in character, though the parish church of St Etienne uses a drystone hut as a font and has in the porch a miniature *borie* constructed by the *curé* with his own hands. Unfortunately the famous picture of Christ on the Cross from whose painted wounds blood was seen to flow on 13, 16 and 20 December 1850, has disappeared altogether and without trace.

Apt, the only town of any appreciable size – 8,000 inhabitants – in this area, its main square just across the bridge on the Avignon N100 road, a rather alarming criss-cross of roads lined by hotels and cafés boasting juke-boxes screeching the most un-melodious of pop music at maximum volume, is a busy little centre with a long history. First it was a Celto-Ligurian oppidum of the Vulgientes tribe, then created a Roman colony by Julius Caesar and named Apta Julia. Today, however, but for the fact that it is one of the best and cheapest shopping centres in Pro-vence – at certain times of the year fruit and vegetables reach a near pre-war price – the town's only attraction is St Anne's Cathedral.

Apt was the first town in France to venerate St Anne, mother of the Virgin Mary. Her body, brought back from the east in Gallo-Roman times, was landed at Marseille and handed over to the Bishop of Apt for safe keeping, but the actual cult of St Anne is not recorded until the twelfth century.

In the meantime the relics like those of the Holy Marys had been buried to prevent them falling into Saracen hands and, in the course of years, forgotten.

They were not hidden for long. On Easter Day 776, Charle-magne himself was in Apt to consecrate the cathedral and the ceremony was just finished when the Baron of Caseneuve's blind deaf-mute son suddenly threw himself on his knees, began scratch-ing at the floor and making signs that the flagstones should be removed. Charlemagne gave orders for this to be done. The result of the ensuing excavation was the discovery of an oratory of St Auspicius, Apt's first bishop. Digging was continued enthusiastic-ally and a second crypt was found, and though, as everyone knew, it had been sealed up for several hundreds of years, there was in it a small oil lamp still burning. Before anyone could even express astonishment the lamp suddenly went out, and at that exact moment the young Caseneuve recovered his faculties – sight, speech, hearing – and his first words were to announce the fact that this second crypt contained the body of St Anne, mother of Our Lady.

'Then the holy relics were seen in a cypress coffer enveloped in a veil on which one could read these words: *Hic Est Corpus Beatae Annae Matris Virginis Mariae*. As soon as the coffer had been opened, as if to confirm the miracle, God perfumed the air with a sweet and subtle odour bathing the two crypts' (*Le Pélérinage de Sainte-Anne-d'Apt* – Abbé Gay).

St Anne's chapel is immediately to the left of the west door, the relics being just above the altar. One sees the bust of the saint (a 'primitive') against the background of a starry dome flanked by that of St Auspice on the left and of St Castor on the right. In this same chapel is also the modern tomb of the Sabran family of the *Château d'Ansouis*.

The 'Treasure' in the sacristy shelters a curious relic: St Anne's veil, also called 'the Arab standard', thought – falsely – to have been worn by the saint in her lifetime. In actual fact it is a light form of *kaftan*, woven probably at Damietta between 1090 and 1100, brought back from the first crusade by Rambaud de Simiane and used subsequently as a wrapping for the relics when they were carried in procession through the town during the great pilgrimages of the seventeenth century when they were popularly supposed to be endowed with miracle-working properties.

It was in fact to Apt that Anne of Austria came in 1623 to pray to her patron saint that her marriage would not be childless, offering a solid gold statuette to adorn the shrine: a prayer answered 15 years later when she gave birth to the future *Roi Soleil*, Louis XIV.

5. Two Rivers – The Durance and the Verdon

With the Rhône, the river Durance, popularly known as one of the 'Three Scourges'* of Provence, has always figured largely in the Provençal story. To follow the roads skirting its banks – being unnavigable one cannot do so on its troubled surface – is not only to sample a wide range of scenic contrasts but to traverse towns and villages whose names history has perpetuated.

From the point, a bare three miles south of Avignon, where the Durance flows into the Rhône, and as far upstream as Peyruis below Sisterton, I am reminded of the Jhelum winding through the Punjabi plains – or perhaps, nearer home, the Po – an immensely wide stony bed, rounded pebbles almost glittering in the sun, a few spiny bushes (Chaste plant) growing haphazard, and the river itself split into small channels, labouring sluggishly as if in agony and threatened with possible extinction. By the time it reaches Sisteron, however, the Durance becomes a classical waterway, admittedly less than half as wide as the Rhône at Avignon but filling the space between its banks, flecked with an occasional flash of white by an inexorable current, soon degenerating into a mountain torrent till the point where it disappears north of Provence's boundaries in the huge artificial lake, the reservoir de Serre-Ponçon, created in the bowl where formerly was its confluence with another mountain river, the Ubaye.

First of the towns on the Durance worth a visit is Cavaillon, a traffic-ridden spot famous for its melons. Being near the river it was the site of a Ligurian *oppidum*, becoming a Roman city under

* The other two being the *mistral* wind and 'the parliament'.

the name Cabellio about 42 B.C. If, however, Cavaillon, apart
from its cathedral, may not seem a place to linger, it is worth while
remembering that it claims to have inaugurated the first regular
European ferry-boat service, and this in the days before the
Roman occupation. The ferrymen are described in modern French
as a *corps d'utriculaires*. Their boats, or rather primitive rafts
were inflated leather hides, *outres*; hence the name *utriculaires* for
the boatmen themselves, who not only made the crossing of the
Durance but navigated these unwieldy craft downstream as far
as the confluence with the Rhône, a trade they continued to exercise until the tenth century.

Continuing past the small town of Pertuis and the village of
Mirabeau, with its four-towered seventeenth-century château or
gentilhommière, home of the Mirabeau mentioned in the previous
chapter, one comes to the confluence of the Verdon and the
Durance, a truly medieval landscape where at the same time one
is brought face to face with the middle to late twentieth century,
the Cadarache dam, beginning of a canal which runs into the
Etang de Berre near Marseille, dotted throughout its length with
hydro-electric works: and the 3,500 barbed-wire enclosed acres of
the Cadarache Nuclear Research Centre. Though these two projects, especially the former, may be necessary to life's evolving
pattern it cannot be said that they embellish the countryside.

Escaping from the revelation of things to be, Manosque is the
next place of importance on the Durance's course.

Until comparatively recent times it must have been an enchanting ancient town in the middle of a rich agricultural area, but as
the *Guide Bleu* admits 'son expansion économique et industrielle
tend, depuis quelques années, à modifier profondément sa vocation
et son caractère traditionnel'.

This *expansion industrielle* has in fact modified Manosque's
aspect so profoundly that one has the impression of a rather nasty
little product of post-1945 mushroom development, one's eyes
being filled with the unedifying spectacle of a succession of bare
and glaring multi-storeyed blocks of flats of the type normally
described as HLM (*habitation à loyer modéré*). The old ramparts

have been pulled down, to be replaced by boulevards, leaving only the fourteenth-century *Porte Saunerie*, battlemented entrance to the principal street, the *Grande Rue*, and the *Porte Soubeyran*, sister to the *Porte Saunerie* but now after restoration surmounted by a wrought-iron campanile.

On his way to Ansouis after the battle of Marignan, François I was received by the town's consul, Antoine de Voland. The consul was the proud father of an exceptionally beautiful daughter, one of the group of young girls selected to presented the city keys to the monarch. Her looks and figure were so outstanding that the king could not keep his eyes off her, his expression clearly betraying his thoughts and hopes. A little surprisingly perhaps the girl, instead of being flattered, was shocked and disgusted, and anticipating that her father would be unlikely to make any objection to royal propositions of an intimate nature, rushed to her room, tore her face with her nails, then rubbing sulphur into the wounds set fire to it. François, genuinely distressed and also impressed, gave the girl a handsome dowry to compensate for the loss of her looks and named the town *Manosque the chaste*!

From Manosque, following a still Punjabian Durance, it is only about 15 miles to Forcalquier, former seat of the Counts of Provence. The ancient city is built round the upper slopes of a conical hill and crowned by a domed church emerging from a circular wreath of immense cedar trees: its main approach one of the most dramatic in Provence.

Here there is nothing to spoil the near-mystic atmosphere of this medieval stronghold brooding silently over the vestiges of a long-past glory. There are no factory chimneys; one is not aware of power pylons. Lying back some four miles from the river it is off the main traffic routes. Well over 2,000 feet above sea level the light is startlingly clear. Trees and buildings remind one of a Breughel background, so sharply are they silhouetted against grey-green slopes. The silence has an endemic quality. Forcalquier is indeed one of the most impressive, at the same time both nostalgic and deeply moving, of all Provençal cities.

Thanks to its position and the natural toughness of the

peasantry the Saracens suffered heavy casualties every time they attempted to storm its rocky heights, though the best-known history of these long wars is one concerning chivalry rather than massacre: that of a beautiful girl, Alaete Nicolai, and a handsome young Emir, Omar Ben-Mansur.

It was in the autumn of the year 1020. Alaete had been visiting relations and was on her way back to Forcalquier when she and her little escort were overtaken by a group of Moorish horsemen. Alaete 'expected that she would suffer the natural fate of a young and pretty girl prisoner in such circumstances. But it happened that the leader of the troop, Omar Ben-Mansur, was a true gentleman. Politely he asked her a few questions, looked her up and down appraisingly, saluted her solemnly, then rode off with his horsemen'.

Alaete reached Forcalquier without further incident, and realising that the Saracens were in the neighbourhood the city was prepared for defence; the water cisterns were filled, the granaries stocked, the moat deepened, the ramparts hastily repaired. Soon afterwards the Saracen hordes appeared and deployed for the attack.

The city held out for several days before the attackers managed to breach the walls and poured in. The last centre of resistance was the parvis of *Sainte Marie* church and commanded by Alaete's father, Marc-Antoine Nicolai. It was shortlived and Marc-Antoine badly wounded. At the sight of her father's wounds Alaete gave a piercing scream. Omar heard the scream, came charging to the rescue, recognised Alaete and immediately took the whole family under his protection. As a local historian, Camille Arnaud, points out, 'What had to happen, happened.' The young couple fell in love and Omar asked the convalescing Marc-Antoine for Alaete's hand. It was Alaete, however, who refused on religious grounds. Whereupon, still according to Camille Arnaud *'le Maure, de plus en plus* gentleman, *prit la main de la jeune fille, y imprima un baiser et partit dignement'*. Alaete for her part took a vow of chastity.

Forcalquier reached its heyday in the twelfth and thirteenth centuries after Raymond-Berenger III of Barcelona became also

Raymond-Berenger 1 of Provence and on his death split his
domaines, leaving Barcelona to his elder son and Provence to the
younger, Berenger-Raymond, who made Forcalquier his capital.
The houses of Catalonia and Provence were finally separated
after the defeat of the Catalans – who had taken up the cause of
the Albigensians – at Muret, and the Counts of Forcalquier became hereditary rulers of Provence from 1209.

These rulers were for the most part liberal minded men. Garcin
(*Dictionnaire de Provence*) records, 'They' (the Counts of Provence) 'held court wherever they happened to be, in the courtyard
of a public building, beneath a pine tree's shade, by a fountain or
on the banks of a stream . . .' Most of the towns enjoyed a certain
degree of autonomy. Count Guillaume abolished tithes. Raymond-
Berenger v, husband of Beatrice of Savoy, was so enlightened that
he is quoted as one of the blessed in Dante's *Paradiso*. He was not
40 when he died on 19 August 1245, but during his lifetime Forcalquier had become a centre for the troubadours and the Courts
of Love. However, he is best of all known for the fact that he was
father of four daughters often referred to as the 'diamonds of
Sainte-Maime': a château near Forcalquier, a favourite country
seat.

All of course were 'exceptionally beautiful and virtuous'. The
eldest, Marguerite, became Queen of France on marrying (Saint)
Louis ix. As noted as her husband for courage and piety she
accompanied him on the crusades and when Louis was captured
at Mansurah it was she who organised and inspired the defence
of Damietta. On her return to France a Catalan troubadour fell
in love with her and was murdered in the *Bois de Boulogne* at the
spot known today, in memory of the unfortunate would-be lover,
as the *Pré Catalan*. Eleanore, the second daughter, married Henry
iii of England in 1236. Provençal historians are not very kind to
the English monarch. André Bouyala d'Arnaud says, '*Elle*'
(Eleanore) '*devient célèbre par sa grande piété. Elle aurait pu avoir
à se plaindre de son épouse, qui était volage . . .*' Sancie, the third,
became wife of Richard Duke of Cornwall and later, when her
husband was crowned at Aix-la-Chapelle, Empress of Germany.

As for the fourth, Beatrice – or Beatrix – thanks to her marriage with Charles of Anjou, Provence became fief of the Angevin family till its unification with France, a union which accelerated the process of Forcalquier's decline.

In 1250 the city numbered over 12,000 inhabitants but after years of comparative peace allied to prosperity it was to suffer from periodical outbursts of violence. During the troubles engendered by the question of 'wicked' Queen Jeanne's succession Forcalquier was subjected to a siege lasting over a year by the forces of Charles of Durazzo. Later it held out against Raymond de Turenne's bandits, *Les Routiers* (Freebooters). It was sacked by the Huguenots and in 1630 over 2,000 inhabitants were wiped out by plague. Today according to the latest census Forcalquier's population is reduced to 2,612, but in this decline – I prefer the word to 'decadence' – the town has preserved the dignity of an ageing aristocrat faithful to lineage and principles, a dignity from which emanates an aura of eternity.

On the main *place* is the cathedral of *Notre-Dame (de la Merci)*. Until the thirteenth century Forcalquier was part of the diocese of Sisteron, but on becoming capital of Provence permission was asked and granted for the church to be known as a con-cathedral, a title which it retained until 1789.

Outside the cathedral's west door is an obelisk with a plaque dated 1935 commemorating the seven-hundredth anniversary of Eleanor's marriage to Henry III. The interior is extremely simple with only one large picture near the font. The nave is ninth century and the apse and choir are Gothic. On either side as one approaches the white marble altar, the original choir stalls are carved with the figures of the apostles, though many have been damaged by acts of vandalism probably the work of the revolutionary mob. Above the west door a small but perfectly proportioned and richly coloured rose window seems to spread a glowing twilight in the general darkness.

Apart from the *Place Saint-Michel* with its Gothic fountain and statue showing St George slaughtering a rather *tarasque*-like dragon, the old town is a mass of narrow streets and it is through

16   Castellane: Notre Dame du Rocher

these streets, becoming steeper every moment, that one climbs to the citadel by a precipitous path up a slope planted with immensely tall cedars which, especially in summer, have both the aspect and smell of a pre-independence Indian hill station: Simla or Murree.

On the hilltop, flattened, known as *La Terrasse de la Citadelle*, is a modern chapel, a mixture of Romanesque and Byzantine, with a cupola supporting a gilded statue of the Virgin, *Notre Dame de Provence*, visible from many miles' distance no matter from which direction one approaches the town. The decoration is entirely on a Provençal theme. Above the altar the crowned Virgin Mary in a long robe has her hands resting, on the right on the red and gold striped armorial shield of Provence, on the left on that of Forcalquier, both being held up to her by kneeling angels. The capitals of the columns are carved with angels playing traditional Provençal musical instruments. The west door, actually thirteenth century, divided into two panels at either side of an elaborate pillar, is crowned by a tympan with a central figure of Our Lady surrounded by local saints.

On the northern edge of the *terrasse* a *table d'orientation* has been set up which goes to the extravagance of giving directions and distances from Forcalquier not only of the principal Provençal cities but also of Paris, London, Madrid, Rome and Moscow. Perhaps it is a justifiable fantasy, for the view is really astonishing, as though such prosaic matters as horizons were non-existent.

Beneath the *terrasse's* overhanging ledge, on the southern face and reached by a narrow path dug into the hillside, is a tiny reproduction of the grotto of Lourdes, the damp walls of the cave covered with votives.

Forcalquier is also blessed by nature in that its air is the clearest, possibly the healthiest, in France, the reason for the building in 1938 of the *Observatoire Nationale d'Astrophysique* on the hill of Saint-Michel to the north of the town. According to statistics the air here is so pure that on an average, 250 nights a year, as against 80 at Mount Wilson in the USA, are suitable for astral studies. This observatory, however, had a predecessor.

17   Fréjus: the cathedral cloisters

Towards the end of the seventeen century a high-ranking officer in Forcalquier, André d'Arnaud, engaged a young Dutchman, Godfrey Wendelin, as tutor for his son. Wendelin, an enthusiastic astronomer, was so impressed by the limpidity of the sky and the extraordinary brilliance of the stars that he obtained permission to build an observatory, one of the first in the country. His chief discovery was the scientific explanation of a natural phenomenon known as *une pluie sang*, till then considered a sign of celestial wrath: in reality a fall of dust mixed with microscopic red organisms.

For so small a town, Forcalquier cemetery is both gigantic and unusually planned. The alleys threading among the tombstones are lined by huge yew hedges clipped to resemble arcades. The work – and expense – involved must be very considerable but the result is that one has the impression of wandering in an immense dark green and peaceful monastery garden. It was in this cemetery that the Drummonds were buried – Sir Jack, his wife and their daughter Elizabeth – after being savagely and mysteriously assassinated in the middle of a night in August 1952 while camping by the banks of the Durance: an apparently motiveless crime still unsolved. The three graves are side by side, that of Elizabeth in the middle, the inscription 'In death they were not divided' on the tombstone. I noticed a pathetic little jam-jar containing freshly-cut wild flowers left by an anonymous hand.

Before leaving Forcalquier one should visit the eighteenth-century *Château de Sauvan*, four miles down the Apt road, which like the *Château d'Ansouis* is still a family home, that of the De Forbins. Built for residential rather than defensive purposes the rooms are considerably larger than those of Ansouis and the interior decoration is more elaborate, particularly noticeable in the vast dining- and drawing-rooms. There is a story that at the time when Marie Antoinette was under sentence of death, the *châtelaine* of Sauvan sent the sum of 100,000 francs to the revolutionary government with an offer to mount the scaffold in place of the queen. The guide told me that the government accepted the money but not the substitution. However, when I asked if there were a picture of the would-be martyr he produced a small picture of a woman in mid-nineteenth-century costume.

Soon after leaving Peyruis the Durance begins to change its character, the river-bed narrows and the river flows in a continuous stream, more turbulent with every mile. On the Sisteron side of Peyruis one should cross to the left bank to the small town of Les Mées lying under the shadow of a long high cliff broken by a series of vertical columns like a rank of petrified guardsmen, some of them more than 300 feet high, known as *Les Penitents*, similar to the Greek *meteora* in the Thessalonian plain. Local inhabitants, however, see in them a likeness not to soldiers but to monks, and go so far as to claim that this is in fact what they are.

During the time of the Saracen wars, the Mountain of Lure on the opposite bank sheltered the monks of St Donat. Donat himself spent his days and nights praying for the victory of the Christian commander in the area, the Sire de Bevon. His prayers were answered. De Bevon routed the Saracens, finding among the many prisoners rounded up after the battle a group of young and highly desirable dancing girls. On hearing of this the austere Donat went to de Bevon and implored him to send away this group of 'she-devils'. Reluctantly – one would imagine – de Bevon agreed. The girls were put on a boat for Arles – still occupied by the Saracens – and the monks ordered to line the river to see that there was no clandestine disembarkation. According to the legend 'this was not a wise move; confronted with the spectacle of these young bodies draped in transparent veils, the monks showed an interest which was too polite to be honest. Donat, revolted by these over-attentive gestures, immediately turned his companions to stone *'dans l'attitude même de leur désir'*. And the chronicler concludes, 'and that is why, beneath their lowered hoods, the penitents of Les Mées continue for all time to look down on the flowing river'.

Another 25 miles on, the river, now an angry flood even at the height of summer, is Sisteron, marking the geographical and ethnical frontier between Provence and the Dauphiné. Being an important road junction and astride the mountain highway linking Cannes with Grenoble, the *Route Napoléon* traffic assumes an alarming density in the summer months. Also because of a certain strategic importance Sisteron was heavily – many consider unnecessarily – bombarded from the air by the US Air Force on 15 August 1944, resulting in the destruction of considerable areas of the old town. Fortunately the ancient citadel though also badly damaged was not beyond restoration and has reassumed much of its former glory.

The Voconces, a Gallic tribe, were the first known occupants of this site, conquered in 25 B.C. by the Emperor Augustus who named the city at the foot of the rock on the river-bank Segustero, the present-day citadel being the capitol. With the fall of Rome Sisteron was involved in continual wars for the best part of 1,000 years: with the Saracens, in the struggles between the house of Aragon and Forcalquier, between the 'Kingdom' and the 'Empire', and finally the merciless wars of religion. It was only after the accession of Louis XII to the outbreak of the Revolution that – as the recorded voice says from the first *point de sonorité* in the citadel – 'time flies away uneventfully'.

Visiting the citadel entails a laborious climb and perhaps hundreds – though I did not count them – of steps before reaching the third and highest of the three tiers of ramparts which give this vast fortress an aspect of impregnability in the face of all but the very latest weapons of destruction. This remarkable feat of military engineering was the work of Jean Erard. It took four years – 1597–1601 – to complete, and can certainly rival anything I have seen by the more renowned Vauban. In fact to quote again the anonymous voice, now assuming that of Erard, 'that system of fortification I devised for Sisterton was to make the future and renown of my successor, Vauban, while ungrateful history forgot even my name . . .'

From the eastern face there is an eagle's-eye view over the town, the river, its confluence with the Buech, and the little suburb of La Baume connected with Sisteron proper by an iron bridge. To linger over this view and that of the surrounding country is a good excuse to rest aching calf muscles, but not recommended to those suffering from vertigo: especially if one ventures along a narrow corridor between high ramparts into the tiny rounded tower known as the 'devil's sentry-box' which, projecting from the main wall, literally hangs in space.

One feels as though all contact with the ground has been lost, looking down on the traffic, the largest lorry the size of a mini-toy, people who have taken on antlike proportions, and the river so far below that it has lost all sense of movement and could well be a static blue-grey tape, its monotony relieved by occasional white specks. Sinister also is the opposite rock face at whose foot the La Baume houses huddle, a bare wall scarred by five deep parallel clefts as if rent by the claws of some gargantuan feline.

Right at the summit of the fortress in a constricted *donjon* reached by a narrow winding staircase in almost perpetual darkness is the tiny room in which Casimir of Poland was imprisoned on Cardinal Richelieu's orders for over a year. His full story may be heard by pressing the button on a *point de sonorité* outside the cell, a story which has much of the romance and adventure of a Dumas novel. He complains bitterly and with reason of the icy winter winds and the summer's stifling heat, adding (in the rather quaint English translation) 'besides I became a butt to the vexations of the low soldiery'. In August 1639 Casimir was removed from Sisteron to be incarcerated for a further six months in Vincennes before being finally released. After this – I quote again from the same English translation (supplied at the entrance) – 'he gets ordained and released from his wows' [*sic*] 'becomes king of Poland, marries his sister-in-law, abdicates, settles in France, marries again there and a widower for a second time, shuts himself up in a cloister where on 24 May 1672 God puts an end to the life that had been so diversely agitated . . .'

In this form of *Si Sisteron m'était conté* another *point de sonorité* explains, and quite rightly, that had the town on 5 March 1815 held out against Napoleon's march on Paris this last adventure of the Emperor's would have ended prematurely by the banks of the Durance.

Sisteron was the birthplace of Paul Arène (1843–1896) a gifted writer too little known outside France who like his successors Jean

Giono and Marcel Pagnol specialised in stories of Provence and
always referred to Sisteron as Canteperdrix, the city whose people
like to say '*Ici les oliviers commencent*'. His best-known works are
Jean des Figues, Au Bon Soleil, and perhaps *Vers la Calanque*.
With Mistral, Paul Arène shared the same passion for the sun, the
Provençal countryside and its people, but his writing is always
gay, even puckish, with none of the fluid pomposity which today
makes *Mireille* rather heavy going in places. Marie Mauron has
described him as *toujours impécunieux, riche partout de poésie*
and has suggested that the inscription on Mistral's sundial could
well apply to him:

> Gai Lesert Beu Toun Souléou
> L'Ouro Passo Que Trop Léu
> E Deman Plouro Beléu*

At Sisteron the Durance steps out of, or rather in the natural
order of things, enters Provence, after mingling its waters with
those of the Ubaye river to form the immense barrage or artificial
lake at Serre-Ponçon, 2,500 feet above sea level, a lake created in
1960 and covering 8,000 acres.

The Verdon, Provence's other famous river, resembles the
Durance in its lower reaches, but for the most its course is a wild
exciting torrent tumbling through superb scenery in a series of
great gorges.

Very soon after its confluence with the Durance just below
Gréoux-les-Bains, a spa still retaining a charming *Belle Epoque*
atmosphere and complete with casino, the Verdon emerges from
the lower gorges split in two – the lower *Canyon de Quinson*, five
miles long, and the *Canyon de Baudinard*, eight miles – by the
village of Quinson and a tiny valley now transformed into a lake.

From Quinson, however, one should make a short detour up
the Verdon's small tributary, the Colostre, across a gently undulating lavender-planted plateau, to the small but historic town of
Riez, very much off what people please to term 'the beaten track'.

* Gay lizard, drink of the sun..Time passes only too quickly..And
tomorrow perhaps it will rain.

Riez, today little more than a large village (1,108 inhabitants), centre of a lavender, olive, wine and truffle-producing area, was once an important Roman city, Reia Apollinaris: later, from the fifth century to 1790 a bishopric. The original city was founded on the site of the present town but with the general insecurity of the Middle Ages moved to the higher slopes of the hill, Mont Ste Maxine, rising a natural fortress from the plateau.

Not being on a main or even secondary road of any importance Riez's large main square is seldom crowded, an advantage in summer if one feels like a meal in one of the two restaurants at the west end of the *place*, which serve the best river trout I have ever eaten.

The typical old town lies to the north of the *place*. The church, a poorly-conceived restoration of the cathedral, so badly damaged during the Revolution that it collapsed in 1812, is squeezed into the south-west corner beside the fourteenth-century *Porte Saint-Sols*. The thickness of its walls would suggest that they were probably incorporated in the ramparts. However, the town's principal tourist attraction – for the rare tourists who pass this way – is the four Corinthian columns, all that remain of a temple of Apollo by the banks of the Colostre. They appear rather forlorn, rather bewildered, as if embarrassedly aware that they do not fit in with the surrounding countryside, but are in such an extraordinarily good state of repair that one wonders why these four columns and these alone should have survived through the centuries while all other traces of the temple have vanished – as if, indeed, they had never existed.

Riez is also connected historically with the site on the Verdon upstream from the *Canyon de Baudinard* known as *Fontaine L'Evêque*. The bishop in question was a Florentine, Monseigneur Doni D'Attichi, a shy man looking for a rural retreat where he could escape from the cares of his diocese.

Exploring the Verdon he discovered a spring known as the *Fontaine de Sorps*, which gushes out from a rock on the Verdon's left bank in a veritable torrent – an average of 4,756 litres a second – splitting into two branches round a little island before rejoining to foam on into the Verdon's stream. The bishop decided to build a country house at this spot, which was begun in 1632 and completed four years later. Only a few walls of this country retreat are left standing today in whose garden 'all the nightingales for miles around had a rendezvous . . .' Even these walls will soon disappear, for, again in the name of progress this pleasantest of little valleys between the *Canyon de Baudinard* and the main and famous *Gorges du Verdon* is soon to be flooded; the *Fontaine*, together with the charming little village of Les Salles will be drowned beneath the waters of a lake which, cold-blooded statisticians tell us, will form 'an enormous reservoir 200 feet deep of 700 million cubic metres'.

Before reaching the main gorge the road from Aiguines, which can be seen on a high ridge to the right, to Moustiers Ste Marie crosses the Verdon by a Gallo-Roman bridge, one-way traffic only, but with seven built-out bays on either side where in pre-motor days individual pedestrians or horsemen could wait for the passage of a cart or carriage. From this bridge, one of the most perfect in the country, it is only four and a half miles to Moustiers Ste Marie town, centre of a 300-years-old pottery – *faience* – industry.

No other place in Provence has a more beautiful, a more dramatic natural setting. The town is built half-way up a wall of rock on either side of a vertiginous gorge through which tumbles a wild cascade: the two cliffs linked by a single-span bridge. The fall of water is so steep that from the northern side of the bridge the stream is not so far below the parapet, but after crossing the road – five or six yards wide at the most – the rock-tormented torrent has dropped so far that one has the impression of staring down over the edge of an abyss.

The town climbs, sloping sharply on either bank north of the main road till halted abruptly by the sheer face of the two cliffs between whose pillar-like rocks is suspended a wrought-iron chain with a gilded metal star of Bethlehem.

In was in 1249 that a Baron de Blacas, Lord of Moustier, was taken prisoner at the battle of Damietta. Thrown into a putrid cell the wretched man prayed for Divine help, promising that if ever again he saw his own country he would hang a star of Bethlehem across the gorges at their very top where every passer-by could contemplate it: visual testimony of God's mercy. Whether he was released or managed to escape is not known but on his return he did not neglect his vow.

How this remarkable engineering feat was accomplished is another mystery, but it must have been brilliantly executed for the original star remained in place for just over 600 years, till on the night of a particularly violent storm it was blown down into the gorge, and strangely enough never found. By then, however, the people of Moustier were so attached to their legend that as soon as possible another chain and star, replica of the originals, took their place.

Hanging in the usually limpid sky I can imagine a necklace adorning the throat of a Wellsian, invisible giantess.

The chain also has its place in legend. It is said that a virtuous village girl pursued by lecherous peasants saved her virginity with Divine aid by running across it with the assurance of a professional tight-rope walker. A few years later, however, another girl, this time of doubtful virtue, attempted the same feat, promptly slipped and was dashed to pieces on the rocks below.

Moustiers was founded by a colony of monks from Riez – hence the name Moustiers or Monasterium – in 432, but it was not till the late seventeenth century (1680) that the first pieces of the now famous pottery, the predominant colour a rich blue, were produced. Several of the works of this period are on show in the small *Musée Historique de la Faience* housed on the ground floor of the *mairie*, with a fifth-century sarcophagus showing the Red Sea crossing in the entrance hall; but the best examples are now in the Cantini Museum in Marseille.

The twelfth-century church with an Italianate-Lombard style campanile, deep reddish in colour, whose body has the peculiarity of being built in a slight curve, is one of the most beautiful of Provençal small-town churches. It has the suggestion of a fortress for though the walls are pierced by windows they are long and narrow and I noticed between them a number of open slits in the masonry which might well have been intended to serve as loop-holes.

Above the church and inevitably involving a steep climb is the chapel of *Notre Dame de Beauvoir*, also known because of its position at the foot of the gorge's unclimbable rock pillars as *d'Entre-Roches*, which local history insists was founded by Charlemagne. It reminds one of a Renaissance canvas set flat against the perpendicular rock on a projecting ledge planted with curiously conventional cypresses, seeming almost black against the cliff's stark glare.

Moustiers is also a good base from which to make a tour of the *Gorges du Verdon*, perhaps the most grandiose natural pheno-menon in Europe and which I have heard a number of people compare with the Grand Canyon. I have made the tour of these gorges probably a dozen times and yet each time there is some-thing new to be discovered, and the almost overpowering beauty never palls.

It is a tour which should not on any account be hurried. A full day is barely enough. The actual gorge is 21 kilometres – about 13 miles – long and at times the sheer drop into the river is a straight 2,300 feet. Another feature which makes the fantastic heights all the more impressive is that throughout its length the gorge is com-paratively narrow; at both entrances it is as though the solid rock had simply been cleft by a giant axe so that the two sides open with the grim simplicity of the two lips of a deep wound, an illusion heightened by the fact that in many places the rock colour-ing is a deep reddish gold that might be due to the sun's rays glinting from a smear of blood. On the northern (right) bank the culminating spot is the *Point Sublime*, marked by a signpost and reached after a five-minute walk. There is a convenient café-restaurant at the opposite side of the road below the village of Rougon built on a ledge 600 feet above, whose schoolmaster, Isidore Blanc, was, with four companions, the first to traverse the gorge from end to end by canoe, an exciting and dangerous feat.

His statue on the highest rock was unveiled in 1937 and dominates the view of the eastern entrance.

The southern (left) bank is even more dramatic. Approaching from Comps one has a first view of the gorge at a point known as the *Balcons de la Mescla* where a little stone terrace has been built out from the cliff-face and looks straight down on the confluence of the Artuby with the Verdon. Here again the narrowness of the two gorges and the absolutely perpendicular walls are phenomenal, while to complete the picture of savage grandeur the canyon faces are prolonged by ledge after ledge of bare but vividly coloured granite mountain masses: gold, red, orange, purple. On one of these ledges opposite the Mescla *balcon* is a large *mas*-type farmhouse, completely isolated and seemingly inaccessible.

Its presence is a mystery – how was it built? How did those who lived there exist? In the days before the helicopter how did its inhabitants make contact other than visually with the outside world? For me, so many, as yet unsolved, enigmas.

After dropping sharply then crossing the Artuby the road rises to 3,000 feet to follow the course of the Verdon through the *Tunnels du Fayet*, blasted through the solid mountain face, before reaching the *Falaise des Cavaliers* with continual dizzy glimpses of the depths. Then after climbing to 4,000 feet comes the most stupendous view of all, the *Cirque de Vaumale* before the descent to Aiguines village.

It is now possible to make the tour of the gorges on foot almost at river level, but it is a tough walk only to be recommended to the very physically fit. It is also possible to imitate Isadore Blanc and hire canoes, while some even hardier have been known to swim the gorges; but as all guide books and pamphlets point out, such an expedition entails certain risks and should not be undertaken by anyone who is not extremely fit and an accomplished swimmer.

If after leaving the gorge one follows the right bank, the town of Castellane is reached some ten miles upstream by a road skirting the river, still a torrent but flowing between low grassy banks, thickly wooded in places and extremely popular nowadays with summer campers.

Castellane itself is a small town of only just over 1,000 inhabitants which gives the impression of being considerably larger. It is also a very dignified little town whose name has figured frequently and never ingloriously in history: its proudest memory, that it was one of the very few towns to hold out successfully in 1536 against Charles Quint.

The first impression of Castellane, however, no matter from which direction one approaches, is not of the town itself but the solid and sheer 600-foot solitary rock rising straight from the flat ground, towering like a skyscraper as one American writer has put it, serving as a plinth to a minute chapel appropriately named *Notre Dame du Rocher*, dating back to 1703 and which like the cupola at Forcalquier is surmounted by a statue of the Virgin. It is a remarkable landmark and one which must have inspired Napoleon with hope, yet – remembering Castellane's citizens' reputation for courage and a belligerent spirit of independence – with anxiety when he looked down on it from the *Col de Luens* on the road now known as the *Route Napoléon* on the morning of 3 March 1815.

The main square, *La Place Marcel-Sauvaire*, L-shaped, is lined with an unusual number of hotels and restaurants for so comparatively small a town, all of them of a high standard and providing excellent value for money. At the head of the L is the twelfth-century St Victor's church and to the left of the church still stands one of the original gates of the medieval ramparts, protected by a battlemented tower. The old streets, with occasional glimpses of all that remains of the ramparts, have like Forcalquier's preserved their sense of a secret life, turning their backs as it were on the main road skirting the western trace of the *enceinte* and its traffic, chaotic during the three summer months.

A song, *La Chanson du Pétard et du Pétardier*, tells the story of how in 1586 a woman, Judith Androu, saved the town from being sacked by a Huguenot army led by the brilliant Marshal de Lesdiguières. Slipping out of the besieged city by night Judith mixed with the troops, pretending she was looking for a fictitious nephew serving in their ranks. Since sixteenth-century armies were not particularly security-minded she was able to discover that the approaching attack would be concentrated on the Annonciade Gate. On getting safely back to her own people 'Judith asked to be allowed to mount guard over this gate; when the Protestants approached to place their explosives she poured a cauldron of boiling pitch over their heads which put them to flight . . .'

Above Castellane, after branching off the main *Route Napoléon* for the *Col d'Allos* and Barcelonnette, is the Castillon dam, built between 1942 and 1947, first of the hydro-electric projects in this part of Provence, converting the Verdon into a clear blue lake six miles long and covering 1,300 acres; the dam is named after the unfortunate flooded village of Castillon, one of the early martyrs to progress.

The lake, however, is not merely utilitarian. It is a popular centre for safe bathing, being currentless and tideless, wide enough for sailing, and being 3,000 feet above sea level always pleasantly fresh on the hottest of summer days. Because of this the little village of St Julien standing on a bluff whose slopes run straight down to the water's edge is filled from June to September with people who cannot afford coastal prices, cannot tolerate coastal crowds, but yet lust for sun and fresh air.

The Verdon reassumes its individuality by the village of St André-les-Alpes, also these days a summer resort, at the head of a small plain covered with orchards and fields of lavender, and where the little Issole river joins it before their waters merge into the lake after the pattern of the Durance and the Ubaye.

The Verdon's source is not far from St André, for it is a domestic river, throughout its whole course racing through much of Provence's finest scenery.

Till recently the road running more or less parallel with the Verdon's last miles was little frequented, but since the French became winter-sport minded and realised that with so many of the best Alpine slopes within their own boundaries there was no need to make the journey to Switzerland, Austria or Italy for their ski-ing, traffic especially during winter week-ends is heavy.

Though strictly speaking in mountainous country the road to

begin with is comparatively level, crossing an undulating plateau, the Verdon now making its course in a mass of small white breakers through a shallow ravine and constantly crossed and re-crossed till the fortified town of Colmar is reached – one of the best examples of Vauban's works, Colmar lies in a hollow sur-rounded by forests and high mountains: a popular centre for those who like mountain walks rather than climbing.

Colmar's ramparts are intact, its crenellated, loopholed walls with a square tower at each corner are reminiscent of Aigues-Mortes, and it is protected by two important works: the *Fort de France* on a rock overlooking the bridge just before arriving at the town itself, and the *Fort de Savoie* on a ridge commanding the main approach from the north.

The *Fort de Savoie* is in such a perfect state of repair that it might almost be mistaken for one of the many similar works which sprang up the length of the Italian frontier when France began to feel herself threatened by Mussolini's yearly swelling megalo-mania, encouraged by the success of his Ethiopian adventure. The immense thickness of the roofs, the angle of their construction avoiding the presentation of a flat surface, the skilful use of the hill-slope both as camouflage and reinforcement of the actual walls, and the semi-subterranean living quarters must have served as a model to Todt and Maginot.

After Colmar the road soon begins to climb, increasingly steeply with only a few glimpses of the new-born Verdon, towards the village of Allos, the ski centre of La Foux d'Allos, and finally the summit of the pass, the *Col d'Allos*, at 7,000 feet above sea level: another visual frontier between Provence and the north, between the Mediterranean and the Alpine scene. The immense view from the top, embracing the Ubaye river valley – which it will be remembered joins the Durance to form the Serre-Ponçon dam – the high peaks of the Parpaillon chain, the Pelvoux *massif*, and the *Aiguille de Chambeyron*, is as definite as a textbook illustration.

To the south, the Provençal side, the upper slopes are almost bare, hence their popularity with skiers: dotted on the approach to the valley with typical squat pines, the occasional ilex, patterned by scattered orchards. The northern slopes, plunging more abruptly, form a sombre mass of giant pines and larch.

Even the sky marks a boundary. Southwards for most of the year it is the deep yet shimmering blue spelling the warmth of almost continual sunshine; while to the north the vault is paler, more remote, as if even when cloudless, shrouded by fine nordic mists threatening at any moment to spread still more enveloping folds.

6. Marseille

'Là on ne voit pas une figure triste' – Stendhal

Though one of the oldest, most historical of all European cities Marseille has very little to offer in the way of ancient monuments, buildings, museums or vestiges of its more than twice millenary past. Today from a population point of view France's second city, its eyes seem fixed so aggressively on the future that one is tempted to say that even the present is neglected. Yet despite this late twentieth-century veneer the name Marseille retains a psychological hold on popular imagination, so that, much as the traditional London Cockney embodies a typically English toughness combined with humour, so the *Marseillais* personifies those traditional meridional faults and virtues immortalised by Pagnol's trilogy – *Marius, Fanny, César* – a character in which generosity and canniness, kindliness and hysterical violence can alternate with alarming frequency.

We have seen in the introduction how the foundation of Marseille by the Phocean Greeks – supplanted in turn by the Romans – marked the dawn of Provençal history, and how as the city passed through turbulent centuries of foreign invasions and internecine struggles between great families lusting for supreme power, its people evolved from their sufferings endowed with an admirable spirit of determined independence which often saved them from irreparable disaster, yet at the same time made them suspicious of any innovation or 'foreign' influence. And this innate conservatism may explain the fact that Marseille was one of the later Provençal centres to be evangelised.

It was not till 228 that one reads of Victor, later St Victor, to whose memory an abbey founded by St Cassien in the fifth century was dedicated.

Victor, a Roman officer stationed in Marseille, became a convert to Christianity – there is no record regarding who brought the word to him – and was promptly thrust into gaol. But his fanatical adherence to his new faith was such that he managed to convert his three gaolers, and later when summoned to burn incense to a statute of Apollo had the courage to overturn the altar. Condemned to death for blasphemy, his right foot was cut off before he was stretched out between two mill-stones, then crushed (slowly) to death. The three gaolers, who also refused to recant, were obliged to watch this horrible execution and then beheaded.

St Cassien founded his abbey in 410 above a cave where, it was believed, an angel had placed Victor's remains and those of his three fellow martyrs. To begin with this abbey was run on such strict lines that it was known as the Gate to Paradise. Like present-day Mount Athos nothing female was allowed to enter its premises, rumour even going as far as to affirm that any creature of the weaker sex that did so lost her sight within an hour. With the passing of time the abbey chapel claimed to house the Western world's most remarkable collection of relics, among them one of Lazarus's ribs, St Cassien's head, one of St Anthony's fingers, a tooth of St Peter, hairs from St Paul's beard, even St Andrew's cross.

A few years later St Cassien also founded a convent – St Sauveur – equally austere, whose nuns made a name for themselves during one of the earlier Saracen raids of the eighth century, when the city's outer defences had been stormed and the Moslem warriors had broken into the convent grounds. Realising that they were completely at the mercy of the Saracens, who enjoyed a worldwide reputation for indiscriminate rape, Eusébie, the Mother Superior, called the nuns together and ordered them to cut off their noses, herself cold-bloodedly setting the example, so that thus mutilated they should appear physically repulsive rather than desirable. It says a lot for the individual toughness of those days

19   Comps: old church

that not one of the nuns hesitated to obey. Their action, according to a contemporary, 'saved their virginity, but not their lives'. From then on the convent was known as the *Couvent des Desnarados* (the convent of the noseless).

Yet in spite of these stories of early fanaticism and heroism – St Victor's abbey was sacked by the Saracens, the monks being massacred, in 923 – the twelfth century saw a curious swing against the ascetic path of life, so much so that in 1209 the Avignon concilium saw fit to issue a decree forbidding 'dancing in the churches', and by 1364 in the *Couvent des Desnarados* things had got to such a state that Bishop Guillaume Sudré was obliged to forbid officially *'L'entrée du couvent aux buffons, sauteurs et voltigeurs'*. A little later the habit of using blasphemous oaths became so current that ecclesiastical authorities had a special law introduced whereby the blasphemers were put into an open rush basket and ducked in the harbour as many times as they had been heard to blaspheme.

At sea the punishment was more severe. Those who had been convicted of making injurious references to the Trinity, the Virgin or the Saints were tied up, thrown overboard and trailed in the ship's wake, first evidence of that often fatal disciplinary measure known in the British Navy as 'keel hauling'.

However, more than wars and fear of punishment it was successive epidemics of the black plague which put a stop to this form of anti-clericalism, many seeing in this deadly scourge evident signs of Divine displeasure.

The two worst epidemics were in 1630 and 1720. That of 1630 reduced Marseille's population from 70,000 to 15,000. The second was brought by the crew of the *Grand Saint Antoine* returning from the eastern Mediterranean after having called in at Sidon, Limassol and Tripoli.

On 26 July 1720, 15 plague cases were signalled in the *Rue de l'Echelle*, a street which within a few days was inhabited only by dead or dying. From then on according to official records 'both sides of the (city) streets are heaped with corpses which because of the summer heat are decomposing and are truly horrible to contemplate'. The only people available to dispose of the bodies were the convicts directed by two very gallant members of the aristocracy, the *Chevalier* de Roze and the *Chevalier* de Mousties. But though the two *chevaliers* survived miraculously there were soon very few convicts left alive.

When the epidemic was at its height a certain Sister Rémusat from the Convent of the Visitation obtained an audience with the bishop, Monseigneur de Belsunce, and assured him that only by constant prayers to the Sacred Heart could the epidemic be stopped. The bishop grasped at the straw. He dedicated his diocese to the Sacred Heart and ordered that a procession through the streets should take place on 1 November. Courageously, considering the truly pestilential conditions, 'wishing to appear as the scapegoat for his people's sins and as if he were the designated victim, he (the bishop) walked barefooted, a rope round his neck, a cross in his arms ...'

From that day the number of victims began to diminish. On 10 December for the first time since the outbreak no fresh cases were reported. The epidemic was over, but 40,000 had died.

Politically over the centuries, as one writer points out, 'the people of Marseille obeyed the central power when it was strong and declared themselves independent when it was weak: a dangerous policy often resulting in collective punishment, sometimes economic, more often physical'. To begin with there was the disastrous error in backing Pompeius against Julius Caesar, an error – provoking the thunderbolts of Caesar's wrath – from which it took centuries to recover. And centuries later after the passing of the Saracen menace another catastrophic mistake was made when the Marseillais decided to resist the power of Charles of Anjou, claiming the city as part of his domaines, resulting from his marriage with Beatrix of Forcalquier. Their resistance smouldered for seven years during which time the city was twice besieged. But in the end the Marseillais were forced to come to terms, and the *Chapitres de Paix*, name of the treaty imposed by Charles to punish these rebels, put an end to the city's jealously cherished semi-autonomy.

The virtual annexation of Provence by the French crown was accepted with indifference and to begin with relations between Paris and Marseille, especially during the Italian wars, were cordial. Marseille built and manned ships which served with the French fleets and often returned loaded with prizes; and when after his victory at Marignane (Melagnano) François 1 made a triumphal tour of Provence he was fêted by the Marseillais and a 'battle of oranges' was staged for his amusement, in which he is said to have participated with great gusto.

Nine years later, 1524, saw one of Marseille's finest hours. Charles Quint's armies commanded by the Constable of Bourbon and the Marquis of Pescaire* crossed the Var river, advanced rapidly and by 19 August was investing Marseille. There was no question, as in Aix, of surrender. Employing a scorched-earth policy as far as the suburbs were concerned men and women alike got to work on improving the defences. The trace of one ditch dug by the women, now a busy thoroughfare, is known as the *Boulevard des Dames*. And though the imperial army submitted the city to severe bombardments every attack was thrown back. This successful resistance evoked the highest praise from the monarch when he re-visited Marseille after the siege had been raised and the imperial army pushed back over the Var. 'Thanks to you,' he said, 'I have retrieved all my county of Provence. I promise to reward you as never before has any prince rewarded his loyal subjects.'

It will never be known what reward Francois had in mind, for only a few months later on 24 February 1525 he was defeated, and taken prisoner, at the battle of Pavia. However, eight years later he was in Marseille for the third time, having chosen the city for the celebration of the marriage of his second son, the Duke of Orleans, future Henri II, with Catherine di Medici.

The festivities, lasting more than three weeks and bringing a fortune to most of the *bourgeoisie*, made probably the most magnificent public spectacle in Marseille's history. 'The *cortège*,' says

---

* The popular Marseillais expression *peuchère* is said to be the result of evolving mispronunciations of the marquis's name.

Nostradamus, 'was headed by 200 mounted men-at-arms and 300 archers of His Majesty's guard, who were followed by His Majesty the most Christian King, being upon a mule draped with a purple saddle-cloth embossed and embroidered with gold which trailed almost to the ground; after came the Swiss Guard, and after them a great host of princes, barons, lords, officers and gentlemen, such a number as to be scarcely believable.' The Pope, Clement VII – Jules di Medici, a former bishop of Marseille – was accompanied by seven cardinals and 35 bishops, and before him 'walked a beautiful *haquenée* (riding mare) white as silk, upon whose back reposed the very august Sacrament.'

The wedding took place thanks to a typically demagogic gesture on the part of the king in the house of a first consul, Jean Blacard, rather than in the cathedral. However, during the ceremony so many salvoes were fired by the artillery, their thunder accompanied by the pealing of every church bell, the blowing of trumpet fanfares, the music of hautbois and the voices of massed choirs that 'it was something never before heard. Such a tumult of sound that for several days after there was not a fish caught or even seen in the neighbourhood of the port . . .'

After another of Charles Quint's abortive attacks a few years later, Marseille was again *en fête* in 1543 for another distinguished visitor, the Sultan Selim I's famous admiral Khair-ed-Din Barbarossa, the Turks having become temporarily France's ally. At the end of this visit ships from Marseille sailed with the Turkish flotillas to harass Nice and Villefranche.

However, despite his flirtations with Provence François I lost much of his erstwhile popularity towards the end of his life when by the *Ordonnance de Villers-Cotterets* (1539) he decreed that French would be the universal language of his kingdom *including* Provence; and it is recorded that on the occasion of the next royal visit to Marseille, that of Charles IX in 1564, the municipality hired a Lyonnais to deliver the welcoming address. Matters improved slightly when Louis XIII toured Provence in 1622, winning over the disgruntled citizens of Aix, Arles and Marseille by the exercise of his personal charm and by seeming to take a personal interest in their problems. However, this unnatural harmony of views was short lived. The Marseillais sided openly with the *Fronde* – that of the princes – irritating Louis xiv to such an extent that he decided that France's oldest city must be taught a salutary lesson.

After a short siege Marseille capitulated on 21 January 1660 and on 2 March the greatest of the Louis' entered the city as a conqueror by a breach in the walls specially made for the occasion. Nothing was left to chance. The citizens had already been disarmed and the carrying of any sort of offensive weapon made a severely punishable offence by decree. Not content with this measure Louis gave orders for the building of a super fortress, Fort St Nicolas, 'to survey', as he said, 'both city and harbour'. Furthermore when six days later he returned to Paris he left behind a garrison consisting of a regiment of Swiss mercenaries and two regiments of Royal Guards.

The Marseillais had now no illusions – though one might say that they bent to the storm like the reed rather than breaking like the oak – for there are no further records of uprisings against royal authority until the Revolution, whose cause they embraced with fervour.

When Mirabeau in his capacity of mouthpiece of the 'new order' entered the city he was given a welcome so delirious that it touched on hysteria, and less than a month later, 11 April 1789, the *Société Patriotique des Amis de la Constitution* was formed in a house in the *Rue Thubaneau* which became the Jacobin club and the Revolution's centre. Soon the Marseillais acquired such a reputation that the mayor, Mouraille, received a letter from Paris saying 'Send Paris 600 men who are not afraid to die'. A battalion of fanatics was straightaway raised which marched the whole distance to the capital and took part in the storming of the Tuileries on 10 August 1792.

News of the abolition of the monarchy on 27 September of the same year was the signal for another outburst of popular rejoicing. An 'Altar to the Fatherland' was set up outside the *Hôtel de Ville*, Mayor Mouraille declaiming: '*O peuple! Te voilà enfin delivré des tyrans qui t'opprimaient depuis tant de siècles'*, superb example of revolutionary jargon.

On orders from General Carteaux, a bloody-minded revolutionary but singularly inefficient commander, a guillotine was installed on the Canebière. Heads fell rapidly; not only those of the aristocracy but also of the *bourgeoisie*. Many churches were converted into 'temples of reason' – the principal 'temple' being the ancient Saint Cannat church, a certain Mademoselle Rivière, an actress whose revolutionary fervour, we are told, far exceeded her dramatic talents, its high priestess – while others only escaped destruction by being used as warehouses. Revolutionary jargon took the place of normal conversation to such an extent that 'words lost much of their sense to form hollow phrases which burst like soap bubbles'.

Robespierre fell a victim to his own excesses on Thermidor 9 of the year II, or more simply 27 July 1794. But though he had inaugurated terror his fall did not end it in Marseille any more than in Paris. The persecuted who had been lucky enough to survive turned on their persecutors. In Fort St Jean alone 127 Jacobins had their throats cut.

After General Bonaparte had more or less put an end to the Revolution by his *coup d'état* of Brumaire 18 – 9 October 1799 – France was divided into *départements*, local power being entrusted to prefects. First *Prefet* of the newly-created *Bouches-du-Rhône*, Charles Delacroix, immediately set up his *préfecture* in Marseille rather than the old capital of Aix, to reward the Marseillais for their revolutionary zeal and to punish Aix for its suspected conservatism.

The Bonaparte family saw a lot of Marseille during the lean pre-glory days. Both Napoleon and his elder brother Joseph were frequent visitors to the house of Monsieur Clary in the *Rue Quatre-Cantons-Saint-Christophe*, attracted by the two pretty Clary daughters, Julie and Désirée. Julie as Joseph's wife became Queen of Naples and later an unhappy Queen of Spain. Napoleon definitely intended to marry Désirée, but early successes going to his head, he decided that the aristocratic Josephine de Beauharnais was a more fitting bride for the man of the future than a *petite bourgeoise* from Marseille: though this did not prevent the rejected *fiancée* from becoming consort of the future king *Charles* xiv of Sweden, formerly Jean Bernadotte.

Marseille became particularly hostile to Napoleon when the continental blockade proved so disastrous for the city's trade that famine threatened. As a result the fervid revolutionaries of 1798 proved to be equally fanatical supporters of the 1814 restoration: proof perhaps that in politics the stomach is more influential than the heart. In fact the Marseillais gave a practical demonstration of re-found enthusiasm for the *ancien régime* and staged a bloody massacre of the Mameluke garrison, loyal subjects of the fallen emperor.

From the time of the 1830 Algiers expedition and later with the opening of the Suez Canal, Marseille's importance as one of the greatest ports for both Africa and the East has never ceased to grow. Later impracticability of the Suez Canal has been more than offset by galloping industrialisation, so much so that with a population already topping the million mark Marseille has supplanted Lyon as France's second city.

This rising tide of prosperity has known only one dark patch: the 22 months from November 1942 to August 1944 when the Canebière was one of the favourite haunts of German occupation troops. During those grim months following on the German entry into the city after Allied North African landings, all the traditional Marseillais characteristics – love of liberty, forceful individualism, refusal to be broken by adversity – came to the fore. In spite of exceptionally brutal repressive measures the Germans were never able to stamp out the highly active resistance groups. Mass deportations under the most appalling conditions were carried out. The *Vieux Port*, rabbit warren of narrow streets, was dynamited. It did not prevent the *maquis* from taking up arms as soon as they heard of the 14 August landings. For four days they pinned down the majority of General Schaeffer's *wehrmacht* units till General Monsabert's leading columns of the 3rd DIA (Algerian Infantry Division) had stormed in from the north.

Perhaps it is the almost breathless industrial expansion that makes the Marseillais of today more aware of the transatlantic model for living than of his own past: to such an extent that in his book *Unknown France* Georges Pillemont writes sadly, 'but I have already stated that the people of Marseille are scarcely interested in art and in the evidence of the past, and it is useless to insist . . .'

The Canebière, pride and joy of all Marseillais whatever their generation, is simply a long wide street of shops, cinemas, cafés and restaurants, opulent one must admit, but no different in any essential from any other great commercial centre of any other great city, even though the odd *jellaba* – or *burnouse* – clad north African hawker of Berber rugs, leatherware and cheap trinkets may still be seen, lending what by a stretch of imagination might be termed a touch of the exotic.

For many older generations of British who spent their lives supporting the white man's burden in Africa or the East, returning on home leave or on his way out for a further tour of duty, the chief memory of Marseille was the basilica of *Notre Dame de la Garde* perched on its 600-foot pinnacle, its bell-tower crowned by a commanding gilded statue of the Virgin.

Though the church is comparatively modern its site is ancient. A chapel on the rock venerated by fishermen existed in 1214 whereas the present basilica was consecrated as recently as 5 June 1864. The tradition that it is still essentially a place of worship for fishermen has been preserved, and the interior is more interesting by reason of the many votive offerings in gratitude for escapes from the sea's perils than for its decoration, despite a clever blending of coloured marble: white from Carrara, red from Africa, green from the Alps. Being well above the city's general level there is a *table d'orientation* on the parvis with a hovering view over an ocean of rooftops, the surrounding hills, the sea and islands, including the *Château d'If*.

This small whitish rock, about twenty minutes by ferryboat from the *Quai des Belges* at the beginning of the Canèbiere – the guide quotes an hour and a half for the return trip and visit – is not much more than a quarter of a mile long and just under the same width, and its fort, built on orders from François i, has always been more important as a prison than as a link in the harbour defences. There is immediate evidence of this. Almost the first thing one sees is a plaque to the memory of the 3,500 Protestants condemned to serve in the galleys between 1545 and 1750, and, near by, one to those, anonymous, who were thrown into cells because of their opposition to Napoleon iii's assumption of power in 1848 and who died there in captivity. There is the condemned cell and on a higher level the larger, more airy cells occupied at various times by such distinguished prisoners as Glandèves de Niozcllcs, sentenced to six years for failing to remove his hat in the presence of Louis xiv; Mirabeau locked up for debt at his father's request, and the unfortunate Casimir of Poland who spent such an uncomfortable year in Sisteron citadel. The château also figures in the 'Man in the Iron Mask' legend, but if indeed this miserable creature existed then it is more likely that he was held in *Fort Royal* on the *Ile Ste Marguerite* off Cannes.

It is to fiction, though, that the *Château d'If* owes its principal claim to fame as the place where Edmond Dantès, hero of Dumas's *Count of Monte Cristo*, was incarcerated on a false charge for so many years. The guide even points out the cells in which Dantès and his companion in misery, the Abbé Faria, are supposed to have occupied.

Oldest of Marseille's public monuments is Saint Victor's church, on the *Place Victor* between the *Rue Sainte* and the *Boulevard de la Corderie*, whose battlemented walls like that of *Les Saintes Maries de la Mer* once formed part of the city's ramparts.

The main body of the church is not of any special interest but a visit to the catacombs is to return to the dawn of Christianity. At the foot of a wooden staircase is the *atrium* of the fifth century basilica *Notre Dame de la Confession*, once lined by nine Corinthian columns, removed by the *Bouches-du-Rhône's* first prefect Charles Delacroix to adorn the city's main squares. Unfortunately not one has survived either time or rough handling by the unappreciative. The basilica was sacked by the Saracens in 923 and the actual church, from 1201, gradually rose from its ruins. No wonder therefore that the idea of a fortress church predominated and the apse walls were ten feet thick!

Beside the basilica, and as though held up by its walls, is the cave in which St Lazarus is supposed to have been buried, later, after being excavated and remodelled in the eleventh century, known as the Confessional of Saint Lazarus, though in this case the Lazarus referred to is a fifth-century archbishop of Aix and not the St Lazarus who landed on the Camargue coast. Deeper in the cave's recesses are still a few sarcophagi, though the more elaborate and better preserved were removed some time ago and can now be seen in the Borély museum.

The opposite (north) side of the *Vieux Port*, the *Place de la Major*, contains the modern cathedral, pseudo-Byzantine in style, built between 1852–59. Far more interesting, however, is the old cathedral, the *ancienne La Mayor*, much of which was pulled down to help in the construction of the newer building. It was a great pity, for this older building was historically a gem which should never have been, as one writer puts it, 'mutilated, dishonoured and disfigured'. Today its skeleton is preserved as a museum which can only be visited after making arrangements with the caretaker – no services are held there. It is an essential visit since it contains the oldest Renaissance statues in France. These are above the altar in the St Lazarus chapel, representing the saint and his sisters, work of Francesco Laurana, an Istrian sculptor invited to Provence in 1460 by King René.* Nearer the apse in a chapel to the left is a *bas-relief* in white faience – the Descent from the Cross – by Lucca della Robbia, while a plaque on the wall marks the tomb of Monseigneur de Belsunce, hero of the 1720 plague epidemic who died in 1755.

However, and this is typical of modern Marseille, this lovely old relic of the past is almost on top of the *Gare Maritime de*

* Two other works by Laurana may be about the same age (1481): the tomb of Charles of Anjou in Le Mans cathedral and the altarpiece in St Didier's church, Avignon.

la Joliette, claimed to be one of Europe's largest and most modern railway stations, with all the attendant din of its ceaseless traffic.

The Marseille *Musée des Beaux-Arts* in the Longchamps palace off the *Boulevard de la Libération*, a prolongation of the *Canebière*, as well as housing a collection of fifteenth, sixteenth and seventeenth-century paintings, most of them qualified as 'the school of' or 'attributed to' rather than credited to a specific artist, has two galleries devoted to Honoré Daumier, celebrated for his caricaturist lithographs of '*La Vie Parisienne*', born in Marseille in 1808, a number of works of Monticelli (1824–86) very much in the Fragonard style but nevertheless greatly admired by Van Gogh, and three *salles* dedicated to the genius of Pierre Puget, who like Leonardo da Vinci was not only a great painter but also sculptor, engineer and visionary. In this collection my favourites are an equestrian medallion of Louis xiv, the frighteningly realistic *bas-relief* of Milan in the grip of the plague, and the canvas, 'The Baptism of Clovis'.

The smaller Grobet-Labadié museum just opposite the Longchamps palace is best known for its tapestries and wrought iron, but in the small *Salle Fragonard* is one of the most charming of this most charming artist's works, 'The Birth of Venus'.

In a corner formed by the *Rue Ferréol* and the *Rue Grignan* is the *Musée Cantini des Arts Décoratifs* housed in the old *Hôtel de Montgrand*, once the Marseille residence of Madame de Sévigné's son-in-law, the Comte de Grignan, at the time when he was governor of Provence. The original heteroclitic collection was presented to the Marseille municipality by Jules Cantini, well-known sculptor who died in 1916, together with a legacy to provide for its upkeep. It includes Renaissance and Provençal furniture, Chinese ivory, Greek Tanagra, seventeenth-century Flemish tapestry, a bust of Washington by Canova – the same Canova responsible for the reclining nude of Napoleon's sister Pauline Borghese* and Venetian, Bohemian and Provençal faience, the

---

* When an indignant Napoleon said, 'Do you mean to tell me you posed in the nude?' Pauline replied, 'Why not? The studio was heated.'

last-named including the finest surviving examples of early Moustiers.

In winter Marseille becomes a Mecca for opera lovers. The original theatre between the *Rue Molière* and the *Rue Corneille* was built just before the Revolution (1787), but the actual building is a modern reconstruction opened in 1928 after the old premises had been gutted in 1919. The policy of recent years has been to break away from the tried favourites – *Faust, Carmen, Manon* – and later performances have included the aggressively modern *Lulu* (in German) and a revival of Donizetti's *Lucrezia Borgia* sung in Italian with Monsarrat Caballé in the title role – on which the toughest critics produced a plethora of eulogies seldom if ever expended on a Paris production.

Roughly half-way between Marseille and Aix is the small town of Aubagne, in itself undistinguished but yet well worth a visit in that it is the home of the *santons*, the little unbaked-clay figures of the true Provençal Christmas *crèche*: and also, since 1962, home of the French Foreign Legion.

Before the Revolution the *crèche* was a normal feature of most churches' Christmas decorations but not until the nineteenth century did it figure in the average home. The idea of producing these *santons en masse* was that of a Marseillais, Jean Louis Lagnel, born in 1764, who, surviving all the Revolution's anti-clerical persecutions, held his first *Foire aux Santons* or 'little saints' in 1803. These figures included not only the Virgin, the infant Jesus, St Joseph and the three kings, but lent the Nativity story a strictly Provençal aspect. The shepherds were dressed in contemporary Provençal fashion and mingling with them a poacher, a *gendarme*, a miller, a fishwife, a musician (*la tambourinaire*), a village simpleton (*le ravi*), and – one is almost tempted to say 'inevitably' – the classical Provençal would-be lovers, Vincent and Mireille. Recently the Seillans parish priest, the late Abbé Viatte, an amateur artist of very considerable talent and most original ideas, went a step farther in localising the scene by enlarging a number of snapshots of local celebrities, mounting them on wooden stands and including them in a background embracing the sanctuary of

Notre Dame des Ormeaux, to frame the traditional group by the manger.

A naïve but very touching gramophone record has been issued based on Yvan Audouard's Provencal nativity which begins: 'What I am about to tell you is the fruit of research I began in childhood. I've hesitated a long time but now I'm categoric. Bethlehem where the little Jesus was born was not in Judaea but at Fontvieille at the foot of Daudet's mill . . .'

On the record the narrator is the angel Boufaréu who, after the singing of the *Gloria in excelsis Deo* announces '*Moi, je suis l'ange Boufaréu. Ils m'ont appellé comme ca à cause des grosses joues que j'ai fini par attraper à force de jouer de la trompette chaque fois que le Bon Dieu est content. Et cette nuit-là jamais Il avait été aussi content de Sa vie, le Bon Dieu, il allait être Papa . . .*' ('Me, I'm the angel Boufaréu. They call me that because of the huge cheeks I've got myself through blowing the trumpet every time the Good God is happy. And that night he'd never been so happy in all his life, he was going to be a daddy . . .')

He then goes on to describe the winter's night, the Virgin Mary and Joseph staggering along a track buffeted by a *mistral* 'strong enough to wrench the horns off the Camargue bulls'; their arrival at the stable after being told there was 'no room in the inn' and their friendly welcome from the ox and the ass (both speaking with a strong Provençal accent), and when the infant Jesus is born all speak alternately the lines of the *Ave Maria* while a choir sings *Il est né le Divin Enfant.*

The action now spreads to the local characters all of whom are, unknowingly, affected by the great event.

The miller, who had fallen into a state of mutinous melancholy, refusing to bake since his wife had left him for a shepherd – recalling the theme of Pagnol's *La Femme du Boulanger* – suddenly hears his windmill beginning to turn although the wind had died down, gets out of bed and goes off with a sack of flour to offer to the *Divin Enfant.* A gipsy who has stolen a turkey has been arrested by the *gendarme,* but the *gendarme* suddenly decides to free his captive and the gipsy to return the turkey to its rightful owner, none other than Roustido, Mireille's cruel father. At this moment Mireille has run off into the night to find her Vincent and we hear Roustido wandering about disconsolately calling 'Mireille! Mireille!' like a lost soul.

Elsewhere a shepherd is weeping over the death of his faithful old dog. '*Tu te souviens*', he recalls wistfully, '*comme tu aimes que je te gratte la tête?*' Suddenly the little dog begins to whine, but happily, and the shepherd, overcome with joy, gathering him up in his arms, determines to offer him as a birthday present to the new-born child. At the same time a fish merchant who has spent his life cheating clients wakes up bitterly ashamed, and swearing to change his ways after he has offered his 'very best fish to the *Divin Enfant.*'

Now all these diverse characters begin to gather round the *crèche* with their gifts, and the *gendarme*, not to be outdone, offers his revolver. Joseph objects that a revolver is hardly a fitting toy for a baby but the *gendarme* assures him that not only has the revolver in question never been fired, it has never even been loaded.

The Virgin then addressing the *gendarme* by name, Colombani – obviously one deduces a Corsican – tells him gently to keep the revolver but to promise never to use it. 'After all a revolverless *gendarme* would seem a bit queer.' And to the shepherd when he offers his dog she says, 'One day like you my son will be a shepherd. He will be the shepherd of men, and men do not need dogs to care for them. They need love.'

Finally Roustido bursts into the stable where he sees the gipsy* with the stolen turkey. But instead of attacking him he says, '*Tu peux le garder, je te le donne*', then bursting into tears gives his consent to Mireille's marriage with Vincent.

At that moment the three kings enter with their gifts and in the words of the good angel, '*Et voilà, c'est bientôt fini.*' He concludes, 'Each one present had taken up his stance, as in a photographer's, but for all eternity . . . and nobody will speak again. And they

* *Broumian* in Provençal.

won't move again till the end of all the centuries. It is the fate of the *santons*.'

One would I think have to be inhumanly blasé not to be most moved by this record. I have noticed too that in villages at any rate there is not a family, no matter what anti-clerical sentiments its members may from time to time express, which does not as Christmas approaches take a genuine pride in getting up its *crèche* on the most strictly traditional lines.

In 1962 when de Gaulle decided that France should quit Algeria there were many who imagined that the 132-year-old Foreign Legion would be disbanded. Very wisely no such decision was reached. A former police barracks, the *Camp de la Demande*, an area covering 70 acres, was taken over as Legion headquarters and depôt to replace the Sidi-bel-Abbès centre, the *Caserne Vienot*.

Today the *Camp de la Demande*, renamed the *Caserne Vienot* after the Foreign Legion officer killed leading his battalion in a counter-attack outside Sebastopol during the Crimean war, is at one and the same time the most modern and yet the most steeped in tradition of any barracks in France. The famous 'Sacred Way' and the monument to the dead unveiled in 1931 to mark the centenary of the Legion's foundation were dismantled stone by stone, brought over from Algeria and re-constructed with meticulous care and are now surrounded by barrack rooms, recreation rooms, messes boasting every modern comfort and convenience: far cry from the lonely mud forts of the *Beau Geste* image.

In 1968 the Legion museum, library and memorial hall, compactly housed under one roof, standing at the head of the 'Sacred Way', were opened officially.

The museum is one which no one who has even the slightest interest in military history should miss. On the ground floor are life-sized models of legionaries in the uniforms of various epochs. There is the famous Saharan silhouette perhaps best known of all: *képi* with cloth protection for the nape of the neck, long heavy blue overcoat pinned back from just above the knee so as not to impede marching, the huge boots which, to toughen their skin to a similar leather-like quality the legionaries used to wear sockless,

the enormous weight of equipment, the *barda*, the cumbersome rifle and extra-long bayonet. Looking at this and realising that thus equipped marches of 40 miles a day in the open desert beneath the African sun were considered normal, one can only be amazed at the limits to which human endurance can be stretched with comparative impunity.

Upstairs is a single enormous hall divided into campaign sections containing also uniforms, models of battles, photographs, relics picked up after actions, citations, standards, a collection which – like the advertisement for the magazine *Tin-Tin* – 'can enchant the young from 7 to 77'.

Most moving too on the ground floor is the Hall of Honour in black marble, the walls engraved with the names of the 59,000 legionaries who from 1831 to 1962 died for France in battle.

When it was known that the Legion was to be installed in Aubagne there were some misgivings on the part of the local inhabitants. Lurid tales were spread about pay-night excesses. Fathers and young husbands wondered if it would be safe for daughters and wives to walk the streets unescorted: or even with an escort. It took only a few months for these unnecessary forebodings to be dissipated. On the contrary the great day in the life of the Aubagnais is now 30 April, the day that the Legion celebrates the anniversary of the battle of Camerone (1863) in Mexico at the time a Foreign Legion regiment was part of the expeditionary force lent by Napoleon III to the unfortunate Maximilian to help him in his struggle with the Juarez 'popular' army.

A company, the 3rd, of the 1st battalion, 63 strong and commanded by Captain Danjou, a Crimean veteran, a wooden right hand replacing that which he had left outside Sebastopol, was allotted the task of protecting a vital supply column (including 2,000,000 francs' overdue pay). Early on the morning of 30 April 1863, they were attacked by a force of over 2,000 Mexicans, and after driving off two cavalry charges took up positions in the semi-ruined *hacienda* of Camerone where they held out till six in the evening. By sunset only two were left; but they had killed or wounded over 600 Mexicans and the convoy was safe.

21 *Nice: looking westwards from the Quai des Etats-Unis*

Some years later it was decided that this example of devotion to duty and self-sacrifice should be remembered yearly as symbolising those very qualities which make the Legion a true *Corps d'Elite*.

The ceremony is open to the public and people flock in their thousands not only from Aubagne but from Marseille, Aix and the surrounding villages. Danjou's wooden hand, in a glass-topped polished wooden coffer, is carried by a veteran Legion officer and escorted by a platoon of bearded pioneers between the regiment's open ranks to the *monument aux morts*. There an account of the battle is read. After the Last Post, followed by the Legion march *Le Boudin* instead of *Reveille*, the hand is escorted off the parade ground and the proceedings close with a march past.

For the rest of that day and the next – 1 May being a public holiday in France – the barracks' grounds are turned into a huge fair with an Algerian, Indo-Chinese and an Alsatian restaurant, several bars and the usual booths. The commander of the Legion offers a buffet lunch (by invitation) and the band plays on the terrace outside the officers' mess.

7. The Var Coast

The meteoric rise in popularity of the Var coast during the last two decades is principally due to that of St Tropez, which in turn owes much of its success to a young film actress, the blonde Brigitte Bardot, often described in the early 'fifties' as the 'Sex Kitten' and one of the first to display her totally uncovered natural charms on the screen. Her villa, *La Madrague*, just outside the village – as it was then – became the centre of the younger set at the time, thus automatically drawing the crowds not only from France but from all over western Europe and even from the United States, hoping to see and copy their idol, feeling too that by breaking new ground and condemning resorts that were fashionable pre-war they were hammering further nails into the coffin-lid of *le monde de papa*.

This popular rush got so out of hand that, as I remember reading, a despairing notice appeared in a local paper that whereas only 3,000 beds were available, at least 40,000 visitors were expected in St Tropez for the month of August alone.

The actual story of St Tropez, however, goes back many centuries. The small town stands – facing north – on the south shore at the tip of the bay now known as the St Tropez Gulf, its small but lately enlarged harbour receiving most of the *mistral's* blast. Formerly used by fishing craft the present port shelters an impressive number of expensive yachts. Originally called Attenopolis by the Greeks it was christened *Heraclea Caccabaria* by the Romans, who turned it into a small naval base auxiliary to Fréjus.

During the Emperor Nero's reign one of the Roman palace

officials, the Pisan-born Torpes, became a convert to Christianity. The Emperor, notorious for his Christianophobia, demanded that Torpes recant publicly. When he refused he was decapitated, and could perhaps count himself lucky to have died so comparatively quickly. His headless trunk was thrown into a small rowing-boat between a dog and a cock, symbol of a parricide, and the boat was taken out to sea to drift at the mercy of wind and current. After an unspecified time the boat grounded on the shores of what was then known as the Sambracitan gulf. Its approach had been revealed in a dream to a pious woman, a Roman Christian called Celerina, who took the body and buried it secretly. The tomb has never been discovered but the martyr's head today reposes in a chapel in his native Pisa and is still an object of considerable veneration.

Like most of the smaller coastal settlements St Tropez, as it was re-named about the year 305, was captured and sacked by the Saracens who later, however, made it one of their principal bases for attacking northern routed shipping. Thanks to the success of so many of these expeditions the town, as it had become, grew prosperous; a depôt for piled-up loot, its inhabitants learning to enjoy certain refinements of life, then exclusive to the East, from their Moslem overlords.

Razed once more before its final recapture from the North African invaders, life for the inhabitants was gradually easing after years of want, when again the town had the misfortune to become a battleground for the rival forces of Louis of Anjou and Charles of Durazzo. Devastation was so complete that it looked as if St Tropez would disappear from contemporary maps, till in 1470 Count Grimaldi, Grand Seneschal of Provence, arranged for a Genoese nobleman, Rafaelle Garezzio, to immigrate with 60 Genoese families. The Genoese agreed to be responsible for re-building the fortifications and for the town's defence against all invaders or intruders. In return for these services King René (the 'Good') promised them exemption from any form of taxation. The bargain was kept, the Genoese families became known as *Capitaines de Ville* and the town enjoyed a semi-autonomy for the best part of 200 years, repelling all attacks and even sending fleets to the help of other coastal towns temporarily in danger.

The greatest victory was won on 15 June 1637 when 20 Spanish galleys, attempting to land a raiding force, were put to flight, a victory commemorated every year by a *bravade*, when the genuine *Tropéziens* – one is sometimes a little astonished to find that beneath the touristic tide such citizens do exist – dress in vaguely *Grande Armée* uniforms and parade the streets firing blank shot from ancient muskets.

In the seventeenth century the Suffren family became the *Seigneurs de St Tropez*, most well-known being the admiral, the *Bailli de Suffren*, who harassed English Atlantic convoys at the time of the American War of Independence.

War was to come again to St Tropez in most devastating form when in August 1944 the town was badly knocked about at the time of the Franco-American landings. Later a contemporary witness noted 'In 1945 St Tropez had not an unbroken window left through which to look at the roadstead; house-fronts like unsteady screens masked the rubble of destroyed buildings . . . the blown-up blocks of the harbour made it nothing more than a heap of rubbish . . .' (*Côte d'Azur* – Pierre Borel).

The nineteenth century, however, witnessed the quiet beginning of St Tropez as a centre of attraction for the art world.

In 1888 Guy de Maupassant cruising along the Var coast in the yacht *Bel Ami* described the town as 'a gallant little city; full of salt and courage' in his book, *Sur l'Eau*. The painter Signac arrived in 1892 on a bicycle, to be followed by such giants of the post-Impressionist world as Matisse and Bonnard, and it was in St Tropez that Gounod put the finishing touches to his *Romeo et Juliette*. Vivid contemporary picture of lazy life in the *midi*, Colette's *La Naissance du Jour* was written at St Tropez and contained the reflection 'a woman may claim as many native countries as she has had happy love affairs; she is also reborn beneath each sky where she recovers from the pain of loving. By this reckoning this shore, blue with salt, decked with tomatoes and sweet peppers, is mine twice over . . .'

Fortunately memories of the passage of so many of the greater exponents of the new art expressions which appeared so startling in the late nineteenth and early twentieth centuries have been preserved thanks to the generosity of a wealthy businessman, Monsieur Georges Grammont, Lyonnais by birth. Himself an avid collector he bought the seventeenth-century *L'Annonciade* chapel which stands at the angle of the *quais Gabriel Péri* and *L'Epi*. The interior was completely redesigned by the architect Louis Sue and in 1955 opened to the public as the *Musée de 'lAnnonciade*, displaying close on 100 masterpieces of modern art: among others works of Dufy, Braque, Utrillo, Vlaminck, Derain, Seurat, and of course Signac himself who contributes two views of St Tropez port and several water-colours. The majority of the subjects chosen are inevitably meridional though two Derains of the *fauve* period represent Waterloo Bridge and Westminster.

This permanent exhibition had only been open six years when 56 of the pictures were stolen (in July 1961). The thieves, however, found it impossible to get rid of their rather cumbrous booty and 16 months later in November 1962 the canvases were found in a deserted farmhouse in the Seine-et-Marne department.

Most of them were damaged. The restoration was undertaken at the Louvre and at last, five years later, they were re-hung in the *Annonciade*.

Another corner of interest, nostalgic memory of the past, is the *Pesquière*, the original fishermen's port, bounded by tall houses with multi-coloured walls, a favourite subject for Sunday painters: reached by an archway leading off the *Place de la Mairie*. Above, a sixteenth-century citadel and three turreted forts with seventeenth-century ramparts remind us that this Mecca of the bikini once echoed to the din of battle rather than of transistors.

The hinterland of St Tropez' squat peninsula produces some of the Var's finest grapes and anyone seeing *Domaine de Pierrefeu* on a wine list is not likely to be disappointed with either the red or the *rosé* bearing the label.

Near by, within eight miles of St Tropez and on the peninsula's highest ground – 470 feet – is Ramatuelle village, also fortified, favoured by those who like to be near St Tropez's turmoil but still welcome an occasional moment of comparative tranquillity. Ramatuelle was the favourite haunt of the talented and charming young actor Gerard Philippe, who was brilliant not only in films of the *Fanfan la Tulipe* variety but also in such a purely classical role as *Le Cid*. Only 37 when he died, he is buried in the village cemetery.

Other Var coastal resorts which have gained ground enormously in popularity since 1945 are Le Lavandou and Cavalaire to the west of St Tropez: and to the east Ste Maxime and St Aygulf. All four started off as cheaper, quieter places for summer tourists, especially British, not so much interested in the social whirl as in a slightly more adventurous extension of the conventional seaside holiday. They made a wise choice since all these resorts can boast of beaches infinitely more agreeable than any I have seen in the Alpes-Maritimes. Ste Maxime, which lies on the St Tropez gulf's eastern side, strives to rival St Tropez. Like St Tropez it began as a fishing village but of much more recent origin, probably about 1820. Thus without historical background it is perhaps something of a *parvenu* in an area where the most humble village is usually steeped in tradition, with at least one monument, a church, a small chapel, a house where some famous figure was either born, died, dined or slept. However, it is a gay little place. The crowds on its quayside are as eccentric as elsewhere, and Ste Maxime has the advantage that, tucked away in its back streets, there are one or two excellent little restaurants where one can enjoy a good meal without risking apoplexy at the sight of the bill.

There is a widespread error – often quoted in books dealing with the South of France – that the range of hills known as the *Massif des Maures* takes its name from the Moors, since in the ninth and tenth centuries it swarmed with Saracens who had established themselves in some of its more inaccessible areas, whence they were able to control the coast from Hyères to the Argens river. The name in fact goes back to the Greek *mavros* meaning dark or black, later adapted in Provençal to *maouro*, so describing the darkness of the pine forests which cover these slopes.

The year 890 was that in which the Saracens' hold on the coast reached its apogee, when they established their headquarters in the village of Fraxinet, today La Garde Freinet, which they soon converted into a quasi-impregnable fortress. It was during this period that St Tropez and Fréjus were razed and Ramatuelle saved itself – though only temporarily – by letting loose swarms of bees on the attackers. The fortress of Fraxinet was not recaptured by Christian forces commanded by William Count of Orange and his brother Roubaud, till 973. After skilful manœuvring, the first assault, actually led by Roubaud – a surprise dawn attack – was completely successful. Seven thousand Saracens were slaughtered. 'I have spared the lives of a few Saracens,' Roubaud noted in his victory dispatch to his brother, 'who may be able to serve in your galleys and these suitably bound I am sending to you.' Generously Rouband also made a present of one Saracen to act as a slave to each of his soldiers, as a set share of the loot. 'Not one,' says a contemporary writer, speaking of the defeated Moslems, 'escaped to bring tidings of the defeat to Spain.'

Today the smaller hill villages, especially those facing south, are prospering. There is a considerable 'foreign' population and the usual summer rush of those who wish to be away, but not too far away, from the coast. La Garde Freinet is now an artists' colony and a centre for cork making; there are vast acres of cork oak forest in the neighbourhood as well as pine. Collobrières, famous for its *marrons glacés*, confectioned from local chestnut trees, is a convenient centre for exploring the *massif*. The most worthwhile expeditions are to the *Chartreuse de la Verne*, founded in 1170 but abandoned at the time of the Revolution and never reoccupied; and to *Notre Dame des Anges*, at 2,500 feet highest spot of the *massif*. Here, legend says, came Nymphe, sister of Maximin, first bishop of Aix, to lead a hermit's life retired from the world, leaving when she died a carved statue of the Virgin Mary, now housed in a small chapel whose origin may be

Roman but which was added to and restored in the nineteenth century, and scene of four yearly pilgrimages: Tuesday of Holy Week, Whit Monday, 2 July and 8 September.

The Maures is also a botanist's paradise. Apart from the forests of pine, cork oak and ilex, the spread Spanish chestnut groves, the climate is such that orange and lemon trees and even date palms flourish. Agave and cactus grow wild. Eucalyptus and casuarina trees have been successfully planted and the village of Bormes is famous for its mimosa.

St Aygulf, named after a saint canonised in the seventh century, is within sight of Fréjus's red tiled roofs and St Raphaël's strangely *Sacré-Cœur*-like church, and has one of the longest stretches of genuine sandy beach between Marseille and Menton, stretching east towards *Fréjus-plage*, and a tiny harbour sheltered from the *mistral*, to the east of the snub peninsula on which the town is largely built. The beach because of its extent is unique in that it is comparatively uncrowded both at the very beginning of the bathing season and the last warm autumn days before winter sets in. The town is framed by low hills covered with the typically Mediterranean umbrella pines. On either side of the Argens river which runs into the sea just to the east of the harbour are vast orchards of cherry and peach as well as stretches of vineyards. In late February and March, blossom time, the drive down from the main N7 road – which runs due east-west some ten miles inland – reminds one of publicity posters of Japan.

Beyond copses, orchards and the highway, the horizon is blocked by the eastern tip of the *Massif des Maures*, with the jagged red rocks of Roquebrune, a striking landmark also from the train, often a dramatic first glimpse seen at dawn. Beyond that again, their outline so often fluid in heat-mist, the purple barrier of hills have on their wooded slopes the upper Var's outpost line of *villages perchés*.

Fréjus is the *doyen* of the coastal towns. Before Roman times the original Fréjus, built on the shores of a lagoon standing back from the sea, was a small Greek (Massilian) settlement. The Romans, looking for a rival to Marseille, were attracted by this site with its comparatively sheltered stretch of shore, a convenient staging post also on the road from Rome to Spain, later famous as the *Via Aurelia*.

In 49 B.C. Julius Caesar founded the Forum Julii and established a small garrison. When the Roman world was convulsed by civil war Octavius, who later assumed the title of emperor under the name Augustus, made Forum Julii into a minor naval base where, we are told, a large number of the great galleys which took part in the battle of Actium (31 B.C.), scene of Antonius's final defeat, were built.

During Augustus's reign Forum Julii became the headquarters of the 8th Roman Legion. In addition a very large number of ex-legionaries with their families were allowed to retire in the neighbourhood, setting up a sort of old soldiers' colony. It was not long, being on the main road to Spain and a major port into the bargain, before the once small garrison town became a prosperous city of over 40,000 inhabitants, nearly double in fact its present-day population; and it was here that Britain's future conqueror, the Emperor Agricola, was born.

Another famous Roman to see the light of day in Fréjus was the actor Quintus Roscius (129–66 B.C.). Cicero, who was his friend, said, 'He is so brilliant on the stage that he should never come off it, but so virtuous that he ought never to have gone on it.' As François Cali states 'Roscius was the forerunner of Raimu and Fernandel.'

Since the port was a good mile inland it was connected with the open sea by a cement canal while, ingeniously, a second canal brought in continually running water from the Argens river to prevent the exit from silting up. The entrance was guarded by two towers. At night a heavy chain was stretched across to eliminate the possibility of surprise attack, while a powerful light, known as Augustus's lantern – still standing today in the ruins of the Roman citadel which can be seen to the left of the level crossing and the *Boulevard de la Mer* – served the double purpose of landmark for mariners and prevention of a potential enemy approach under cover of darkness. Ships seldom put to sea during the winter months. They were dry-docked – the harbour could shelter some 400 galleys – and usually refloated about mid-April.

This major port, however, did not survive Roman times. The city was sacked by the Visigoths and later by the Saracens. Untended, the canals and docks became silted up, never to be restored. Ironically one of the most respected Fréjusiens in history, Bishop Riculphe (tenth century), largely responsible for rebuilding the city after Saracen ravages, was also responsible for the despoliation of much of the remaining vestiges of Roman presence, using the stones of still standing edifices for his own rebuilding programme. Bouyala d'Arnaud says, 'Fréjus has been called the Pompeii of Provence. one can also add that Bishop Riculphe was its Vesuvius . . .'

Today the most striking Roman remains are the aqueduct and the arena.

To be sure of an adequate watersupply for so considerable a city the Romans built an aqueduct 50 kilometres – 31 miles – long which captured the waters of the Siagnole river near the little mountain village of Mons, following first the course of the Siagnole valley, then that of the Riou Blanc and finally that of the Reyran river. The sector of this major work which entered the city can be seen to the left of the *Avenue de Cannes*, the main inland route crossing the Esterel hills.

The arena, to the right of the main N7 highway as one leaves Fréjus in the direction of Aix-en-Provence, is in a remarkably good state of preservation. Though very much smaller than the arenas of Arles and Nîmes it could seat up to 12,000 spectators. Today like its bigger brothers it is the setting for bullfights – El Cordobes appears there frequently – and sometimes at the height of the summer season for one of the more spectacular operas.

A few years ago an enterprising promoter put on what must be considered as the most original of all performances of *Carmen*. After the fourth act overture and the Carmen-Escamillo duet *Si tu m'aimes, Carmen,* soloists and chorus withdrew and the audience was treated to a genuine *corrida* in which the bull was put to death by a *matador* – replacing the baritone – by the name of Georges Bizet. The bull was indeed successfully killed but one wonders what would have happened to the production had the *matador* rather than the bull met his end in the arena . . .

On 2 December 1959, Roman architectural skill was submitted to the severest possible test, surviving triumphantly. Due either to some structural error or geological miscalculation the dam on the Reyran river at Malpasset, five miles upstream from Fréjus, gave way at about ten o'clock at night after 48 hours of continual rain. It let loose 55 million cubic metres of water which hurtled down on the city at the speed of a fast train and in a wave of 200 feet high.

All over the low-lying quarter to the west of Fréjus isolated farms and villas were swept away, leaving only the foundations. I was on the scene myself next morning, eye-witness of the flood's murderous power. But though the wave's full force struck the arena the blow had no effect; not a stone moved. On the other hand the railway station, rails torn up and twisted, offices demolished, looked as if it had been hit by a minor atomic explosion. From a near-by bare plane tree branch some ten feet above road level hung a Renault *quatre chevaux*. Details made grim reading: 403 dead, 52 buildings and 253 farms destroyed, 4,000 acres of cultivated land – mostly orchards – ravaged.

Old Fréjus, untouched because of its position on rising ground, is grouped round the cathedral, dedicated both to Our Lady and St Stephen. Finished about 1200 – Fréjus became a bishopric in 370 – the cathedral was a precursor of the Gothic style in Provence, but the baptistery, an octagonal building, is considerably older and dates back to the fifth century.

One feels that the cathedral, too, small but immensely solid, might well have resisted the Reyran flood-waters. The west door, embellished with 16 carved panels, the most beautiful being those representing the marriage, annunciation and coronation of the Virgin Mary, is particularly striking. The altar piece is by Jacques Durand (1450) of the Nice school and represents Ste Marguerite surrounded by saints. There is also a picture, to the right of the altar, of St François de Paule with Fréjus in the background. St

François, to whom is dedicated the church on the *Place d'Agricola*, is the patron saint of Fréjus. He came to the town in 1483 at a time when plague was killing an alarming number of *Fréjusiens*, but on his arrival the epidemic ceased miraculously, an event celebrated yearly by a *bravade* on the sixth Sunday after Easter.

Tickets have to be obtained to visit the baptistery, the cloisters and the little archaeological museum.

Granite Roman pillars with Corinthian capitals at the walls' eight angles support the baptistery's cupola. In 1926 excavations brought to light the baptismal pool in which catechumens were immersed, and the terracotta basin or *dolium* which held the liturgical oil.

The museum, leading off the cloisters with their well-kept lawns and delicate marble columns, is devoted almost entirely to archaeological remains. In the first of the three rooms there is a particularly striking mosaic, a leopard in its centre, and a marble head of Jupiter. Coming to a more modern era, however, there is a portrait in the second room of Cardinal Fleury, Bishop of Fréjus till 1715, in which year he was called to Paris to become minister to Louis xv, and letters from Napoleon and the Abbé Sièyes. The latter, well-known revolutionary figure who was in turn member of the Convention, of the Directorate, and finally Senator and Count of the Empire, was born in Fréjus in 1748 and one of the few leading personalities of that turbulent period to live to a ripe old age: not dying till 1836. Fréjus was of course the scene of Napoleon's disembarkation after his hazardous flight from Egypt, and of his embarkation – after having narrowly escaped assassination at Orgon – for his brief Elban exile.

The new quarter – *Fréjus-plage* – is really a continuation of St Raphaël: a Hove to St Raphaël's Brighton. It consists of a long sweep of shops, hotels, arcades, cafés and restaurants facing the sea, while between the road and the sea itself the narrow greyish *plage* is dotted with bathing establishments which do little to embellish a strictly banal scene.

St Raphaël, youthful neighbour of historic Fréjus and now a town close on 20,000 inhabitants, was 'discovered' by the highly

republican-minded French author Alphonse Karr, who had been
obliged to leave Paris after his unpleasant remarks concerning
Napoleon III's taking over the running of the country. After a
stage in Nice when he temporarily abandoned writing to become
a horticulturist – 'plant a stick in my garden,' he wrote to a friend
in Paris, 'and when you wake up the following morning you will
see roses growing from it' – he wandered westward along the coast
till in 1864 he came to St Raphaël and bought land to the east
of the town. There opposite the two islets known as *Lion de Terre*
and *Lion de Mer*, he built himself a house he named the *Maison
Close* – The Whoreshop – a touch of twisted humour since Karr
was as inveterate a misogynist as he was republican. On the other
hand he did keep more or less 'open' house for his friends of the
art world, the composers Gounod and Berlioz, the painters Hamon
and Fromentin, the novelists Alexandre Dumas and Jean Aicard
all being frequently his guests, as well as the *poète maudit* Guy de
Maupassant.

Although looked upon as rather a second-class resort by the
wealthy, and very much not 'with-it' by the young, St Raphaël
had increased its population from a mere 900 to 9,000 by 1930.
The post-war era brought about another spectacular rush of
holidaymakers, and later of secondary home-makers; but a rush
which remained nevertheless within more sober limits than that
which swamped St Tropez. In fact St Raphaël, on whose coat of
arms figures the archangel, has always been quiet, despite a casino
built on the point overlooking the small harbour. It is more sought-
after by the middle-aged than by the adolescent: by those who
prefer to take the sun on the promenade rather than bake nine-
tenths nude on the *plage*.

The town has little of historical interest to offer, and heavily
damaged at the time of the Allied landings at near-by Le
Dramont, its villas, shops and hotels affect one adversely by their
blatant newness. Nevertheless St Raphaël is a good place to eat
fish without spending a fortune!

The 20-mile *Corniche d'Or* linking the town with Cannes and
the classical Riviera is the most dramatic of the *midi's* coastal

roads. For most of the 20 miles it clings to the side of the Esterel hills and the astonishing porphyry cliffs which from a distance on a normal sunny day give the effect of being steeped in blood, while the rock face takes on a deep purple, even at midday, as if submerged permanently in the gloom of a sad twilight.

The guide-book tells us that this road is *'large et bien entretenue mais sinueuse et très fréquentée, où s'impose une attention soutenue'*. The warning should be taken seriously. With the amount of traffic encountered on all but the wettest of winter days, to take one's eyes off the road to admire the scenery is tantamount to suicide It is better to stop and climb to the vantage-point of *Cap Roux* at the foot of the *Grand Pic du Cap Roux* – this latter can be climbed by those not afraid of a rough walk of about an hour and a quarter – from where there is a view of the coast from the approaches to Toulon in the west as far east as the Italian frontier.

Le Dramont, only five miles east of St Raphaël, with its porphyry quarries, was the scene of the Allied landings known by the code names 'Dragon' and 'Anvil', on 14 August 1944. A force of some 150,000 men came ashore after an intensive bombardment by a fleet including six capital ships covered by 5,000 aircraft: an operation described by contemporary correspondents as 'apocalyptic'. In his memoirs General de Larminat says that he cannot understand how it was that all the forests of the Esterel and Maures were not set ablaze. It was indeed a miracle when one considers that these same hills are yearly ravaged by fires consuming tens of thousands of acres, started in many cases by a carelessly discarded cigarette or by campers heating up a meal (a practice strictly forbidden by law).

A monument commemorates this important step towards France's final liberation, but today the beaches are so covered by camping sites that it is apt to be passed unnoticed.

Another war episode is recalled by a plaque in the wall of the *Phare de la Baumette* in memory of the aviator and writer Antoine de St Exupéry (*Le Petit Prince*) near Agay, a small *plage* beyond Le Dramont where his sister had a house which he often visited. Over it he flew on 31 July 1944 heading out to sea on a mission from which he did not return.

Going westward from St Tropez one soon comes to the Var's most built-up area, the agglomeration formed by the old resort Hyères and the huge naval base, Toulon.

In spite of Hyères' proximity to Toulon (200,000 inhabitants) it has always been popular with those who wish to combine coast, quiet and warmth. One might say that Hyères is really a more mellow, more retiring, more traditional counterpart of St Raphaël. It is in fact the oldest resort of France's Mediterranean coast to be frequented by the British.

As an ideal place for a rest cure its reputation dates back to the Roman occupation, a reputation preserved throughout the succeeding centuries. Catherine de Medici and Henri IV were among its royal devotees, and as a port, too, it was famous. It was at Hyères that St Louis disembarked on his return from the seventh crusade in 1254; then, as the historian Bonde says, one of the main ports of departure for the Holy Land. From the port St Louis went straight to hear mass in the church now called St Louis and then only just completed, a church still standing though badly damaged by the 1944 bombardments.

In April 1946 I returned to the *midi, en route* for the Middle East. I spent five days in a transit camp between Toulon and Hyères after a journey by troop train from Dieppe which had taken no less than four days. Every evening I managed to escape from the camp to Hyères town. The shops were empty, food and wine scarce. Life had not regained its normal rhythm and coffee was still very much *ersatz*. Yet the charm of the old city, the beauty of the date-palm avenues – especially the *Avenue Gambretta* – so much more lush than any I remembered in North Africa, the quiet hills and meadows, a blazing glory of spring flowers, combined to achieve that magic which draws people in their millions to the *midi*. It was overwhelming; it made material considerations appear trifles to be ignored even before their impact had been felt. Of this countryside, I felt convinced, Ambroise Thomas must have been thinking when from his villa just outside

the town he composed the opera *Mignon* and the touching little aria: *Connais-tu le pays où fleurit l'oranger? . . . où dans toute saison butinent les abeilles . . .*

Hyères port no longer exists, having been, like Fréjus, silted up. The town now stands back some four miles from the sea and *Hyères-plage*, backed by umbrella pines curving round the western shore of Hyères roadstead. Beyond the *plage* is the small port of Saint-Pierre from where one can sail, not for the Holy Land as in St Louis's time, but for the *Iles d'Hyères*.

These islands, *Porquerolles*, *Port Cros* and *Ile du Levant*, the largest barely five miles long (east to west) and a mile and a half wide, resemble emerged ridges, as though the stretch of water separating them from the mainland were purely accidental. Well wooded, with sandy beaches facing the mainland and cliffs dropping steeply to the open sea *Port Cros*, whose vegetation is almost tropically luxuriant, was declared a national park in 1936, which means no shooting, no camping, and above all – wise precaution – no fire-lighting by picnickers. The *Ile du Levant*, most easterly of the group, has acquired fame because of its nudist colony, founded by Doctor Durbille in 1931. Today the naturists have to share the island with the Navy who have commandeered the north-east promontory for a guided missile trial and experimental centre – to which no layman is allowed access.

Toulon's importance as a naval base coincided with the secession of Provence to the French monarchy. Louis XIII took the first steps towards fortifying the harbour but it was Henri IV who ordered the building of a second ring of defences completely surrounding city, arsenal and dockyards, thereby displaying an admirable foresight. During the war of the Austrian Succession Toulon was besieged by an Austro-Sardinian army commanded by Prince Eugène, and blockaded by an Anglo-Dutch fleet. Thanks to the enlarged and improved fortifications, the work of Vauban, Marshal Tessé was able to resist this double threat till a relieving column led by the Comte de Grignan, then Governor of Provence, forced Prince Eugène to raise the siege.

During the reign of Louis XIV, even well on into that of Louis xv, most of the navy's ships were galleys rowed by convicts, political prisoners, those condemned because of their religious beliefs, or slaves captured as a result of forays along the North African coast.

The living conditions of these wretched individuals were quite inhuman. Each of the enormous oars was handled by five men, the benches to which they were chained being their sole accommodation. But for the fact that the spectacle of human and animal suffering has always drawn crowds one would be astonished to read that the sight of the galley-slaves' misery, their foul environment and utter degradation was a highly popular tourist attraction, particularly of a Sunday afternoon: one of the sights of Provence, in fact.

The *Bagne** of Toulon was particularly infamous. Up to 1838 there were 4,305 *bagnards* of whom 1,193 were serving a genuine life sentence. They were lodged, some in six 'halls' each consisting of a ground floor and upper storey, and others in four floating prisons: obsolete and condemned men-of-war. Prisoners wore red caps and their yellow cloth trousers were slit up the sides to allow chains to be fixed the more easily to their legs. They were chained two by two, the chain weighing 16 pounds. Rations consisted mostly of bean soup, biscuits – there was never a meat issue – and 48 centilitres of wine a day per man.

After some years a *bagnard* careful and tough enough to survive could be employed by the prison authorities and paid for his labours: baker, assistant cook, chain-welder, lamp-lighter and trimmer. By far the most sought-after post, however, was that of executioner. We have a record of the tariff paid to these amateur torturers: 20 *livres* for a hanging, 15 for a burning alive, six to slice off the ears, two to cut off a nose or slit a tongue.

On the outbreak of the Revolution Toulon royalists got the better of the mob and called for British aid. Between them British and French turned the harbour area into an almost impregnable

---

* The word *Bagne* comes somewhat obscurely from the Italian *bagno* (bath) due to the fact that a prison for slaves had been built in Istanbul on the site of the 'Turkish' bath of a pasha's harem.

position, able without difficulty to resist the revolutionary army's ill-led, unco-ordinated attacks directed by General Carteaux. Although Carteaux was replaced by the slightly more talented Dugommier the city might have held out indefinitely but for the fact that the besieging army included a young artillery captain, Napoleon Bonaparte, to whom Dugommier had the somewhat unethical good sense to give a free hand for the planning of the assault. Thanks to Captain Bonaparte's genius, energy and courage under fire the key point of the defence, a redoubt known as *Petit Gibraltar*, was stormed in a downpour of rain on the night of 18 December 1793.

After the torment of the Napoleonic wars it was from Toulon in 1830 that the French expeditionary force to Algeria sailed to inaugurate 132 years of occupation; and enjoying the reputation of being France's greatest naval base it was to Toulon that a Russian naval squadron paid an official visit in 1893, after the alliance between the two countries inspired by mutual fear of the Kaiser's increasing aggressiveness. In honour of this visit the *Darse* Vieille* was renamed the *Quai Cronstadt* . . . today with undiminished Russophilia the *Quai Stalingrad*.

After the 1940 disaster the French fleet was again concentrated in Toulon, then in the unoccupied zone, overrun by the Germans after the Allied 1942 landings in North Africa. Arrived in Toulon the Germans tried to negotiate with the French naval authorities, then, losing patience, they attempted a *coup de main* on the night of 27 November. Despite his rabid anglophobia Admiral Laborde at once gave orders for his ships to be scuttled. As a result 72 vessels, including two battle cruisers and seven cruisers, went to the bottom, effectively blocking the harbour.

Before its liberation by General de Lattre de Tassigny's columns on 25 August 1944 town and harbour were severely damaged by American bombers, whole areas being razed. After the war they were replaced by a modern city which has a functional rather than a Provençal aspect. In this 'new look' Toulon two museums are worth a visit: the *Musée Naval* on the *Quai Stalingrad*, containing

* *Darse* – a purely Provençal word for dock.

models of famous men-of-war from *Duquesne* (1787) to *Colbert* (1928) as well as pictures of interest to students of French naval history. The *Musée d'Art et d'Archéologie* on the *Boulevard Général Leclerc* holds a collection of Egyptian *figurines* considered to date back to 1000 B.C., and paintings mostly by lesser-known artists but including *Proverbes Flamandes* by Breughel, a Joseph Vernet and a Monticelli.

Though Toulon is not a place in which I care to linger it has one great sentimental link. It was the birthplace of Jules Muraire, better known as Raimu, incomparable interpreter of Provençal roles on both stage and screen.

8. The High Var

Till recently the Var was the poor relation of the departments making up modern Provence, ignored by tourists visiting the Riviera and without the historical and archaeological interest of the Vaucluse or the Bouches-due-Rhône. Apart from the naval base at Toulon and the fact that the not-so-wealthy were in the habit of wintering at St Raphaël rather than Cannes or Monte Carlo, the country beyond the coastal strip limited by the Estérel and Maures hills was as unknown as nineteenth-century darkest Africa. It did not even tempt the normally adventurous Romans who concentrated on making Fréjus a major port and adorning the settlement with an impressively solid arena.

In aspect the Var, covering over 4,000 square miles and largest of Provence's departments, is rugged and at first sight unfriendly. It is striped by parallel east-west ridges of scrub, stunted pine- and ilex-covered rocky hills (whose highest peak, Mont de la Chens, overlooks the Logis du Pin on the Route Napoleon), split by narrow rivers whose courses are usually waterless during the summer months. The Provençal peasant's traditionally hard life has always been at its hardest in the Haut Var, growing even harder paradoxically with the introduction of machinery and the gradual disappearance of home industries before the onslaught of manufactured goods; and as has been mentioned, after the terrible slaughter of male youth in the 1914–18 war. For the best part of 40 years after the 1918 armistice the despair of villagers with their lot, the fight to scratch the barest living from the soil, led to a veritable *sauve qui peut* of the young to the towns. Entire villages became totally deserted; others of a normal population of 500 to 1,000 dropped to a few scores of inhabitants, the majority approaching old age. In fact within the last ten years one could read: 'It (the Haut Var) is poor and mountainous and the population of its little towns and hill-top villages, unable to live on scenery alone, is steadily dwindling . . .' (Archibald Lyall – *The Companion Guide to the South of France*).

The change that has come about since those words were written is little short of miraculous and is due to a large extent to outside influence, not only from abroad but also from other regions of France.

Since the war the sun has become a necessary element in the lives of so many. In spite of rising prices and air travel's annihilation of distance the south of France is still one of the best investments for the holiday budget, weighing in the balance such main factors as accessibility and local amenities. Not everyone, however, is afflicted with gregarophilia and by the '60s the coast's very popularity was posing problems. Individuals began to study the possibility of being nearer, instead of on, the sea front. It was soon found that this was not only a possible but a happy solution. Then, as near-coastal towns and villages in turn became overcrowded, so the inland trend became the more pronounced. It was discovered that a distance of even 30 miles inland was within easy drive of a beach, that the average height at such a distance being 1,500–2,000 feet the climate was healthy and refreshing, the countryside well worth exploring for its own beauty, and that there was escape from one of the age's greatest scourges – noise. Such a revolution led to a further school of thought: that the Haut Var was the ideal area for a secondary home.

As a result the region's economic present and future has changed radically. Villages which were crumbling have been resuscitated. Populations have increased by as much as 150 per cent in the last five or six years. Village teenagers on leaving school no longer flock to the cities. The boom in the building trade has been phenomenal and local masons have swapped their bicycles for the latest Porsche or Alfa-Romeo.

Despite this gold-rush atmosphere, however, the only inland town of any size is Draguignan, which in spite of the fact that its population is less than a quarter that of Toulon, is the seat of the department's Prefecture.

Draguignan is a pleasant non-touristic town of some 20,000 inhabitants, unpretentious, a good and cheap shopping centre; but built in a hollow, it can be a refrigerator in winter and a furnace in summer.

The old town – traces of the original ramparts still stand – was built up the slope of a bare rocky hill and culminated at the *Tour de L'Horloge*, dating back to the seventeenth century, on the site of the original tower built in 1230 by the city's governor Romeo de Villeneuve, and destroyed on Cardinal Mazarin's orders in 1649 to punish the *Dracenois* for having joined with the *Semestre* (the Provençal *Fronde*) revolt against royal authority. Today this tower with its wrought-iron campanile, though not of great beauty, serves as a useful landmark.

Draguignan, earlier known as Dracoenum, does not figure largely in history other than in the story of how its patron saint, St Hermentaire, who later became first bishop of Antibes, slew a dragon, as fearsome as Tarascon's *Tarasque*, which had been swept by a tidal wave from the Iles de Lerins and settled in the marshy country in the Nartuby river valley from where it terrorised the city population, and again in Louis XIII's time when there occurred an incident which is not often mentioned in Draguignan's history. There was apparently a shortage of professional executioners, and Draguignan was ordered to produce a number of temporary *bourreaux* to perform such duties as breaking on the wheel, tongue-slitting, beating and hanging, in return for which they would receive 36 *livres* per year as well as being allowed to draw a weekly ration of a calf's head or lung, or a portion of tripe.

In 1797 Draguignan replaced Brignoles as seat of the Var Prefecture, but even so its centuries-old tranquillity was not really disturbed till mid-August 1944, when the town was cleared of its German occupants by a mixed force of American paratroopers and local *maquis*.

Speaking of the town in the early years of the century André Hallays* said: 'It is threefold and fourfold Provençal, it is delightful. It has stone foundations, admirable plane trees, large avenues . . .' But in spite of this appreciation it must be admitted that for the tourist Draguignan has little to offer. It remains a typical market town, shopping Mecca for the neighbourhood, especially on a Saturday morning when the plane-tree-shaded market square is at its busiest, its stalls weighed down with sweet red, green and yellow peppers, tomatoes, aubergines, huge peaches and golden melons, whole smoked mountain hams, spiced sausages and goat cheeses, or as Christmas approaches sad immobilised ranks of turkeys, geese, ducks and chickens, cases of pathetic rabbits, and even guinea-pigs, all waiting resignedly to appear on the table.

In the new town, opposite the Prefecture, the public gardens boast a Rodin bust of Georges Clemenceau. Though the 'Tiger' was born in the Vendée he was 25 years Draguignan's representative in the *Chambre des Deputés* before becoming Senator of the Var.

However, if not of great interest Draguignan has two advantages: it is a good place to eat and drink comparatively cheaply and an excellent excursion centre, in particular for the spectacular Gorges du Verdon.

For this tour one leaves Draguignan by the Comps road, heading almost due north. While still in the suburbs, a bare kilometre from the centre, there is an over-discreet signpost with an arrow pointing left, which simply reads *Pierre de la Fée* (Fairy Stone). Few people ever take the trouble to follow the direction in which the arrow points, and yet this *Pierre* is in fact the only genuine dolmen in Provence.

It stands on a small hillock and is formed by four massive crude stones, three uprights covered by a fourth horizontal some 20 feet long and about 15 feet at its widest; it is sheltered by three

* According to François Cali, Hallays was an amiable creature whose *bête noire* was restoration and who 'at the sight of Avignon's restored walls trembled with fury and could not get this out of his mind . . .'

trees, an oak, a *micocoulier* and a juniper, the three symbolic trees of the southern Celts. It is thought that this dolmen was used ritually by the Druids of the region, who existed until the fifth century, but this is only a surmise and nothing is known of its origin.*

A few miles beyond the dolmen the road enters the Nartuby river gorges, ending with a dramatic view of the village Château-double to the left. The village walls, like those of a fortress and of a rich red colour, always remind me of a Grand Atlas Kasbah. They rise straight from a cliff-edge with a sheer 500-foot drop to the torrent, and a diversionary visit entails a steep climb ending with a short tunnel cut through the solid rock.

Continuing through the valley one comes to Montferrat surrounded by orchards, then climbing steadily, the scenery changing dramatically, to the *Plan de Canjuers*, with a left turn to Aiguines, a small village dominating the valley formed by the exit of the Verdon river from the main gorge.

This *Plan* – or plateau – has been very much in the public eye of recent years and the subject of a bitter dispute between local authorities and Paris.

The plateau covers roughly 75,000 acres: a bare, rolling, utterly waste land with a few isolated farms dotted over its surface. Flocks of sheep wander the iron-hard ground searching optimistically for the occasional blade of grass. Of all Provence's desert regions this, with the Crau, is the barest. Stretches bring back for me further North African memories of the Moroccan *Sebkha*, that stony desert that used to be referred to by French settlers as *la mer de cailloux* (the sea of pebbles). Not even the hardy olive seems able to survive.

Because of this general desolation the War Ministry decided

---

* In Provençal the dolmen is known as the *peyro de la fado*. Throughout the country it is usual, if wishing to suggest that an individual is a little dotty, to say 'Il est *fada*,' at the same time pointing the index finger to one's temple and slowly rotating it. Villagers were in the habit of explaining that someone slightly simple had been 'touched' by a fairy (*la fado*) at birth, and the expression is now so commonplace that the word *fada* is looked upon as French.

that the *Plan de Canjuers* was to be used as a rocket range and proceeded to issue expropriation notices not only to the isolated farmers but also to the inhabitants of a couple of peripheric villages. The resulting outcry – especially from the villagers – was far greater than expected and has since been taken up by both local and national newspapers. However, it is unlikely that the government's scheme, even if retarded, will be abandoned, and proof of this can be seen in the fact that by the Comps-Aiguines fork in the road a military camp has been installed, built by the Foreign Legion's bearded pioneers with the same skill and speed that in a past era they showed in constructing the Beau Geste type forts which formerly silhouetted the Moroccan and Algerian Sahara horizons.

It is worth while making the run to Aiguines, only 15 miles, since the road may well be closed to the public at some not too distant date; and the *Plan de Canjuers* has a strange arid beauty that may be aptly described as lunar – so denuded that the very idea of existence of any form of living matters seems paradoxical. Aiguines itself, apart from a small multi-coloured tile-roofed château built during the reign of Henri IV and restored in 1911 is pleasant but featureless. But the view just as its first houses are sighted is one of those vast wide-open-spaces vistas rare in western Europe. On a clear morning or evening particularly in late winter one can look across no less than five departments, the apparently boundless plateau losing itself to the west from which, like islands from a purplish sea, emerge the spinal ridges to the south of the Sainte Baume and Sainte Victoire and a good 60 miles as the crow flies, Mont Ventoux's menacingly volcanic 6,500-foot snow-capped peak.

Complete contrast to the stark savagery of the *Plan de Canjuers* is the valley of the Artuby river – not to be confused with its tributary the Nartuby – which curls through green meadows, then laps the foot of the rocks at the head of a gorge on which is the typical Provençal village of Comps. It clusters round the base of a hill surmounted by an austere chapel whose lines are so elongated that one might well imagine it had been designed by a spiritual ancestor of Bernard Buffet. Since the original village was built on the higher slopes for defensive purposes against Saracens and roving robber bands the chapel formed part of the integral plan, but with the passing of these threats the villagers preferred to be spared the drag of climbing to their houses after a long day's toil in their fields and moved down to the present site. Now a summer camping ground Comps is a road junction for the southern left-bank circuit of the Verdon gorges.

Most fascinating of these fortified communities, however, is Bargème village, five miles east of Comps on the Logis du Pin road through a countryside of an extraordinary medieval aspect: long rolling green slopes crossed by the Artuby's silver ribbon, a strange unexpectedly formalised landscape with small seemingly petrified copses which gives me the impression of a time machine image, and where I would not really be surprised to meet a group of mail-clad horsemen, pennants fluttering from their lance tips.

Bargème, which may have been a staging post for Greek traders from Antipolis, sits on the top of a 4,000-foot hill, not huddling round but actually within the ramparts of a castle whose tall cylindrical towers, like a Wagnerian décor, command the surrounding valleys and lower ridges. The only entrance is through what must have been the main gateway facing south, and here the walls are so thick that a number of houses have been built into them, some of which, restored after decades of neglect, are now occupied by artists. The village, a thriving community in 1914, was so crippled by First-War losses and Second-War restrictions that by 1950 it was almost totally deserted, only three or four ageing couples clinging obstinately to their homes while surrounding houses decayed and crumbled.

Today, however, restoration of castle and church – the latter containing an impressive 'Martyrdom of St Sebastian', work of an unknown early sixteenth-century artist – are in the hands of the Beaux-Arts. Houses are being rebuilt privately and at the last census the population had risen to 58. It is not surprising that most of the new inhabitants are connected with the arts; the extreme beauty of the countryside viewed from this peak, the purity of the air and the almost positive quality of the silence make it highly conducive to creative work.

Below Bargème is Brovès, one of those condemned periphery villages of the *Plan de Canjuers*, now qualified somewhat pathetically as *Le village qui ne veut pas mourir*. Evacuation date has been put back from 1972 to 1974 but appears inevitable. It is sad for the inhabitants, for they too were beginning to recover from years of depression, and the village baker is reputed to produce the best bread within miles.

Heading south from Brovès either by the Col de Belhomme or the Col de la Glacière – the latter a *maquis* stronghold during the German occupation – one reaches the stretch of *villages perchés* now becoming increasingly well known: Montauroux, Callian, Fayence, Seillans, Bargemon and Callas.

These six villages have known an extraordinary boom in the course of the '60s, because of their ideal position: 30 to 40 miles only from the coast or nearest ski-ing resort, their pleasant healthy climate due to their altitude, an average of 1,500 feet, and the beauty of the countryside, fringed to the north by wooded hills, looking south across olive-grove-filled valleys and the jagged Maures and Estérel ridges to the Mediterranean.

All have certain common features. Conceived with an eye to defence they are built either on the upper slopes or the crest of a hill. The outer line of houses forms an unbroken rampart four or five storeys high, sheer and without balconies, pierced only very occasionally by low arches whose heavy gates have today vanished, but many of whose massive iron hinges remain. Water being an essential for survival, fountains and *lavoirs* – open troughs where even today many of the older women prefer to do the household washing, gossiping with their neighbours rather than switching on the washing-machine – were as integral a feature of the military system as halberds, bows and arrows, and boiling oil. Streets are narrow, barely wide enough for two loaded donkeys to pass each other. The individual house is non-existent, each street forming, like the exterior, a high and continuous wall broken only by tiny doorways and loophole-like windows set well above the ground level.

By contrast the interiors of these village houses are remarkably spacious, and as most now have running water and modern plumbing they can be made extremely comfortable. The walls, never less than four feet thick and of solid stone, effectively keep out both heat and cold. The principal disadvantage – especially for those not in the first bloom of youth – is the stairway. Antithesis of the bungalow principle the village houses are built upwards and may in some cases consist of five superimposed rooms connected by slippery banisterless stairs.

Driving west along the main Grasse-Draguignan road which keeps mostly to the valleys these villages can be seen to the north, strung out, each on its little hill-top in a quasi-defensive line guarding the approaches from the coast.

Though Callas and Fayence are the *chef-lieux* of the two *communes* concerned, they are perhaps the two least interesting either to visit or as a possible temporary residence. Fayence is in fact expanding so rapidly that it is now a small town rather than a large village. The silhouette of the original structure cannot be touched but so many houses are springing up all round that the general outline changes yearly. Much of this popularity is due to the glider field on the *Plan de Fayence*; the sport of sailplaning is growing in favour not only locally but is attracting large numbers of non-French, especially from West Germany. Sometimes one may see as many as 15 gliders hovering silently like giant storks above the hills, or swooping down to land, skimming roof-tops, the air making a weird rustling in their wings.

Callian just to the east of Fayence is overawed by its fifteenth-century castle – the original village was destroyed in 1391 – dwarfing houses and church. In the typically Provençal cemetery is the tomb of Christian Dior who died in 1957. It is at Montaurox, a neighbouring village, however, where the fashion king's annual memorial service is held: an act of gratitude for the gift of a considerable sum of money donated to restore one of the village chapels.

From Fayence a minor road runs due west crossing a small ridge, *Le Peyron*, from where there is a first sight of Seillans, one of the Haut Var's most attractive sites. Not crouching on a summit, the village falls down the hillside, a shimmer of red-tiled roofs, in near triangular form, like a masonry cascade. Particularly these days this original view is the best, for at a distance of a couple of miles the village stands out as a clear-cut entity, folds in the hills and scattered copses hiding the violent outcrop of small modern villas which erupted in the years 1965–70, many of them painfully out of tune with old Seillans's eleventh-century charm.

Just before reaching the village and on the left of the road is the chapel of *Notre Dame de l'Ormeau*, a classified historical monument. The original building, on the site of a pagan temple, sheltered a reputed miracle-working statue of the Virgin. Unfortunately during the ninth and tenth centuries Seillans was frequently the target for Saracen raids, on one of which the chapel was razed to the ground. However, before this particularly damaging attack an anonymous villager removed the statue from its niche and buried it at the foot of an elm (*ormeau*) in a near-by field. Two hundred years later when Saracen incursions were no more than evil memories a peasant tilling, felt his ploughshare jar on some hard object, and discovered that he had unearthed the legendary statue which, brought up on folklore, he recognised immediately. By then the chapel had been restored in Romanesque style, and after due ceremony the Virgin re-found her place.

Today, however, the chapel is chiefly known for its reredos.

In 1350 an Italian monk, strangely enough anonymous, had been obliged to leave his native land as a result of trouble (unspecified) with the local authorities, and on arriving at Seillans asked the *seigneur* of the village for *droit d'asile*. The *seigneur* after discovering that he had been a pupil of the celebrated sculptor Nicolas Pisano, struck a bargain: provided the monk decorated the apse his request would be granted. The monk got to work and after two years produced the primitive masterpiece which still occupies its original place behind the altar.

Many a stern Anglican complains that it is 'fussy', even gaudy, though personally I find it enchanting. The work is sculpted on wood, gilded and vividly coloured, and the facial expressions combine a fascinating mixture of the truly primitive with a life-like veracity.

The presentation is in the form of a classical four-column doorway resting on a gallery. Between the two central columns is the most dramatic of the composite details, '*L'Arbre de Jesse*'. The tree, with its 18 gilded-robed figures, was carved from a single piece of walnut. To the right is represented the Adoration of the Shepherds, to the left the Adoration of the Kings. Old and New Testament motifs are mixed haphazard on other panels so that one finds side by side the Burning Bush and the Calf of Gold with an unusual subject, the Marriage of the Virgin: the Virgin flaxen-haired, rosey-cheeked, dressed in voluminous medieval robes, the celebrant a combination of Orthodox priest and Victorian maharajah.

Although services are usually held in the village church, also Romanesque and dating back to the twelfth century, soberly and artistically restored in 1962 under the supervision of the Abbé Viatte, a much-loved priest who died suddenly in 1967, marriages are sometimes celebrated in *Notre Dame de l'Ormeau*, and the Seillans annual fête – last week in July – is always inaugurated by a Mass in Provençal, often followed by folk-dancing on the parvis beneath the shade of the cypresses – no longer the elms – surrounding the building.

Bargémon, to the west of Seillans, is reached by a continuation of the same secondary road, climbing to a little *col*, St Arnoux, where in May and June Spanish broom (*genêt*) grows in such profusion that one has the impression of traversing a narrow street of golden walls before descending gently through woods reminiscent of the approach to a Punjab hill station. In some ways Bargémon, its hub of life centred round the village square with its fountain, seems the most welcoming of all, and for a community of barely 800 inhabitants it must hold a record in that it boasts five first-class restaurants.

Callas, most westerly of this line of hill-top villages, stands on the fringe of a vast stretch of vineyards extending almost to the coast and crossed by a road known as the *Route des Vins* and spreading westward to the Bouches-du-Rhône, an even greater area of wild foothills covered by mixed pine, ilex forests and olive groves.

Just as the coconut palm is symbolic of tropical shores, the sad giant pine or larch the dark reflection of nordic mists and schizophrenic heroes with antlered helms, so the olive tree is the very image of the Provençal soul, evocative of civilisation's cradle and the dawn of the Christian era. At the same time it is intensely individual, intensely nostalgic, an essential element in any composite Provençal mental canvas, together with the hot sun's slanting rays scorching the thirsty earth around the oasis of its shade sheltering a recumbent peasant at midday, his wine-flask, loaf of bread, hunk of goat's cheese, a tomato, a clove of garlic, and of course a handful of olives beside him, a living reflection of Provence's profound antiquity and the irrefutable statement that 'the vine and the olive tree are symbolic of the world's most ancient and most beautiful civilisations'.

In the heart of this olive country, less than ten miles from Draguignan, is Thoronet Abbey, one of Provence's three Cistercian abbeys – the other two being those of Senanque and Silvacane – known as 'the three sisters of Provence'. Thoronet is hidden deep in a forest, in the hollow of a valley, a site chosen deliberately by the Cistercians as a sign of humility to mark their disapproval of other monastic buildings built ostentatiously – in their opinion – on hills where they were visible for miles around. All three were founded by permission and with the help of Raymond Berenger, Count of Provence, and built between the years 1176 and 1190.

The beauty of these Cistercian abbeys lies in the pure austere dignity of their lines, at Thoronet in particular those of the library and dormitory, unadorned since, in accordance with Cistercian rules no sculptural ornamentation or statuary was permitted.

One of the abbots began his life on a very un-Puritanical note. Foulgues of Marseille was, in his youth, a troubadour. Son of a rich Genoese merchant he had given up commerce for poetry.

24   *Vence: rue du Marché*

25 *Coursegoules and Cheiron mountain*

26 *Olive trees, centuries old*

After being a favourite at the court of Richard Cœur de Lion and Count Raymond v of Toulouse he fell in love with the wife of Barral, Lord of Marseille, although by then he was married and father of several children. The lady not only rejected him but died shortly afterwards – perhaps of a broken heart? – whereupon Foulques entered the Cistercian order, became eventually Abbot of Thoronet and later Bishop of Toulouse.

The monks were driven out by the revolution and the deserted abbey would undoubtedly have fallen into ruin but for the fact that the writer Prosper Merimée – author of *Carmen* – visited the area in his capacity of Inspector of Historic Monuments in 1834 and was so impressed that he managed to obtain a government grant for the restoration.

The area west of Draguignan is still the most unknown and off-the-beaten-track in Provence. There are no urban centres and its many picturesque villages are too far from both winter sports resorts and the coast for the liking of the average tourist, though there are signs that those who seek the latest – and hardest to find – of the latter twentieth-century's luxuries, freedom from noise, have cast their eyes in the direction of this backwater. Smaller towns such as Aups, Cotignac and Barjols now have their foreign residents or wealthy French businesmen's holiday or secondary home.

Aups, happily situated at 2,000 feet above sea level, though cold in winter, is comparatively spared by the *mistral*. It is an agreeable little town with quiet streets; within easy reach of the Gorges de Verdon beauty spots and Sillans-la-Cascade, a walled village of only 141 inhabitants, popular with summer campers because of its long stretches of shady meadows fringing the Bresque river, noted for its trout-fishing. One will not find Aups mentioned in history's annals, which probably means that its inhabitants have generally been happy; but Julius Caesar himself, for some unexplained reason, is supposed to have said: 'I would rather be the first in Aups than the second in Rome.'

Barjols, a centre of the tanning industry sometimes described as the Tivoli of Provence, enjoys the same green and tranquil setting, standing at the confluence of two small rivers with the picturesque names of *L'Eau Salée* and the *Ruisseau d'Ecrevisses*. Its fifteenth-century church tucked away in a corner of the Place Emile Zola is more than worth a visit.

Immediately to the left of the entrance can be seen a bust of St Marcellus (St Marcel), a fifth-century bishop and martyr known for his severity towards any form of moral laxity. Unlike most high-ranking ecclesiastics of his time St Marcellus, his face pale, with staring black eyes, is portrayed as clean-shaven, a fact which lends his features an exaggerated harshness. But the saint's reliquary is not the church's only interest. The stained glass – never mentioned in guide-books – is the most beautiful I have seen in the Var. Particularly behind the altar, reds and deeper crimsons have a rich glow almost recalling Carcassonne.

Another surprise is the *Chapelle des Demoiselles* to the right of the nave. On entering one is confronted by a brilliant image of the Virgin Mary in pale robes surrounded by a choir of putti whose head and shoulders emerge from white plaster clouds. It is only when one's eyes dazzled by the brightness become re-attuned to the rest of the chapel's shadows that one realises that this is a reproduction in light filtering down from an overhead glass pane reflecting the sun and colour, of a very old and dark canvas hung in the gloomy recesses to the left of the chapel's entrance.

Half-way up the nave, also to the right, is a huge picture executed in the 'old master' style as recently as 1820 portraying the assumption of the Virgin Mary with the fortified outline of old Barjols in the background, painted in accordance with the testamentary wishes of a rich Barjols citizen.

Once every four years St Marcel presides over a strange half-Christian half-pagan fête, held usually on 16 January. The saint's bust is brought down from its niche at vespers and carried outside the church on to the square where an ox is blessed in its presence. After this rather strange blessing the unfortunate animal is 'sacrificed', its carcass slung on a cart and then paraded through the streets following behind the saint's bust and accompanied by the clergy, the town's butchers, the *tripiers* and cooks.

The origin of this rather barbaric fête goes back to 1350. At that time the remains of St Marcellus were kept in the monastery of Saint Maurice between Aups and Barjols. One January night in 1350 the saint appeared in a vision to the monk in charge of his relics, demanding that they be moved but not stating where. When this was known both Barjols and Aups claimed them, quarrelling so violently that the Count of Provence ordered that the exact distances between the monastery and Aups and Barjols should be measured and the relics confided to the care of whichever community happened to be the nearer. However the Barjolais, more cunning and go-ahead – if less honest – than their rivals, literally kidnapped the relics one night while the Aups representatives were painstakingly engaged on the business of measuring. This happened on a January 16, the day when Barjols traditionally sacrifices a fat ox to commemorate an ancient famine which had been staved off by the miraculous arrival of a (presumably) heaven-sent animal. The smoking entrails were distributed to the population to the accompaniment of songs and dances. In the middle of these strange festivities arrived the kidnappers of the saint. Straightaway the Barjolais decided that the two festivals should be combined, expresing their joy in an ironic little song:

> *Nautro leis auren*
> *Lei tripeto, lei tripeto*
> *Nautro leis auren*
> *Lei tripeto de Sant Maceu.**

We are told that a Bishop of Fréjus, and later Revolutionary authorities, both tried to put a stop to these activities but without success.

For the statistically-minded Barjols has another attraction. At the lower end of a sloping *allée* is an enormous Roman fountain, so moss-covered that it now has the appearance of a neolithic mushroom, and just below it is a plane-tree which, states the

---

* *(Ce sont les nôtres qui les ont, les tripettes de Saint Marcel.)* Guide de la Provence Mystérieuse *(Tchou).*

Guide Bleu, claims precedence as the 'biggest plane-tree in Provence'.

Running due east-west across the Var and acting as a frontier between the Haut Var and the Var coast is the main road, N7, linking Nice with Paris, a road with the sinister reputation of having Europe's highest accident rate due to the appalling density of traffic. It is a road I avoid whenever possible, but straddling it are three places of very great interest – Les Arcs, St Maximin and Brignoles. All three fortunately can be approached by side roads.

Les Arcs, nearest main line railway station for Draguignan, is also a modern road junction chiefly distinguished by solid ranks of petrol pumps, but the old town built up a hillside stands sadly aloof, topped by a dilapidated castle of the thirteenth century, birthplace of Rosseline (later St Rosseline) de Villeneuve, about whom is told the charming story of the miracle of the roses.

Rosseline's father Arnaud de Villeneuve had no sympathy with the poor whereas his daughter spent her time trying to help them. This annoyed the baron so much that he forbade her to continue with her good works under pain of death.

One morning Rosseline had collected a basketful of loaves and was hurrying across the courtyard when she was surprised by her father.

'What have you got in that basket?' he asked menacingly.

'Roses, my lord.'

Arnaud de Villeneuve wrenched the basket from her hands, opened it – only to find that it was indeed filled with roses.

Twelve years later Rosseline became the mother superior of the convent Saint Rosseline, four miles to the east of Les Arcs. On her death her body was preserved in a glass shrine which was lost during the religious wars but found a century later by a blind man, brought back to Les Arcs by him and re-installed in the convent chapel. Even in this rather prosaic age the relic preserves its reputation of miraculous healing powers, especially for children.

At first sight Brignoles is a characterless modern town, though in fact it figures largely in Provençal history. It was in 1274 in the château of Brignoles that Princess Marie of Hungary gave birth to a son, Louis, great-nephew of Saint Louis and great-grandson of Blanche of Castille, who at a very early age seemed destined to tread the same paths of sanctity as his great-uncle. Refusing even to contemplate the idea of marriage he was sent to Rome by his father, given an audience by the Pope and admitted into the Franciscan order in 1296. The following year he is said to have worked his first miracle, when a dying monk – Pierre Scarrasson – drank out of his bowl and was healed immediately. Unfortunately because of his incredible self-imposed austerity Louis died at the age of 23. Legend insists that when the candles were blown out by a violent mistral during his funeral they were re-lighted by celestial fire. Twenty years after his death he was canonised by Pope John XXII and adopted by Brignoles, his birth-place, as the town's patron saint.

Brignoles church contains a sarcophagus stated to be not only the oldest in France but in the whole Christian world: *le sarco-phage de la Gayole*. Work of a second-century Greek sculptor it represents St Peter the fisherman. On the end of his line can be made out a dolphin while in his left hand he holds a rush basket. Behind the saint there are two rams, an anchor and a tree, while beside him a seated Christ is preaching to a young girl.

Eleven miles farther west on the N7 but again more conveniently approached by side roads, is St Maximin with its basilica of St Mary Magdalene – pronounced Maudlin by confirmed Oxonians – whose crypt contains the sarcophagi of St Mary Magdalene, St Maximinus, St Marcellus and St Sidonius. Though the exterior of this vast church possesses a certain monotony – it has neither spire, belfry nor tower – it has a monolithic grandeur which dominates not only the featureless little town but the countryside for many miles around. Architecturally the interior is pure Gothic and gives an extraordinary impression of towering grandeur, dwarfing the individual. The present edifice dates from 1295 but before the church as it stands today was completed, just over 200 years of intermittent toil had passed.

Probably the original site of the basilica was a small oratory containing the relics of the four saints, which by the fifth century had become a sanctuary watched over by Cassianite monks.

However, when the Saracen menace took shape the monks decided to fill in the crypt so as to make sure that the precious relics did not fall into Moslem hands. A thousand years went by, when rumours began to circulate that the relics had been found again. Charles II, nephew of St Louis, went in person to St Maximin and supervised the excavations round the high altar which in the midst of general excitement eventually disclosed the lost tombs, the first being that of St Sidonius in which, according to Father Valuy, 'the tongue, in spite of the absence of the lower jawbone, was found intact'. From then on St Maximin became one of the most popular centres of pilgrimage. Anne of Brittany, wife first of Charles VIII then of Louis XII, had a gold statue of herself placed at the foot of the Magdalene reliquary. *François Premier* held a thanksgiving service in the church after his victory at Marignan. On one day no less than five kings were assembled to pray before the shrine – Philip de Valois of France, Hugh IV of Cyprus, John of Bohemia, Robert of Sicily and Alfonso IV of Aragon.

The Revolution brought a threat almost as great as that of the Saracens. St Maximin was re-named Marathon. Most of the exterior figures on the basilica walls were smashed and the church itself was scheduled for demolition. The most popular story concerning its preservation is that it was saved by Lucien Bonaparte, married to one of the local innkeeper's daughters, a Madamoiselle Boyer, who frustrated the iconoclasts by making it a military stores, at the same time saving the organ by finding someone who could play the *Marseillaise* on it to visiting Revolutionary dignitaries, among others, Barras.

After the restoration of the monarchy St Maximin was visited by Prosper Merimée who was, as with Thoronet abbey, deeply impressed by the church though in general he disliked Provence and particularly the town of St Maximin but nevertheless obtained a government restoration grant. Finally the church returned to the Dominicans some twenty years later.

The crypt entrance is half-way up the nave and to the left, and can be lighted by a *minuterie* at the top of the descending stairs. On the first landing is an undistinguished statue of Mary Magdalene, then on the lower floor a fourth- or fifth-century funeral vault contains the sarcophagi. At the far end in almost total darkness is the recumbent marble figure of St Mary Magdalene and a reliquary containing a skull venerated as that of the saint herself.

In the church there is a magnificent altar-piece in the fourth chapel to the right of the nave, work of the Flemish-born sixteenth-century painter Francesco Ronzen, depicting the Passion in a series of 22 panels whose backgrounds vary from the earliest known reproduction of the papal palace at Avignon to the Colosseum at Rome and the Piazzetta of Venice, while in the neighbouring chapel is preserved a gold-embroidered cope worn by St Louis of Anjou and dating back to the thirteenth century.

Still travelling west by side roads towards the Var's boundaries with the department of the Bouches-du-Rhône one reaches a small backwater-type village standing on a bluff: Pourrières. It is a village which does not of itself call for a halt but the first time passing through I was struck by a street name – *Rue de l'An 102*.

It was not until some months later that I realised the year thus commemorated was 102 B.C. – that of the Marseille Pro-consul Marius's great victory over the Teuton and Cimbrian hordes marching towards Rome, one of those battles which left a profound imprint on the course of history.

In 105 the Teutons, engaged on a vast ethnical migration with Italy their avowed objective, had defeated the Romans near Orange but then inexplicably swung west towards Spain. They did not turn east to resume their march on Italy till three years later, by which time Marius had had the time to prepare a new defensive-offensive strategy, and chose as the spot to give battle the long flat east-west plateau between what today are known as the Sainte-Baume and the Sainte-Victoire

Heading east the barbarian hordes crossed the Rhône near

Tarascon and advanced unopposed till they were in the neighbourhood of modern Aix. In those days opposing armies were
frequently not only within sight but sound of each other, and as
the Teuton columns, estimated by some to be close on half a
million strong, passed near Roman outposts they would call out to
the Roman soldiers that the first thing they intended doing on
arriving in Rome was to rape their wives.

'Don't worry,' Marius spread the word to his men, 'we've got
them where we want them.'

Just below the Pourrières ridge Marius ordered one of his
generals, Claudius Marcellus, to attack the head of the column
with 3,000 men while he himself, with the bulk of his forces,
charged the enemy rear – made up mostly of women, children and
heavy baggage carts . . . 'Their (the women and children's) screams
of terror made the men try to rush to their help. It was hopeless.
Already reinforcements for Marius were arriving from Marseille; Ligurians, Celts, Greeks, joined with the Romans to say
"no" to the savage invaders. The very heart of the Cimbro-Teuton
camp was overrun; women and children captured to be sold as
slaves. The 300 barbarian priestesses strangled themselves with
their blonde tresses so as to escape Roman fury, rape and slavery.
The men fought on. The battle raged three days and three nights.
The plain was heaped with corpses, weapons. The river (Arc) ran
red. Only the death of the last barbarian stopped the slaughter'
(Plutarch).

According to Nostradamus 'the conflict was so bloody and so
bitter that 200,000 Ambrons lay dead while 80,000, including
their king Teutobochus, were made prisoner'.

The village of Pourrières is supposed therefore to have taken
its name from the appalling stench of rotting corpses (*pourriture*)
left unburied after the battle – as a result of which, Pope-
Hennessy says, 'the sack of the antique world was deferred for
four centuries'. However, in this age of de-bunking there is a
counter-theory that the name Pourrières is merely derived from
the unromantic word *poreires*, meaning fields of leeks, which
abound in the neighbourhood.

Another of the Haut Var's charms is that it remains the area in which comparatively unchanged traditional village life can be best studied, despite encroaching industrialisation, television and growing outside influences.

Here one might say the year is divided basically not into four but two seasons – *la saison de boules* and that of *la chasse*, overlapping in the month of September.

Social distinctions in France can be subtle and though the Provençal is basically so stout a republican there are often basic feuds, a local snobbishness affecting the division of certain trades, and more recently a tendency, trend of the present day, to worship too freely at the altar of Mammon. The game of *boules* is, however, a great social leveller.

In Seillans for instance I have seen a world-famous painter, the butcher, an art critic, the doctor, the baker, a couple of mechanics and a retired Paris businessman engrossed in their game of *boules*, after which the losing side pays for drinks all round in a long-drawn-out get-together at the nearest bar. And although the individual members of such heterogenous teams may not mix in normal circumstances there is no lack of *camaraderie* while the match is being discussed over a glass of *pastis*.

The game is really the equivalent of English lawn bowls but played on any surface, and most popularly on the village square beneath the shade of the ever-present giant plane-trees. It has the added advantages that it can be played by anybody roughly from the ages of 9 to 90 and practically any number a side, and while being a leisurely game it can, and frequently does, give rise to the most heated post-mortem arguments.

La chasse is more dramatic. Even if he has never heard of Daudet I do not know of a single Provençal who is not an embryonic Tartarin, and as with the immortal of Tarascon it is not only the sport but dressing the part which figures largely in the overall *mystique*.

Today the favoured garb is the parachutist's 'leopard' canvas camouflage suit, heavy hobnailed boots, and the slightly sinister peaked canvas cap suggesting some Middle-Eastern terrorist, cartridge belt and bandolier. Furthermore in Provence shooting is not the privilege of the wealthy and just as to be a non-*boules* player is to have oneself classified as a freak, so not to own a sporting rifle is an eccentricity.

Till comparatively recent times the high Var swarmed with game – hare, pheasant, partridge, wood-pigeon and wild boar. But with the increase in population and of individual mobility the guns are getting the better of wild life. Too many sportsmen, not wishing to return empty-handed, have got into the habit of blazing away at any living creature within sight, including robins and finches – even on occasions fellow-sportsmen's gun dogs or the fellow sportsman himself, these latter aberrations being explained away by the statement, 'I mistook the movement for that of a wild boar'.

Fittingly the village fête is the great event of the year. There is not a village however small that would not feel itself dishonoured if it did not hold such a fête, and these events always taking place between May and the end of September, may last from one to four days according to a community's size and importance.

They follow a traditional pattern: inauguration with Mass, preferably sung in Provençal, an *apéritif-concert* given by a visiting professional band or orchestra, a *boules* competition with money prizes for the winners, a variety show, a *bal*, and ending with a *monstre aïoli*.* Displays of Provençal dancing usually feature on the programme, though unfortunately some villages in the name of progress have substituted displays by *majorettes* – surely one of the world's most ridiculous spectacles as well as one of the most boring – and bicycle races.

Often one finds that the smaller the village the more attractive the fête. Quite the best of the many *aïoli* I have eaten was at Brovès, the village doomed to disappear when the army takes over. Long wooden tables had been set up bordering the only road through the village. One chose one's place haphazard. The local teenagers acted as waiters and the masses of vegetables,

* . . . A dish made from dried cod and garlic mayonnaise.

boiled fish and hard-boiled eggs making up the main dish were brought straight from the *auberge's* kitchen in small bath-tubs. The *aïoli* itself was followed by perfectly roasted beef and cheese. Wine was free and unrationed and every passer-by received a free glass of *rosé*. Price: seven francs, children under ten free.

9. The Côte d'Azur

On visite Nice pour une semaine, on y reste toute la vie
(Theodore de Banville, 1862)

The *Riviera* of one's grandparents which begins at Menton and runs west to Cannes, a distance of a bare 40 miles, acquired fabulous wealth and world renown in well under 100 years. Discovered by an English nobleman, Lord Brougham, it reached its apogee of elegant popularity at the turn of the century, by which time it had become the winter playground for Europe's reigning families and aristocracy. Today, if opinion can be based on sheer numbers, its popularity has increased. Result of the upheavals of two world wars, however, the 'Age of Elegance' and 'Gracious Living' belong to the past, while the annihilation of distance due to air travel and the development of 'package tours' combined with the staggering increase in the number of private cars, mean, for the British, that a holiday in the South of France is less of an undertaking than one in the North of Scotland, and, for Americans, that Côte d'Azur beaches are but a few hours flying time from main east coast airports.

In many ways this revolution in travel has been a disaster. Beautiful villas have been pulled down to be replaced by soullessly ugly blocks of flats. Once moderately secluded beaches now boast camping sites and super-markets.* Traffic is such that on coastal roads progress may be limited to a mile an hour if one is

* Recently an American remarked, 'These are just the sort of places we left America to escape from. . . .'

lucky. The beaches are not overclean; they are hopelessly over-crowded. Even the sea is threatened with pollution.

It was in November 1839 that Lord Brougham and Vaux, heading for Italy's winter sunshine, was stopped at the frontier post on the Var river, then marking the boundary between France and the Kingdom of Sardinia. There was an epidemic of cholera in France, and to try to check its spread the Sardinian authorities had set up a *cordon sanitaire*. Despite his angry protestation, his lordship was forced to turn back. Disconsolately following the coastline, he reached the little fishing village of Cannes by evening and decided to spend the night at the local *auberge*, the *Pinchinat*.

Finding the spot agreeable, he made up his mind to break his journey for a few more days. It was a *coup de foudre*, a case of love at first sight.

There would be no more Italian sunshine for Lord Brougham. He bought a plot of land and built a superb villa – the Villa Eleanore – overlooking the Fréjus road beyond Le Suquet, where he spent the remaining winters of his life, dying there the 7 May 1868 at the age of 90.

During his lifetime, and thanks to him, Cannes changed from an obscure fishing village into Europe's 'smartest' winter resort, profiting from this heritage till one could read in 1890 that no less than 60 crowned or princely heads had taken advantage of its winter sunshine. Till post-1945 no one would have dreamed of staying on the coast after mid-May at the latest, and on the walls of one of the older hotels one can still read the very faint inscription – 'This Hotel remains open in the summer'.

Modern Cannes, a city of well over 59,000 inhabitants, would seem to be best known for its harbour and the two-mile-long sea-side promenade, La Croisette.

The harbour, overlooked from the east by the Municipal Casino and beneath the shadow of the Le Suquet hill to the west at whose foot runs the Quai St Pierre, is chiefly a *Port de Plaisance*. In over 14 years of occasional visits, I have seldom noticed any vessels other than private yachts of varying sizes anchored there. Till recently the largest and the most striking was a miniature single-stack liner – the stack being covered with gilt sparrows – owned by an ex-music-hall star married to an astronomically wealthy South American, who called herself *La Môme Moineau* (hence the sparrows) and abroad was always dressed in an admiral's uniform.

No other yachts I have seen, with the exception of those of Niachos and Onassis, are, however, anything like this tonnage, and I have often thought that many of the smaller craft must be extremely cramped even for two. In addition, the moored yachts are tightly jammed the one against the other. The rather narrow quays are hemmed by main traffic-surfeited thoroughfares, and in the evenings and on holidays, crowds of strollers gather to stare over the open sterns as if the yachting folk were zoo exhibits.

To the east of the harbour and the Casino stretches the 'Croisette' with its luxury hotels, referred to locally as *palaces*, such as the Carlton – dating from 1912 and still retaining its supreme 'snob appeal' – the Miramar, the Majestic, and the Martinez. One can pay as much as 200 francs (about £15) a night for a room, and up to 50 francs for a meal at such establishments, but though not the *genre* of hotel which appeals to me, they seem to represent the Mecca of many a tourist who has formed certain ideas of 'high society'.

Particularly the *Croisette* comes to life during the annual film festival at the beginning of May. It is true that other cities stage similar festivals, but it is probable that Cannes awards still carry with them greater publicity and financial value than those of its rivals. One could never say that the *Croisette* was deserted at any time, but during this fortnight it would appear to be in the grip of a permanent international rush hour.

The *Iles de Lérins* – Sainte Marguerite and Saint Honorat – respectively 15 and 30 minutes by ferry boat from the harbour, are of far more interest than Cannes town.

Legend insists that the two islands were once one, the haunt of the Devil, and infested with horrible and poisonous reptiles. Determined to put an end to this state of affairs, God made the island sink beneath the waters thus drowning the reptilian population and purging the land of its evil aura. But on rising again to the surface the island split into two separate masses, banished the one from the other by a wide channel.

It was on the smaller of these masses that Saint Honorat, son of King Andrioch and Queen Helenbore of Hungary who had left the court to lead the life of an ascetic, landed with a group of devoted disciples in the year 395, there founding a monastic colony which soon became one of Europe's most important ecclesiastical centres. Saint Honorat himself was appointed Archbishop of Arles in 426. By that time, however, the *Ile Saint Honorat* had acquired a reputation as a nursery for saints which continued to flourish many years after his departure; amongst these saints one finds St Patrick of Ireland, and St Loup who later inspired the resistance organised by Aetius, Mérovée and Theodoric which eventually halted, then defeated Attila and his Huns at Chalons in 451.

By the seventh century St Honorat monastery was a favourite meeting-place for theologians; its library reputed unrivalled. The monks had spread their influence inland and, in the name of the monastery, owned territory not only in Provence, but as far afield as Italy and Spain. Any city considered itself privileged if its bishop came from Saint Honorat. The monks minted their own coins. Salt, fishing, even 'shipwreck' rights in the gulf were theirs.

The great weakness of this monastic empire was that the island, its capital, was more or less indefensible and one can only be surprised that its soil remained so long inviolate.

The Saracens who, naturally, had no scruples regarding Christianity's holier places, were the first invaders. Because of them the island was untenable for over 200 years. In 1073, as the Moslem threat passed, a militant abbot, Adalbert, set about building a new monastery which would, at the same time be a fortress. There were no more Saracen razzias, but it is sad to note that from then on the island was frequently attacked by Christian pirates, mostly Genoese, and later became a target for foreign invaders, being attacked and overrun by the Spaniards – Francois I spent the night of 21–22 June 1525 there as Charles Quint's prisoner – and finally in 1746 by the Austrians. By then the former great colony of monks had been reduced in number to four, a fact which prompted Louis XVI to secularize the monastery and order that the islands should be included in the diocese of Grasse.*

Revolutionary authorities sold the island to a well-known actress, Blanche Sainval, who lived there in highly unplebeian style. She made her residence in the monastery's fortified tower, decorating the walls with murals depicting Arcadian love scenes involving scantily clad shepherds and shepherdesses. However, this secular period did not last long. The island was eventually bought back as church property by the Bishop of Fréjus and taken over, in 1869, by the Cistercian Order who set about the work of restoration. The resuscitated monastery can be visited, but like Mount Athos, only by members of the male sex.

The shore, on the other hand, does not come under this stern ban and has become a favourite haunt of bathers seeking a modicum of sea-space.

Closer inshore and the larger of the two islands, Sainte Marguerite, sometimes known as Lero, takes its name from Marguerite, Saint Honorat's sister, also dedicated to the life of a religious community. She had the human weakness of being devoted to her brother, but the austere Honorat forbade her to pay him a visit except when 'the cherry trees were in bloom'. This ruling so upset the affectionate Marguerite that God took pity on her and miraculously one of the island's cherry trees blossomed once a month throughout the year. Honorat recognised Divine intervention and made no objection to these monthly meetings.

Of far greater strategic significance than the smaller *Ile Saint Honorat*, Sainte Marguerite was occupied in 1617 on the orders of the most unspiritually, but highly politically, minded Cardinal

* One of the monks during this time was a certain Raymond Féraud, born in the country of Nice in 1245, who started life as a troubadour, but ashamed of what later he termed a *'lasche et oltronne vie'* retired to a monastery cell where he composed a detailed history of St Honorat in *langue d'Oc*. It is suggested that the reason for this 'repentance' was his lack of amorous success with the Lady Alix of Les Baux.

Richelieu and work begun immediately on its fortification which was still uncompleted when in 1635 the Spaniards overwhelmed the defence and remained masters of the island for two years, before being driven out by the Comte d'Harcourt. Again in 1746 a mixed Spanish-Piedmontese expedition, backed by the bombardment of a British flotilla, got the better of a weak garrison, but this occupation was short-lived, as the occupiers were in turn overcome the following year by the Chevalier de Belle-Isle.

Perhaps Sainte Marguerite's greatest claim to international fame is the fact that in one of its fortress cells was incarcerated the 'Man in the Iron Mask'.

There are several theories concerning this wretched individual's identity, but certain facts are irrefutable, namely that a masked captive was brought by night (in 1679) to the fortress of Pignerol, from there transferred to Exiles, and finally to Fort Royal on the Ile Sainte Marguerite in 1687.

The most popularly accepted solution of this mystery is the original, supported at the time by Voltaire, that the prisoner was a twin brother of Louis xiv – born at a two-hour interval – and that his imprisonment was decided upon so as to avoid possible dynastic complications. The present century has, however, seen a number of variant theories advanced. According to Funck-Brentano, the unknown was a certain count Hercule Antoine Mattioli, minister at the Duke of Mantua's court who, after negotiating a secret treaty between the Duke and the French King, disclosed the terms to the public with the result that, much to the annoyance of the two signatories, the transaction had to be abandoned.

In the '30s' two more suggestions were put forward. The first by the historian Emile Laloy that the victim was an over-zealous priest, Eustache Dauger, who denounced Louis xiv's liaison with Madame de Montespan in the strongest terms. The second by Maurice Duvivier, that he was a former page of Louis xiv, Eustache de Cavoye, involved in a case of poisoning. The comparatively mild (for those days) sentence was due to the fact that three de Cavoyes had been killed in battle while another brother was the King's most trusted friend.

Finally there is the theory – qualified as *la plus ingénieuse de toutes, la plus démente, et la plus comique* – that after the autopsy on Louis XIII, it was evident that the monarch could never have been a father. The doctor who made this discovery very wisely kept his mouth shut in public, but his son-in-law enjoyed dining out on the story and, not surprisingly, was arrested and thrown into a cell on the island fortress. There – the theorists do not tell us how – the prisoner became father of an illegitimate son who was smuggled off the island, confided to a Corsican family and baptised Buonaparte. In 1804 this same Buonaparte's great grandson, Napoleon, was crowned Emperor of France.

Basically, however, one may say that the mystery remains unsolved. Only two facts stand. There was a masked prisoner: the mask was not of iron, but of leather.

Two other notable prisoners were housed in this same fortress. In 1773, a young naval lieutenant, the Marquis de Jouffroy d'Abbans, was committed for a two-year sentence for duelling. During his enforced inactivity he drew up plans for a vessel that rather than relying on sail would be propelled by steam, an experiment tried out after his release on the river Saone at Lyons. A hundred years later, Bazaine, stripped of his Marshal's status, condemned first to death then to twenty years' imprisonment for his cowardly surrender of Metz, shut up in the fortress, managed to escape the night of 9/10 August 1874.

Today the fortress is no longer a prison, one wing having been converted into a youth hostel. It serves also as a background for a yearly midday banquet given in honour of visiting stars and magnates at the time of the film festival, a banquet sometimes enlivened by *ad hoc* strip-tease acts by would-be stars.

Cannes to Menton is these days a megalopolis. The visitor making his first acquaintance with the Côte d'Azur would be rather hard put to decide, for instance, where Antibes begins and Juan-les-Pins/Golfe Juan ends, or what in fact are the limits of Nice, Villefranche, Beaulieu. In most agglomerations, though, some relic of the original may be found huddled timidly within, and dwarfed by, forests of skyscrapers.

One such is Antibes, the Antipolis of the Phoceans, created as a bastion against Ligurian aggression and later more intensively fortified by the Romans. The château, the old town's principal attraction, is a sixteenth-century stronghold of the Grimaldis, now a museum and dedicated almost exclusively to paintings, faience and drawings, work of Pablo Picasso in 1946, constituting one of the world's most concentrated and most varied collections of this modern master's art.

Continuing east by the route known as the *Bord de Mer*, parallel with the N7 and Côte d'Azur motorway, one reaches the triple town of Cagnes; Cros de Cagnes, Cagnes-sur-Mer, and Haut de Cagnes.

The Cros, once like St Tropez a drowsy fishing village, now has a sea frontage which is an almost uninterrupted rampart of small hotels, restaurants and traffic jams. A mile and a half inland after passing the attractive Cagnes race course, Cagnes-sur-Mer is a thriving but featureless little town which none the less strives to put up some resistance to general inflationary tendencies, while Haut de Cagnes, built on a bluff, preserves the advantage of proffering one of the few medieval silhouettes still visible from the coast. Its château has so stylised an aspect that one might be tempted, in ignorance, to doubt its antiquity suspecting the feudal dream of some Hollywood producer of the booming twenties. However, like so many of the châteaux in this area, it was built by a Grimaldi, in this case Rainier I, after the village had been ceded to him by Count Robert of Provence in 1309.

In common with all habitations along the Côte d'Azur, Cagnes has suffered from a succession of invasions, counter invasions, and foreign occupations; for a brief period – 1746–1747 – it was in English hands. But one of the most curious incidents took place in 1710, when a Captain d'Artagnan of the King's (Louis XIV) musketeers arrived at the château with a warrant for the arrest of the Marquis of Grimaldi on a charge of minting counterfeit currency. More extraordinary was the fact that the accusation was proved to be just, when a search-party discovered all the apparatus for the production of false coins in a room which is today the *Musée de l'Olivier*, inaugurated in 1946.

Severely damaged by revolutionary mobs, the château was bought eventually in 1875 for 8,000 francs by a rich Ukrainian landowner, Markovitch, who undertook the work of restoration. Deprived of all sources of income from Russia after 1917, Markovitch's daughter, Elizabeth, was obliged to sell to the Cagnes municipality in 1937 for a sum of 250,000 francs – roughly £25,000. Classified as an historic monument, the château is now well known because of frequent modern art exhibitions.

Near Cagnes, as though passed by in the general rush and yet too close to the coast to become an oasis for jaded tourists, is the village of Villeneuve Loubet, on the left bank of the Loup river. Comparatively quiet, typically Provençal in aspect at the foot of a hill surmounted by the thirteenth-century castle of the famous Seneschal of Provence, Romée de Villeneuve, it would not really merit a detour but for the fact that, tucked away in a side street, is the memorial to one of the world's greatest culinary artists, the *Fondation Auguste Escoffier*.

This *Fondation*, or museum, could be described as a temple to good living set up in the house where Escoffier, who lived to the ripe age of 89, was born in 1844. For even the least appreciative of the table's pleasures, it is a fascinating exhibition. No schoolboy could fail to be overawed by the monumental cakes whose icing-sugar coatings take on the proportions of Baroque sculpture. To read the menus is to be seized by gnawing hunger while marvelling at our forebears' digestive powers. A pamphlet issued at the entrance reminds us that 'The classical language of the art of cookery is French but international in scope'. Personal touches are lent by a signed portrait of the great soprano Dame Nellie Melba acknowledging Auguste Escoffier's creation of the *Pêche Melba*, and a gold watch and chain, gift of the Czar Nicholas II.

Though 'cookery's tongue' may be French, the Society of Gourmets gives its annual dinner in London, the 13 December. Auguste Escoffier who founded the society chose 13 December as the most auspicious date for this meeting since it is the birthday of

St Fortunat, born 530, who as Bishop of Poitiers wrote a number of treatises extolling the joys of good fare, thus becoming nominated by Escoffier, patron saint of chefs.

Nice, to the east of the Var river, a city of over 300,000 inhabitants, is my favourite town on the 'Riviera' for the simple reason that it is the only one which can be said to exist in its own right, independent of foreign, above all touristic, influence. Traffic may roar along the now rather brash Promenade des Anglais and Quai des Etats-Unis, but behind this veneer is Nice, a living entity with a long, tormented, yet at the same time romantic, history.

The name is generally supposed to stem from the Greek *Nikáia*, 'Victory', to commemorate a naval battle won by the Massiliot Phoceans over the Etruscans in the fourth century B.C. There is another version, however, that it comes from this same basic word (Nikaia), but from that in which the stress is on the first, and not the second, syllable, and which signifies a source of fresh water. Nikaia therefore denoted the spot where the Phoceans disembarking found a supply of drinking water enabling them to implant one of their 'counters'.

The Romans, essentially a land power, moved from the port area to the hill some two miles inland, which they named Cemenelum – present-day Cimiez – there building a new city complete with an arena, a pygmy compared with those of Arles and Nîmes seating only 5,000 spectators, but whose ruins still form an impressive background to summer open-air operatic performances.

When the barbarians destroyed the Roman Empire, the port again became Nice's centre, and it was on the low but steep hill dominating the harbour that was built a fortress, generally considered to be impregnable, 'proud of its towers, its massive walls, and its garrison of picked troops'.

Studying the city's history, one feels that the inhabitants – the *Niçois* – are termed *Provençaux* rather arbitrarily. In 1338, they refused to acknowledge the authority of Louis d'Anjou, Count of Provence, claiming the protection, instead, of the Count of Savoy, thus openly opting for the Empire rather than the Kingdom, indicating a preference for Italian as opposed to French influence.

In 1543, backed by a Turkish fleet and land contingent, François I attacked Nice, successfully storming the lower town, but failing to subdue the citadel, or château, was eventually obliged to fall back across the Var, leaving the Savoyards to reoccupy the city unopposed.

Legendary heroine of this defence was an Amazonian flower-seller, Catherine Ségurane. Worn down by constantly renewed assaults, the morale of the Niçois was flagging. A group of the Turkish mercenaries, the Janissaries, succeeded in placing scaling ladders and their leader had already planted the crescent banner on the ramparts, when Catherine Ségurane hurled herself on him, sent him toppling backwards into space with a blow on the head from a wooden pestle. Grabbing the standard, she broke it over her knees and hurled it after him. Then in a sublime gesture of mingled triumph and contempt, she hitched up her skirts, and turning her back on the enemy presented them with the spectacle of her ample bare bottom. History would have us believe that this act of sublime exhibitionism had a more devastating effect on the besiegers than a salvo from a hundred guns.

Probably because of offensive weapons' technical advances, the château's legend of invincibility became a thing of the past after being stormed by Marshal de Catinat in 1691, and again by the British Marshal Berwick, in the service of France, in 1706. Having gained possession of the citadel, Marshal Berwick* decided to play safe and blow it up. It was a final gesture, for the great ramparts were never restored. Today the hill is a semi-tropical park in which flourish date palms, cactus and agave, as well as typically Mediterranean umbrella pines, and a shaded path leads to the highest point (300 feet) with its *table d'orientation*, looking up to the peaks forming a near semi-circle and down on to old Nice's dark narrow alleys.

* Marshal Berwick was, in fact James Stuart, Duke of Berwick, illegitimate son of James II born at Moulins in 1670, naturalised French, later created Duc de Fitz-James.

The city became French officially when it was annexed on its own request, so it is said, by the new-born Republic, and it was from Nice that the young General Bonaparte in 1796 set out on his first great Italian campaign with his ragged scarecrow soldiers after promising them *'Honneur, gloire, et richesse'* under his leadership, a promise more than fulfilled after the victories of Arcola, Castiglioni and Rivoli, and the final triumphal entry into Milan.

This French period was, however, short-lived.

After the Emperor Napoleon's defeat and exile, the Congress of Vienna handed Nice (and Savoy) back to Sardinia. It was not until 1860 when Napoleon III had backed Victor Emmanuel in his struggle to throw the Austrians out of Italy and French troops had borne the brunt of the decisive battles of Magenta and Solferino, that as a result of a plebiscite Nice and Savoy returned to France.

Yet links with Italy remain strong. Italian influence can be discerned in both the local dialect and local *cuisine*. The western limit of old Nice is the Place Garibaldi, named after the hero of Italy's fight for independence, born in a house on the Quai Lunel looking on to Nice harbour (Port Lympia) in 1807. It may be deliberate, or through subconscious atavism, but many *Niçois* youths still favour red shirts.

Old Nice streets, which have to be visited on foot, suggest Naples rather than a French *ambiance* with their tall five- or six-storeyed houses, balconies overhanging and almost meeting, brilliant displays, of multi-coloured underwear drying in slanting sunrays, noisy but cheerful crowds. Though the interest here is principally human and gastronomic – there are a number of cheap and excellent restaurants – Sainte Reparate Cathedral and the *Chapelle de la Miséricorde* (or of the *Penitents Noirs*) should not be missed.

Reparate was only fifteen years old when she was put to death in Caesarea for refusing to abjure the Christian faith. Her arrival in Nice reminds one of the story of Torpes (or Tropez). 'One autumn evening in the year 250, fishermen were hauling in their nets when they noticed a tiny boat piloted by a dove. Aboard, a young girl, almost a child, covered by a sheet of the purest white and lying on a bed of lilies and roses, appeared to be sleeping. The fishermen towed the frail bark to the shore and installed its precious contents beneath a dome of leaves. Thus was born Reparate, saint and martyr, patron saint of Nice . . .'

The present cathedral was completed in 1650 and largely restored in 1901. It is in neo-classical style, not often found in this part of the world. Beneath the high altar can be seen a coffer containing the relics of Saint Victor – not to be confused with the Saint Victor of Marseille – gift of a Portuguese bishop in 1685, and to whom the Niçois used to pray at times of protracted drought or severe floods.

Nice has always rivalled Avignon as a centre for Penitent Orders.

The most ancient, the *Penitents Blancs de Vieux Nice* was founded in 1306. They were flagellants and used to whip themselves till they drew blood during their processions through the streets, a custom which was continued till well into the eighteenth century. The *Penitents Noirs de Notre Dame de la Miséricorde*, were recruited mostly from the upper stratas of Niçois society, their mission being 'to honour the dead, both poor and rich . . .' Their chapel – *Notre Dame de la Miséricorde* – which opens on to the winter vegetable market on the Place Pierre Gautier, contains a remarkable altar piece, that of Our Lady of Pity, one of the most beautiful works of the fifteenth century 'primitive' Jean Miralhet. Miralhet (or Mirailhet) was a leading exponent of *École Niçoise*, also referred to as the *École Bréa* after its most famous representative, Louis Brea, and which included also Louis's two brothers, François and Antoine, and Jacques Durandi. This school, like that of Avignon, has produced masterpieces sadly neglected by the world in general, their works overshadowed – unjustly to my way of thinking – by the Italians.

The heart of modern Nice is the wide thoroughfare, for many years known as the *Avenue de la Victoire*, rebaptised recently the *Avenue Jean Medecin*, leading off north from the Place Masséna, a most impressive square built in the Genoese style in 1835, whose principal building is the Municipal Casino. The centre of the square is now occupied by a vast car park, but to the west and fringed by the sweep of the Avenue de Verdun is the *Jardin Albert I*, whose formally laid-out flower-beds have a distinct turn of the century atmosphere. However, the bandstand is no longer occupied by hussar uniformed instrumentalists. On the contrary, the garden's centre is taken up by an open air *théatre de verdure*, holding some 5,000, today one of the principal stages on 'pop' singers' summer tours.

The *Avenue Jean Medecin* is itself almost entirely commercial. Resaurants are mostly in side streets, such as the Rue Paul Déroulède or expensively along the Quai des Etats-Unis, while the great hotels face the sea from the north side of the Promenade des Anglais which now runs from the *Jardin Albert I* almost as far as Nice airport. The promenade owes its name, originally to a freak of nature. The winter of 1822 was marked by exceptionally hard frosts which destroyed most of the fruit trees with the result that unemployment and subsequent indigence became an acute problem. It was the Reverend Lewis Way, first chaplain of the British Anglican Church, 'opened for worship' on 1 December 1822, who had the idea that these unfortunates could be well employed (and paid) to build a little seaside road.

The Ruhl and the Negresco were the most renowned of the Promenade's hotels. Unfortunately the Ruhl, uneconomic by modern standards, has been demolished, but the superbly baroque Negresco still stands – it was built just prior to the First World War for the then fabulous sum of 6,000,000 gold francs – its cockaded top hatted flunkey waiting to welcome arrivals (nonfunctional reminder of a bygone age) still a symbol of defiance in the face of the jet and press-button era.

Though Nice may not be as rich in historical monuments and art treasures as Arles, Aix, and Avignon, the Masséna Museum, on the Promenade and close to the Negresco, is, of its kind, one of the finest in Provence.

The original building was put up on orders of Victor Masséna,

Prince of Essling and grandson of Napoleon's marshal, André Masséna – 'The spoilt child of victory' – Prince of Essling and Duke of Rivoli in 1900. Handed over to Nice municipality in 1919 by Victor Masséna's son André, this palace, as it could be called without undue exaggeration, became a museum in 1921 known either as the *Musée Masséna* or the *Musee d'Art et d'Histoire de la ville de Nice*.

The first Masséna was born at La Turbie, near Monaco, the 6 May 1758, son of a soap manufacturer. Nobody at his birth, unless gifted with second sight, could have foreseen his ascendance to princely rank. His father died young, and at the age of 13 André went to sea as a cabin boy on a merchantman, then in 1775 enlisted as a private in the Royal Italian regiment. Returning to civil life, he became a successful smuggler. Having made a considerable amount of money by this hazardous trade, he married an Antibes surgeon's daughter, Mlle Lamarre, and started an olive oil and dried fruits business. Revolution and war brought him back to the army and the foot of the ladder of promotion up which he was to climb to the topmost rung. At his very best in the Italian campaigns and later, in 1809 at Essling and Wagram, he is blamed by many, including General Marbot who served under him at this time, for French disasters in Portugal. In the confused days following on Napoleon's return from Elba, he adopted a fence-sitting policy justifying perhaps Marbot's criticism – 'As he grew old he pushed caution to the point of timidity, in fear of compromising the reputation he had earned.' And, because of this, after the second restoration of Louis XVIII and only narrowly escaping the same fate as Marshal Ney, 'the marshal lived in retirement at his château of Rueil and ended his glorious career in misfortune and solitude on April 4, 1817.'

Students of military history and admirers of Napoleon will be chiefly interested in the *Salle Premier Empire* and *Salle Masséna* on the first floor, and the *Salle Militaire* on the second floor. They form, however, only a small part of a most catholic collection.

Also on the first floor is a wonderful exhibition of Bréa School primitives, of which an altar piece 'St John the Baptist' is a striking, if somewhat grim, example. On the predella one sees the martyred St Agatha smiling despite the fact that her breasts have been hacked off, St Lucy carrying her torn-out eyes on a plate, and St John the Baptist's headless body lying in a pool of blood while his head is being held up by a hunchback. Coming to more recent times, there is a gallery of 'impressionists' (*Salle Centrale*), and on the second floor galleries devoted to *Provençal* furniture and ceramics, a pictorial record of Nice's reunion with France, and to Garibaldi. Near by, at No. 33 Avenue des Baumettes, is the smaller *Musée Jules Cheret*, named after an early twentieth-century artist who died in Nice in 1932 at the age of 96, and in which can be seen Rodin's *Le Baiser*, and an important collection of Dufy's work presented by the painter's widow in 1962.

Nice's most famous spectacle is the Carnival.

The first, echo of the great Venetian eighteenth-century carnivals, was staged in 1878, and from that year to the present day the same ritual with but few modifications has been followed.

The proceedings open with a procession in which *Sa Majesté Carnaval*, a gigantic *papier-maché* figure with a sinisterly round, rubicund, jovial face is preceded and followed by a mixed cortège of horsemen in medieval costumes and wheeled floats (corsos) bearing grotesquely clad groups weighed down by enormous masks, often gross caricatures of leading lights of the world political scene, or else of birds, animals, natural or mythical, yet all with that slight exaggeration of design which envelopes each individual with a vaguely nightmarish quality, an impression heightened by the deafening accompaniment of over-amplified brass band type music, blasting one from a legion of loud speakers.

After making the round of the streets, King Carnival is enthroned on the Place Masséna, turned for the occasion into a vast grandstand, where he remains for the whole period of Carnival, a fortnight, till the final firework display the evening of *Mardi Gras* before the Niçois begin Lent's theoretical austerity régime.

Although Carnival is generally looked upon as an excuse for an outburst of uninhibited gaiety, the original Italian conception dating back to the sixteenth century, was symbolic. *Sa Majesté* is, in effect, the effigy of the populace's collective sins during the past year, and his destruction by fire during the culminating pyrotechnics, a general absolution whose efficacy is valid for the next twelve months.

The best place from which to watch the procession is the grandstand on the *Place Masséna*, but the seats are dear, and provided one does not object to a little horseplay, the streets themselves can be more amusing. But the unsuspecting tourist should be careful. Literally tons of confetti are hurled light-heartedly at any and everything, and it is safer to maintain a trappist silence as one is quite likely to be cut off in the middle of a sentence by having a handful of these little coloured pellets thrust vigorously down one's throat by some exuberant masked merrymaker. In the past raw eggs were more popular missiles than confetti. Like Tarascon's *Fête du Tarasque*, it would seem that Nice Carnival has lost something of its primitive robustness!

Finally why the mask?

According to Varagnac, 'Masks suggest phantoms. Those who go masked wander amidst phantoms. Between those who are merely disguised and masked ghosts there is a certain identity which one would imagine to be only temporary, but which can prove to be permanent. In the country districts, we hear weird stories of carnival festivities infiltrated by strange revellers who disappear at the cock's crowing, and of young men who, masked, after mixing with these strange intruders, themselves vanish, never to be seen again, having been dragged by their nocturnal companions into the beyond.'

East from Nice, in the direction of Monaco and the Italian frontier one may make one's choice of three coastal roads named, according to their height above sea level, the *Inférieure*, *Moyenne*, and *Grande Corniche*. The lower (*inférieure*), and most traffic bound, skirts the shore, passing through Villefranche, Beaulieu, and Eze-sur-Mer, a solid built-up area offering few attractions to the non-gregarious, while the upper, though affording views of the Alps and a plunging wide sea vista is winding, in parts precipitous and not to be recommended to the nervous traveller. The Middle (*moyenne*) does indeed strike the happy medium and has the advantage of running past the foot of *Eze-village*, a walled village built on the site of a Ligurian oppidum, reminding one of the *villages-perchés* of the upper Var and the Vaucluse. With an eye to the tourist, shops and restaurants within the ramparts are far from inexpensive but the church, chapel of a White Penitent brotherhood dating back to the fourteenth century and containing a wood carved figure of Christ – the 'Christ of the Black Plague' – bearing the inscription, in Catalan, 'As you are so was I, as I am so will you be', is certainly worth a visit.

After Eze, one should turn up to the *Grande Corniche* to La Turbie to see what remains of the great Roman monument, now known as *La Trophee des Alpes*, raised in the year 7 B.C. to commemorate the Emperor Augustus's final victory over the Ligurian hill tribes, a vast column crowned by a huge statue of the Emperor. When Rome fell this monument to Rome's glory was largely destroyed, but the Guelphs impressed by the site's strategic advantages used the original stones to build a fortress. As such it remained for the best part of 600 years till demolished – at the same time as the Nice château – by Marshal de la Feuillade, acting on the orders of Louis XIV.

In 1929, financed by an American, Edward Tuck, work on restoration directed by Monsieur Jules Formigé was begun. As a result one can today form some slight impression of this monument in all its glory, an impression enhanced by a visit to the little museum, also financed by Edward Tuck, at its foot.

A small boy once said to me, 'Wasn't it naughty of that man to break the Bank !' He made the remark after listening to my not very melodious version of the old music hall hit 'As he walks along the *Bwaw de Boolong* with an independent air . . .', not realising that the 'break' had a financial, and not a purely demolitionary, significance.

Charles Wells, the professional gambler whose exploits inspired the song, did in actual fact break the Monte Carlo casino 'bank' in the Spring of 1887, not once but three times in two days. Having

started at the roulette tables with 10,000 francs, he left with close
on 3,000,000. He returned in 1892, but luck was no longer with
him. He lost all his own money, a considerable amount of money
that was not his, was arrested at Le Havre on his way back,
extradited and condemned in England to eight years' imprisonment. He died in Paris: penniless.

In actual fact Monte Carlo is only a part of the little Principality
of Monaco, and the renown of Monte Carlo overshadowing all else
by its reputation as a gambler's Mecca is of comparatively recent
date.

At the time the territory east of the Var river became reunited
with France (1860), the reigning Prince of Monaco, Charles III
was in dire financial straits. It seemed to him that his only chance
of solvency was to play on the human weakness which tempts
countless millions – then as today – to gaming tables in the hope
of gaining a fortune overnight. Luck was with the Prince, as the
concessions he offered were taken up by a Monsieur François
Blanc, former director of the Bad-Homburg casino.

The company they founded which bore, and still bears, the title
of *La Société des Bains de Mer*, was even more successful than
had been anticipated, making the fortunes of both Monsieur Blanc
and *Son Altesse Sérénissime*.

The name Monaco is derived from the Latin, *Portus Herculis
Monoeci* since Monaco was supposed to have been the last stage
of Hercules's westward journey prior to his encounter with the
giants of the Crau.

The present reigning family, the Grimaldis, became rulers of
Monaco in 1297, when Francesco Grimaldi, known as the
Malizia (the cunning one) stormed the city by a surprise night
attack, after which he was able to negotiate a measure of independence with the Genoese, an independence finally conceded to
the descendants of Charles Grimaldi who died in 1363.

But for a brief period during the Revolution, Monaco has
remained in Grimaldi hands ever since, though the family history
has been one of vicissitudes, violence, and strife.

In 1505 Jean II was assassinated by his brother Lucien. In 1523 the fratricide Lucien was struck down by his nephew Bartolomeo Doria. After this murder Monaco was placed, more or less voluntarily, under the tutelage of Charles Quint and a small Spanish garrison established on the rock. In 1621, however, the reigning Prince, Honore II, signed a secret treaty exchanging Spanish for French protection. Strangely enough the Spaniards departed without a fight on being presented with the *fait accompli*. The new protectorate was officially recognised by the Treaty of Peronne, a treaty which also accorded to Monaco's princes the title of Marquis (and the fief) of Les Baux, a title now bestowed on the reigning prince's heir.

At the time of Louis XIV's death, it seemed as though the Grimaldis, with no male heir, might die out. But a marriage was arranged between the eldest son of the Norman de Matignon family and the eldest Grimaldi daughter, by which de Matignon not only became Prince of Monaco but also took on the name Grimaldi for himself and his descendants.

The people of Monaco, the *Monagesques*, proclaimed their attachment to the Republic in 1793, after chasing out the Grimaldis, but their revolutionary fervour was short-lived. With Talleyrand's connivance, the princely régime was restored in 1815 under Honoré V as a Sardinian protectorate. Honoré, however, was a lover of *la vie Parisienne* and everything French. In 25 years he only visited his domaines three times, but as the sort of life he liked to live in Paris was costly, he heightened his unpopularity as an absentee landlord by levying extortionate taxes to meet his gallant expenses.

His grandson Charles III, as we have seen, was still bearing the crushing burden of the old man's extravagances – despite the sale of Menton and Roquebrune to Napoleon III for the sum of 4,000,000 francs – when he had the genial idea of converting Monaco into Europe's 'smartest' winter gambling resort, thus laying the foundations of the family fortune and the happy position of *Monagesques* passport holders in being exempt from all forms of taxation.

Although covering so small an area – a bare three square miles

– the principality is made up of three distinct zones: Monaco itself, built on a rocky promontory, a tiny district embracing the Palace, the cathedral, the oceanographic museum, and the town hall; La Condamine which is the commercial quarter overlooking the port, and Monte Carlo, the true international community with the casino, the Sporting Club, and the Hotel de Paris much favoured in his old age by Sir Winston Churchill.

Because of its world-wide reputation, there would be little point in visiting the principality without passing through the casino's swing doors. Yet on so doing one's first impression is of surprise at not being hemmed in immediately by gambling tables. The original rather baroque building was inaugurated in 1879 as a theatre, its designer Charles Garnier. It is a delightful miniature of the Paris Opera, designed by the same Charles Garnier, a plush and gold affair whose stage is framed by five huge, pseudo-classical panels representing Drama, Song, Poetry, Dance, and Music.

Rather discreetly, the gaming rooms open off to the left of the entrance. The stories they could tell could fill several volumes: tales of fortunes lost and won, the foibles and characteristics of famous gamblers and famous men and women who enjoyed either serious gambling or a 'flutter' at the tables. Perhaps the saddest – and most sobering – is that told by Carlos d'Aquila in his recent book *La Côte d'Azur*, when he mentions that the famous *Bel Epoque* beauty and *demi-mondaine*, La Belle Otero, admitted when old, penniless, and eking out a miserable existence in a Nice garret, that she had lost the best part of 20,000,000 gold francs at Monte Carlo.

In Monaco itself, I always enjoy the 'Changing of the Guard' ceremony at midday outside the Palace, a building dating back to the thirteenth century, but much embellished in Victorian Gothic style after the financial success of the launching of the *Société des Bains de Mer*.

The Monaco army, known as 'The Prince's Carabineers' is really a household Guard and as such was raised in 1817. It comprises 60 'other ranks', 10 sergeant-majors, and three officers; a commandant (major), a captain and a lieutenant. All ranks must be well educated men, in perfect physical condition and of 'irreproachable' character. Their uniform, dark blue tunic with lighter blue slacks, is colourful yet strictly military with no hint of 'operetta', and the drill on the guard-changing ceremony is precisely carried out.

The Oceanographique Museum was founded by Albert I, reigning Prince from 1889 to 1922 and officially opened by him in 1910. Oceanography was his hobby, and most of his time free from cares of State was spent on board his yachts the *Princesse Alice* and *L'Hirondelle*.

The museum contains an unique collection not only of skeletons, embalmed fish, including a 70-foot whale, sea birds, a polar bear, swordfish, giant crabs from the tropical oceans, but also of model small craft (notably of *L'Hirondelle*), marine zoological instruments, and various objects, both artistic and practical, fabricated from products of the sea; mother-of-pearl, coral, amber, shark skin.

Even more fascinating for those who prefer things animate, is the aquarium with its tanks of brilliantly hued tropical fishes, brilliant in colour as any bird of paradise, bulbous-eyed octopods and, perennial charmers, sea lions. ·

The museum is run by the pioneer under-water explorer Commandant Cousteau, who hopes in the near future to open a 'Monagesque Underwater Park' three hundred feet beneath sea level.

What a pity that with such a universal appeal of fantasy, of the mundanely exotic and blend of history and frivolity, the development of La Condamine has been allowed, visually in any case, to ruin this somewhat roseate illusion for the visitor of today and tomorrow. For vast blocks of flats of almost unbelievable hideosity now sprout like evil weeds to ruin not only the traditional *cachet* but the cherished view enjoyed by older inhabitants of the lower town, the harbour with its millionaires' yachts, and the sea.

Supreme irony; the harbour's west side is now completely dominated by a coca-cola factory!

Five and a half miles east of Monaco the 'Riviera' ends at

Menton, popular resort of the Edwardians and of the 'twenties' when it was usually known as 'Mentone'. Understandably, for barely have Menton's last houses been passed than one arrives at the Italian frontier.

Menton's old town is also distinctly Italianate in appearance, and looking up from the harbour towards the cathedral-crowned hill brings to mind an exuberant setting for *Rigoletto*'s second act. Again this is hardly surprising, for the town's history has been considerably more influenced in past centuries by Italy than by France.

Menton's founders were probably Lampedusan corsairs who disembarked on the shores of Garavan Bay towards the end of the eighth century. Frequently occupied by the Saracens, it became the property of the Dukes of Ventimiglia after the Moslems' final defeat, till ceded by them to a Genoese nobleman, Guglielmo Vento.

And it was not until the 13th century, in 1273 to be exact, that the first Frenchman set foot in Menton when Vento, at war with Genoa, called on Charles of Anjou, Count of Provence, to come to his aid.

Eventually after a series of most involved negotiations the town was bought by Charles Grimaldi in 1346, after which it became 'looked upon as a piece of furniture, in turn to be sold, swapped, divided by a half, a quarter, a tenth. A number of sovereigns had a share in it, the Grimaldis, the Del Careto, the Lascaris, the Dukes of Savoy . . .'

Though French during the Revolution years and the first Empire, it returned to the Grimaldis at the same time as Monaco after Napoleon's fall, till 1848 – the year of revolutions – with near-by Roquebrune it declared itself *ville libre et indépendante* under the protection of the King of Sardinia till becoming purely and simply a French town in 1860.

Climatically, Menton is probably the most favoured spot on the whole of the French Mediterranean coast during the winter months. It is at this point that the Maritime Alps are at their closest to the sea, surrounding the town like a wall, sheltering it from the cold winds – the *mistral* and the *tramontana* – so that it is indeed a sun trap.

Nowhere else in France does semi-tropical flora bloom so luxuriantly. The *Mentonnais* claim that their lemons – the first tree was planted, so they will tell you, by Adam and Eve after they had been driven out of the garden of Eden – are the best in the world and can be picked at any time of the year between New Year's Day and New Year's Eve. They are proud, too, of their enormous olive trees which seem like hot-house growths, their great shade spreading branches heavy with fruit, when compared with the tough gnarled specimens of the Rhône valley which so appealed to Van Gogh, whose existence is a long battle with the screaming *mistral*, and alternating periods of torrid drought and bitter frost.

The old town, sometimes likened to a North African Kasbah, is the most attractive on the coast and built, rather like Tangier's Kasbah, on a promontory. Its hub is the cobbled Place Saint Michel with the Eglise Paroissale of St Michael, and the White Penitents Chapel, also known as the Chapel of the Immaculate Conception, both in Baroque style.

The church has a grandiose altar-piece figuring St Michael, St Peter and St John the Baptist, work of Andrea Manchello (1565). One should also ask the Sacristan to see a curious processional cross. The shaft, unusually thick, according to church records was once that of a Turkish lance captured during the battle of Lepanto (1571) by Prince Honoré 1 of Monaco. This theory is rejected by some who insist that the shaft is in fact centuries older, being that of the lance with which St Michael himself slew a dragon.

During the height of the summer season, the parvis of the church becomes an open-air theatre for a series of chamber music concerts at which some of the world's greatest instrumentalists and *lieder* singers can be heard.

The Menton Hotel de Ville, with its pleasant 1860 façade, stands on the corner formed by the Place Ardoino and the rue de la République. Its *salle des mariages* was redecorated in 1957 by Jean Cocteau and must be counted as one of the most curious in the country. The poet has certainly let his fantastic imagination run riot. I am not myself a great admirer of this form of 'art' – no man I have ever met has had fishes instead of eyes – but one must admit that Cocteau's frescoes, mixed modern and classical themes, including, of course, Orpheus and Eurydice, provide a welcome contrast with the grim functional bleakness of the normal registry office.

Though life in the *Alpes Maritimes* centres mostly on the coast, the inland triangle of towns formed by Grasse, St Paul de Vence and Vence is becoming increasingly popular because of the generally healthier climate and as an escape – though nowadays a dubious one – from the scourges of noise and crowds.

Chiefly because of its perfume industry, Grasse at just over 1,000 feet above sea level, has always been well known. In the 'Riviera's' golden age, the hillsides round the town were dotted with villas whose pergolas dripped bouganvillia and wistaria and from whose terraces rose pseudo Taj Mahal style gazebos. There were so many English wintering along the millionaire's lane to the west of the town in the direction of Maganosc, that the boulevard by which one leaves Grasse is named the boulevard Victoria, and on a bluff, to the left, one finds a small English church, architecturally reminiscent of Indian hill stations of British Raj days, one of whose stained glass windows was a gift from the Queen herself. Today the suburbs have spread cancerously, especially to the south and west, but apart from the old town with its early Gothic cathedral of Notre Dame, and arcaded squares, like the *Place aux Aires*, the pre-1939 quarter, its main thoroughfare the plane tree shaded *boulevard du Jeu de Ballon*, has managed to preserve its discreet air of quiet prosperity.

The simplified version of the origin of the town's name is that it was called after the Roman consul Crassus, but it now seems probable that it was founded by Jewish refugees from Rome who had escaped from Sardinia, Rome's Devil's Island, and on reaching the mainland made their peace with the locals and settled in the neighbourhood of the hamlet of Maganosc. After years of tranquillity, Jewish persecutions began, whereupon the early settlers' descendants embraced Christianity, thereby obtaining their '*Grace*'.

It was a Florentine, Tombarelli, who settled in Grasse towards the middle of the sixteenth century to study the question of obtaining perfume essence from petals, making his first experiments with lavender and rosemary. Originally these experiments were carried out for the benefit of Catherine di Medici who loved to smother herself with perfume, but Tombarelli was so successful that his concentrated products were soon in demand all over the country, above all at the great Beaucaire fair.

Three major '*Parfumeries*' exist in Grasse today; Fragonard, Gallimard and Molinard. They use not only rosemary and lavender in their factories – open to the public – but also roses, specially grown in the *Alpes Maritimes* and the Var, mimosa, violets, tuba roses, jasmin, and even the yellow petals of Spanish broom. One hears complaints that these Grasse perfumes cost a great deal of money, but it should be remembered that it takes a ton of petals to produce one kilo – two and one-fifth pounds – of *essence*.

The city's most illustrious son was the painter, Honoré Fragonard.

This most agreeable of individuals, a pupil of Boucher, described as the *Peintre de l'amour, des plaisirs d'amour sans hypocrisie ni prétentions d'intellectualisme*, known to his friends as *Le galant Frago*, was a special favourite of the du Barry. To the twentieth-century eye, the work of this painter of rosy fleshed nudity set against temples of Eros, may seem stylised and artificial, singularly lacking psychological depths, yet it never offends while suggesting a comfortable, yet naïvely romantic, irreality, often fringing idealism. It is difficult not to agree with L. Hourticq's judgement – '*La génerosité* (of Fragonard's work) *a dépouillé l'amour des insolences de la galanterie*'.

The Fragonard Museum, created in 1921, is installed in the former residence of the Marquise de Cabris, sister of the famous Mirabeau, opening off the *passage* Mirabeau below a small public garden with a statue of the painter by A. Maillard at the foot of the *boulevard Jeu de Ballon*. It contains a number of his works, including the 'Three Graces', bought by Madame du Barry in 1770, as well as canvases by his son and grandson, Evariste and Théophile. Equally interesting are the rooms devoted to local history with their reconstructions of family life after the style of those found in Arles' *Muséon Arlaten*.

The silhouette of St Paul de Vence crowning a spur thrusting out into two narrow valleys, which is the apex of this triangle of inland towns, suggests a miniature Carcassonne, but with the advantage that no modern quarters lap round the foot of its sixteenth-century *enceinte*.

The fortified town we see today took ten years to built (1537-1547) and was the work of a forerunner of Vauban, François de Mandon de Saint-Rémy. Determined not to let anything stand in the way of his efforts to make the place impregnable, de Mandon ordered 700 houses to be demolished. Their disgruntled inhabitants, homeless but unwilling to wander too far afield, founded the village of *La Colle-sur-Loup* a little to the west and slightly lower down on the slopes leading towards Cagnes and the sea.

As well as being a 'protected site', St Paul is also a modern art centre thanks, in the first place, to a Monsieur Paul Roux, late owner of the restaurant *L'Auberge de la Colombe d'Or*. Talented amateur collector, loving artists' company, Paul Roux acted as a magnet. For the often hungry spiritual sons of Rudolfo and Marcello, *La Colombe d'Or* gained a reputation as a spot which provided excellent food, accorded limitless credit, or else was prepared to accept a canvas in lieu of cash payment. After many years Paul Roux's *auberge* became famous not only for its *cuisine* but as an art gallery, the diner finding himself surrounded by works bearing the signature Matisse, Dufy, Picasso, Miro, Signac, Bonnard, to mention but a few.

Though the streets are too narrow for motor traffic, the existence of *La Colombe d'Or*, and the fact that St Paul is a favourite haunt of both film and stage stars and producers, has meant that the generally pervading atmosphere is what might be termed 'arty-crafty'. The main street and the square immediately within the principal gate, are filled with *boutiques* crammed with *objets d'art*, the inevitable souvenir, 'antiques', and local materials whose prices maintain a steady upward trend. Perhaps one cannot be really surprised by this commercialisation on learning that this town of roughly 1,500 inhabitants is yearly swamped by well over a million tourists. However, one can still turn one's back on this less attractive aspect, and make the tour of the ramparts, unchanged since the days of the Sieur de Mandon.

In 1964 the *Fondation Maeght* – a temple to modern art – was opened on a hillside half-way between St Paul and Vence by the art dealers Aimé and Marguerite Maeght. The buildings seem to belong to the twenty-first century, yet in some strange way appear to harmonise with this ancient countryside in their cleverly blended employ of light and contour. There is a wall in ceramics and a *girouette*, both works of Miro, pools in mosaic by Chagall and Braque, while the gardens are peopled by Giacometti's rather terrifying statues – note particularly the nightmarish *chien de chasse* and the *promeneur solitaire*.

Vence, only 20 miles from Cannes and 15 from Nice, ancient capital of the Salyens one of the first Gallic tribes to be subdued by the Romans, is only three and a half miles uphill from St Paul. Named Vintium by the occupiers, it was promoted to the dignity of 'Roman City' by the Emperor Augustus.

The people of those days were in some ways fortunate to benefit by the *Pax Romana*, for the term was no euphemism; a fact eloquently proved by the bald statement in the *Guide Bleu* that after this 'promotion' – '*Elle* (Vintium) *connut cinq siecles de paix et de prospérité....*'

A bishopric in the fourth century, Vence became known for its famous prelates: the saints Véran (late fifth century) and Lambert (mid twelfth century), Andrea Farnese the future Pope Paul III (early sixteenth-century) and the remarkable Bishop Godeau who died in Vence in 1672, often called in his day the 'wittiest man in France', one of the first twelve members of the *Académie Française*, for whom none in his youth and early manhood, would have predicted a sacerdotal vocation.

Though no Adonis, his mind was so brilliant, his tongue at the same time so barbed and honeyed, his verses so suggestive, that women found him irresistible. His liaison with Julie d'Angenne, known as the *déesse* of the brilliant *salons* held at the Hotel Rambouillet, meeting-place for Paris's most exclusive aristocratic and intellectual circles, was no secret. One would often hear him referred to as 'Julie's dwarf'.

Tiring of the social round, he travelled south, became enamoured of Provence – rather than Julie – entered the priesthood, and it was Cardinal Richelieu himself who nominated him Bishop of Grasse and Vence. Since the touchy *Provençaux* would not agree to sharing a bishop between two cities, he eventually took up office in Vence, devoting himself with rare zeal to his flock's well-being, yet losing nothing of his literary brilliance.

Only a few days before his death from a stroke the Marquise de Sevigné wrote about him – 'C'est un Prelat d'un esprit et d'un mérite distingué; *c'est le plus bel esprit de son temps.*'* While some 200 years late the critic Emile Faguet said – 'Avant de dire *beau comme le Cid*, on a dit longtemps d'un poème que l'on jugeait admirable, "*C'est du Godeau*" '.*

Old Vence reminds me of a rocky island surrounded, but not submerged, by an ever-spreading tide. New buildings crowd right up to its walls. Modern suburbs encroach on the once wooded hillsides. One has only to drive a short way up the road towards the Col de Vence rising steeply to the north, to get an aerial view of the town, picking out the form of the old red-tiled *enceinte's* sturdy mass still holding out against the enemy as stubbornly as one of Wellington's 'squares' at Waterloo.

The most impressive entrance into this old city is from the *Place du Frene*, called after the giant ash planted in 1528 to commemorate the visit of Pope Paul III and François I, by the *Porte*

---

* In both cases in italics in the original text. ('He is a prelate endowed with great wit and talent; he has the finest brain of today' ... 'For sometime now rather than complimenting a poem by saying *as fine as Le Cid*, one says, '*Its worthy of Godeau*'.)

du Peyra – flanked by a square tower, relic of the seignioral castle – leading on to the *Place* of the same name, ancient forum of Vintium. The comparatively modern but very harmonious fountain (1822) in its centre, is fed by the waters of the old Roman source of La Foux on the hill to the north-east. It is much appreciated by hydrophiles. Personally I am inclined to agree with the famous gourmet Dr Besançon's judgement '*L'eau pure est un mythe*' and much prefer the excellent local sparkling wine as a thirst quencher.

A narrow shopping street, one of the most typical and most delightful in the Maritime Alps, leads to the *Place Clemenceau*, with the *Mairie*, a rather lamentable edifice built on the site of the bishop's palace, and the cathedral which has the distinction of being the smallest in France, originally raised on the ruins of a temple to Mars, probably in the early eleventh century.

Inside, St Véran's Chapel, the third on the right, contains a fifth-century sarcophagus considered to be that of the saint, but it is the choir stalls, work of Jacques Bellot of Grasse carried out in 1445, which should not be missed.

Bellot was more interested in portraying daily life at the time of Louis XI than biblical history or the lives of saints. Thus one discovers a magician with his long pointed cap, a woman with a pet monkey, a cobbler, and strangest of all, a contortionist with his head sticking out from between his thighs. The frieze also extols nature rather than faith, with its carvings of monkeys' heads, snakes, bats, pigs and ferociously gaping-jawed hounds.

Five hundred years later, a modern painter, Henri Matisse, whose work was usually of a markedly secular nature, reached on his own estimation the apogee of his art in a spiritual outpouring, when he decorated the Dominican *Chapelle du Rosaire* on the St Jeannet road to the north of the town. Consecrated in 1951, the chapel and its decoration were by way of being a votive offering on the part of the octogenarian painter, self-styled 'free thinker', who had been nursed by Dominican 'white sisters' during a serious illness.

As might be expected there is little to remind one of classical ecclesiastical art, the dominating motif being based on the exploitation of light combined with the severest economy of line. Figures are outlines in black on a white background; the Virgin, St Dominic, the fourteen stations of the Cross. Two walls are almost entirely in glass, geometrical designs of green, blue, and yellow, Matisse's conception of Provence's basic colours in terms of light. This, even today, ultra-modern style, may not be to everyone's taste, but there can be no doubting of the genuinely devout spirit of its inspiration.

Leaving Vence by the St Jeannet road one looks up to the hotel Château St Martin on the Col de Vence road, former site of a Templar Commandery whose restored main gate still serves as the principal entrance to the hotel grounds. The view from the terrace is one of the most grandiose in the *département*, but the hotel being in the luxury class – a room alone can cost up to £20 a night – the price even of the simplest *apéritif* is correspondingly high.

A short drive past St Jeannet village overlooked by two savagely abrupt peaks, the *Baous* whose rock faces serve as nursery ascents for budding alpinists, and one reaches the compact walled village of La Gaude. From there, turning one's back on the vast I.B.M. construction to the south, there is a long view up the Var river valley, even more Jhelum-like at this point than the Durance, till it vanishes into a veritable wall of mountains blocking the horizon.

Though the two popular ski stations, Auron and Valberg, high up in this world of snow-capped peaks, are included in maps of Provence, this great mountain barrier is as much one of Provence's frontiers as the climatic divide found at Sisteron and the great waterway of the Rhône which once separated 'Kingdom' and 'Empire'.

East of the Var river, the chaotic Alpine world symbolises the torments of a land whose possession over the centuries has so often and so recently been disputed. It was not in fact till 1947 that the village of Tende and neighbouring communities on the Italian frontier finally became French, while from the coast at Menton to as far north as Briançon, all slopes facing east are still scarred by vestiges of fortifications, fief of France's crack *Chasseurs*

Alpins, reminder of the not so long past Mussolinian menace; a world as foreign to the general conception of 'The South of France', as the Rhône's right bank wilderness of factory chimneys.

One of these many aloof peaks would, indeed, be a fitting place to turn one's face again to the south and the sun, remembering, perhaps echoing, Mignon's wistful complaint:

> *C'est là que je voudrais vivre*
> *Aimer, aimer et mourir.*
> *C'est là que je voudrais vivre*
> *Oui, c'est là.*

Index

Abd-er-Rahman, 15
Agricola, 195
Aigues-Mortes, 42, 109
Aiguines, 152, 207, 208
Aix-en-Provence, 13, 14, 21, 24, 29, 39,
    Chap. 4
Alberon, 102
Algeria, refugees from, 25
Alpilles, 75, 82, 92
Amboy, Château d', 82
Andreos and the Devil (legend), 58, 59
Anne, Saint, 135
Ansouis, Château d'
Antibes, 12, 234
Apt, 15, 128, 130, 134, 135
Aqueducts, 57, 191
Arausi (Arausio), 59
Argens River, 189
Arles, 14, 15, 20, 21, 27, 39, 40, Chap. 3,
    106
Alyscamps, 77–79
Arts, the, 30ff., 186
Artuby River, 155, 208
Aubagne, 175
    Christmas crèche at, 175ff.
Aucassin, 96
Augustus, Emperor, 59, 148, 190, 245
'Augustus's Lantern', 190
Aups, 217, 219
Auron, 258
Avignon, 14, 15, 16, 20, 32, Chap. 2
    The Bridge of, 40, 41, 49

Balcons de la Mescla, 155
Baous, 258
Barcelonnette, 35, 157
Bargème, 35, 209
Bargémon, 210, 213
Barjolo, 217
    Festival and sacrifices at, 218
Bauxite, 93
Bazaine, Marshal, 234
Beaucaire, 95, 96, 100
Bénézet, 40
Benoit XII, Pope, 43
Berwick, Marshal, 238

Béziers, 42
Black Death, 44, 164, 193
Bonaparte Family, 169, 174, 222
Bord de Mer, 235
Bories (shepherds' huts), 134
Bormes, 189
Boules, 225
Brea family (painters), 240, 242
Bresque River, 217
Brignoles, 205, 220
Brougham, Lord, 24, 228, 229
Brovès, 210, 226
Bull-fighting, 27, 105, 191

Cadarache Dam and Nuclear Research
    Establishment, 138
Cadenet, 127
Cagnes, 235
Cagnes-sur-Mer, 235
Callas, 210, 211, 213
Callian, 210, 211
Calvet, Dr. Esprit, and Museum, 50
Camargue, 35, 75, 80, 101ff.
Cannes, 24, 229
    Film Festival, 230
Canteperdrix, 150
Cap Roux, 195
Carpentras, 67
Casimier of Poland, 149, 172
Castellane, 35, 155
Castillon Dam, 157
Catalonia, 19
Catherine de Medici, Queen, 87, 196
Catherine of Sienna, Saint, 44
Cavaillon, 15, 66, 67, 137
Cavalaire, 187
Celts, 12, 13, 207
Cézanne, Paul, 32, 119ff.
Chagall, 33
Chant de Marseillais, 23
Charlemagne, 135
Charles Martel, 15, 16, 40, 72
Charles of Anjou, 19, 20, 165, 173
Charles Quint, 22, 73, 113, 156, 166,
    167, 232
Charonton, Enguerrand, 54

Chartreuse de la Verne, 188
Christianity, 14, 103
Christmas crèche, 175
Cimiez, 14, 237
Cirque de Vaumale, 155
Col Bayard, 34
Col d'Allos, 157, 158
Col de Belhomme, 210
Col de la Glacière, 210
Collobrières, 188
Collostre River, 150
Colmar, 158
Comps, 155, 208, 209
Comtat Venaissin, 45
Costume, 79, 80
Côte d'Azur, Chap. 9
Cotignac, 217
Coulobre, the, 66
Count of Monte Cristo, 172
Couvent des Desnarados, 164
Courts of Love, 40
Crau, the, 75, 106, 207
Cros de Cagnes, 235

Daudet, 28, 33, 81, 85
    windmill, 82
De Bevon, 147
De Lisle, Roger, 23
Dentelles de Montmirail, 61
Dior, Christian, 211
Domaine de Capitaine Danjou, 123
Donat, Saint, 147
Draguignan, 205
Drummond Family grave, 146
Dumas, Alexandre, 194
Durance River, 127, Chap. 5

Embrun, 19
Erard, Jean, 148
Ernst, Max, 33
Escoffier Museum, 236
Estérel, 35, 191, 195, 210
Etang de Berre, 108, 138
Eugène, Prince, 199
Eze-sur-Mer, 244

Fairs, 95
Falaise des Cavaliers, 155
Fayence, 210, 211
Felibrige, Palais, 79
Felibrige Society, 29, 88
Fondation Maeght, 255
Fontaine l'Evêque, 151
Fontaine de Sorps, 151
Fontaine de Vaucluse, 64, 65, 67
Fontvieille, 28, 73, 81
Forcalquier, 19, 94, 139ff.
    William and Adelais of, 40
Ford, Ford Madox (qu.), 41, 42

Fort de Savoie, 158
Fragonard (painter), 32, 253
    (perfume), 235
François, 1, King, 166, 167, 172, 238
Franks, 14, 15
Fraxinet, 188
Fréjus, 188, 203ff.
    destruction by flood (1959), 192
French fleet, scuttling of (1940), 201
French Foreign Legion, 175, 208
French Revolution, 23, 47, 52, 81, 113,
    151, 168, 175, 178, 181, 200, 222
Fromont, Nicolas, 31
Funerals, 27

Galleys, 200
Gallimard, 253
Gardians (Camargue cowboys), 105
Gassin Castle, 30
Gauguin, 32, 73, 88
Giono, Jean, 33, 150
Glanum, 91, 92
Gliding, 211
Godeau, Bishop of Vence, 255
Gordes, and Château, 134
Gorges de Verdon, 33, 152, 206, 217
Gounod, Charles, 33, 91, 185, 194
Grasse, 35, 252
    Parfuneries, 253
Great Schism, 45
Greeks, 11, 91, 162, 183, 187, 189, 209,
    221
Grenoble, 34
Gréoux-les-Bains, 150
Grimaldi Family, 235, 246
Grimaud, 30
Guesclin, Bertrand de, 44
Gypsies, 104

Hallays, André (qu.), 206
Hannibal, 13
Haut de Cagnes, 235
Henri II, King, 166
    IV, 196, 199, 208
Holy Roman Empire, 40, 73
Honorat, Saint, 231

Iles de Lérins, 230
Ile du Levant, 199
Inguimbert, Malachie d', 67

Jeanne, Queen, 20, 43
Jouffroy d'Abbans, Marquis, 234
Juan-les-Pins, 234
Julius Caesar, 13, 14, 60, 165, 190, 217

Karr, Alphonse, 194

La Baume, 148
La Ciotat, 12

La Foux d'Allos, 158
La Garde Freinet, 188
La Gaude, 258
Lamartine, 82, 83, 85
Languedoc, 15, 16, 19
Lattre de Tassigny, General de, 25, 201
La Turbie, 245
Le Dramont, 194, 195
Le Lavandou, 187
Les Arcs, 220
Les Baux, 73, 93
Les Mées, 147
Les Saintes Maries de la Mer, 14, 94, 102
Les Salles, 152
Literature, 31, 33
Logis du Pin, 203
Louis, Saint, 196, 221, 222
Louis VIII, King, 42, 199, 205
   XIV, 22, 168, 172, 199
Luberon, 127, 129

Maganose, 252
Maillane, 82, 83
Malpasset, 191
Man in the Iron Mask, 182, 233
Manosque, 138
Marcel, Saint, 218
Marignane, Battle of 139, 166
Mario (Marion), 60
Marius, 60, 72, 122, 223
Marseille (Massilia), 12, 20, 22, 72, Chap. 6
Martha, Saint, 96ff.
Martiques, 23
Masséna Family and Museum, 242
Massif des Maures, 187ff., 210
Matisse, 185, 257
Maupassant, Guy de, 185
Mauron, Marie (qu.), 87, 150
Menton, 234
Mérimée, Prosper, 33, 217, 222
Merindol, 129, 130
Meynier d'Oppède, Baron, 22, 130
Mignard, Nicolas, 32, 67
Mirabeau, Count Honoré-Gabriel, 113, 168, 172, 253
Miralhet, Jean, 240
Mistral, the, 28
Mistral, Frederic, 29, 33, 79–85, 88, 150
Mitre, Saint, 117
Molinard, 253
Monaco, 246ff.
Mons, 191
Montagne Ste Victoire, 13
Montagnetta, la, 100
Montauroux, 210
Mont de la Chens, 203
Monte Carlo, 246

Montferrat, 207
Monticelli, 174
Montmajour Abbey, 73, 74, 81
Mont Ventoux, 61, 208
Mount Andaon, 53
Moustiers Ste. Marie, 252
   Star Legend of, 253
Museums, 50, 54, 79, 118, 153, 174, 178, 241
Music, 33

Napoleon I, 23, 27, 149, 169, 170, 174, 193, 201, 239
Napoleon III, 24, 194, 239
Narbonne, 16
Nartuby River Gorge, 207
Nice (Nicaea), 12, 14, 22, 237ff.
Nicolai Family, 140
Nîmes, 16, 27, 58, 106
Nostradamus, 30, 31, 86, 87, 167, 224
Nôtre Dame de Beauvoir, 154
   de L'Ormeau, 212
   des Anges, 188
Nouguier, François, 40

Olives, 214
Orange, 59
Orgon, 27, 193
Ostrogoths, 14
Ouvèze River, 62

Pagnol, Marcel, 33, 150, 170
Painting, 32ff., 47, 51, 67, 185, 240, 253, 257
Parrocel family, 32, 67
Penitents, The, 51, 240, 244
Petrarch, 31, 64ff., 67
Peyruis, 147
Philippe, Gerard, 187
Phoceans, 11, 162, 237
Picasso, 33, 47
Pierre de la Fée, 206
Pioch, 102
Plan de Conjuers, 207, 208
Pompeius, 13, 165
Pont du Gard aqueduct, 57, 58
Popes, 42ff., 57, 128, 167
Porphyry, 195
Porquerolles, 199
Port Cros, 199
Posidonius, (qu.), 11, 28
Pottery, 152
Pourrières and Battle of, 13, 60, 223, 224
Prison, 200
Provençal, character of the, 26
   language, 29, 167, 213
Puget, Pierre and François, 32, 174

Puyloubier, 123
Pytheas, 12

Quinson, 150

Raimbaud d'Orange, 30
Rainfall, 28
Ramatuelle, 186, 188
Raoulx de Gassin, 30
Raymond Berenger, Count of Provence,
    19, 42, 141, 214
Raymond de Turenne, 94, 142
Raymont, Count of Toulouse, 62, 95
Remoulins, 58
René, King of Aragon and Provence,
    21, 54, 94, 96, 98, 103, 111ff., 173,
    184
    Castle at Tarascon, 96, 99
Reperate, Saint, 239
Reyran River Dam, Collapse of, 192
Rhône, River, 12, 39, 40, 49, 74
Riez, 150
Rigaud, Hyacinth, 32
Riou Blanc, 191
Robert, Hubert, 51
Roman remains, 57–59, 74, 91, 92, 151,
    190, 191, 193, 237
Roquebrune, 189, 245
Rosseline, Saint, 220
Rougon, 154
Roumanille, Joseph, 29, 88
Route de Vins, 214
Route Napoleon, 34, 147, 203
Roux, Paul, 254
Ruisseau d'Ecrévisses, 218

Sabran, Elzéar and Delphine de, 128
Sade, Marquis de, 64, 96, 114
St. André-les-Alpes, 157
St. Antonin, 122
St. Aygulf, 187, 189
Ste. Baume, 14, 124, 208, 223
    Hostellerie de, 124
St. Cassien Lake, 35
St. Exupéry, Honore de, 195
Ste. Marguerite, 230, 232, 233
Ste. Maxime, 187
St. Maximin, 220, 221
St. Paul de Vence, 35, 254
St. Raphaël, 25, 193
St. Rémy, 15, 29, 80, 86ff.
    Asylum at, 88
St. Saturnin d'Apt, 134
St. Tropez, 12, 183
Ste. Victoire, 33, 208, 223
Saints, Early Christian, 14, 103, 124,
    135, 223
Salon-en-Provence, 86

Santons, 80
Sara (Gypsy saint), 103, 104
Saracens, 15, 16, 19, 40, 72, 103, 140,
    147, 163, 173, 184, 187, 191, 212,
    222, 231
Sauvan, Château de, 146
Segobrigians, 12
Ségurane, Catherine, 238
Seillans, 210, 211, 225
Senanque Abbey, 214
Serre-Poncon reservoirs, 137, 150
Siagnola River, 191
Sidonius, Saint, 222
Signac, 185, 186
Sillans-la-Cascade, 217
Silvacane, 214
Sisteron, 19, 137, 147
Sorgue River, 65, 66

Tarascon, 14, 80, 95
    Castle, 54
Tarasque, the, 80, 96ff.
Tartarin de Tarascon, 100, 225
Teutons, 13
Tholonet, 122
Thoronet Abbey, 214, 222
Torpes, Saint, 183
Toulon, 22, 34, 196, 199ff.
    The *Bagne* (prison), 200
Trophime, St., 75, 76, 78
Troubadours, 30, 40
Tuck, Edward, 245
Tunnels du Fayet, 155

Ubaye River, 137, 150, 158
Urban VI, Anti-Pope, 45
Utriculaires, 138

Vaison-la-Romaine and Hautville, 61,
    62
Valberg, 258
Vandals, 39
Van Gogh, 32, 73, 80, 86, 88, 91, 174
Van Loo family, 32
Var Coast, 127, Chap. 7
Var, Haut, Chap. 8
Vaucluse, 127, 134
Vaudois, Massacre of the, 22, 129
Vence, 255ff
Verdon River, 138, 150ff.
    Gorges, 33, 152, 206, 217
Vernet, Joseph, 32, 51
Victor, Saint, 163
Vidal, Peire, 31
Villages perches, 210
Villefranche, 244
Villeneuve-les-Avignon, 49, 53ff., 93
Villeneuve-Loubet, 236

Viollet-le-duc, 45
Visigoths, 14, 61, 191
Voconces (Germanic tribe), 61, 148

Wars, 1st and 2nd World, 24, 170, 185,
    195, 210, 205, 209

Wells, Charles, 245
William of Orange, 61, 188
William the Liberator, 19
Wine, 186

Zola, Emile, 33, 82, 120